BUILD YOUR OWN 80386 IBM® COMPATIBLE AND SAVE A BUNDLE

AUBREY PILGRIM

To Dolores

FIRST EDITION
FIRST PRINTING

Library of Congress Cataloging-in-Publication Data

Pilgrim, Aubrey.
Build your own 80386 IBM compatible and save a bundle / by Aubrey Pilgrim.
p. cm.
Includes index.
ISBN 0-8306-9131-6 ISBN 0-8306-3131-3
1. Microcomputers—Amateurs' manuals. 2. Intel 80386 (Microprocessor)—Amateurs' manuals. I. Title.
TK9969.P56 1988
621.391'6—dc 19 88-19111
CIP

TAB BOOKS Inc. offers software for sale. For information and a catalog, please contact TAB Software Department, Blue Ridge Summit, PA 17294-0850.

Questions regarding the content of this book should be addressed to:

Reader Inquiry Branch
TAB BOOKS Inc.
Blue Ridge Summit, PA 17294-0214

Contents

Acknowledgments

Writing a book is not an easy thing to do. It takes long hours and a lot of research. It can practically isolate you from your family, friends, and loved ones. Please don't misunderstand; I am not complaining. I loved every minute of it.

I want to thank my family, especially Dolores, for the encouragement and moral support they gave me. They sometimes said, "Aren't you ashamed of yourself, lying around loafing? Get back to work so you can make some money to pay the rent." I'm just kidding. They didn't really say that. (They might have thought it, but they didn't say it.)

Introduction

This book shows how to assemble a powerful 80386-based computer. This computer is more powerful than many minicomputers. Although it is a very sophisticated and advanced computer, it is very easy to assemble. Except for the motherboard, most of the components needed to assemble an 80386-based machine are basically the same as those used in the PCs, XTs, and 80286s. No special expertise or special skill is needed. Soldering or special tools are not required. A pair of pliers and a screwdriver will be all that you need.

This book has a lot of photographs and easy-to-understand instructions for assembling an 80386-based computer. It shows the components needed and gives detailed descriptions of most of them.

COST TO BUILD

Just a short time ago the 80386 was much too expensive a chip to use in a personal computer for the homeowner. It was even too expensive for some businesses. The IBM PS/2 Model 80 still costs up to $10,000 or more. Many of the other name-brand clones cost almost this much. A 386 Compaq might cost about $8000, but with options such as a 300M hard disk and lots of memory, the price can go up to almost $24,000.

Except for the price of the 80386 chip itself, prices of the no-name motherboards and other components are coming down. You can now assemble an 80386-based machine that will do everything that the Model 80 does for less than $3000, or about one-third the cost of the Big Blue box.

Even if you don't want to assemble an 80386-based microcomputer yourself, you can buy a ''barebones'' system and add to it. This book will help you make informed decisions on what to buy as well as help you save money and time.

APPLICATIONS FOR A 386

In this book, I describe some of the many applications and ways that the 386 can be used to great advantage at home, in schools, in churches, in large and small businesses, and by doctors and lawyers. An 80386-based machine can be used at home or in a business office to manage investments and portfolios. It can be used by real estate agents, bankers, and farmers. Architects, design engineers, manufacturers and managers will find many advantages in using Computer-Aided Design/Computer-Aided Manufacturing/Computer-Integrated Manufacturing/Computer-Aided Engineering/Computer-Aided Software Engineering (CAD/CAM /CIM/CAE/CASE), desktop publishing, network file serving, and many other areas. I include short reviews of hardware and software and offer suggestions for certain applications.

One of the great advantages of the 386 systems is that they can be configured almost any manner desired. So that you can make informed choices, this book goes into detail regarding the operation of some of the peripherals needed, such as the disk drives, monitors, and printers.

I also list a few of the hundreds of applications for which the 386 system can be used. I recommend some standard off-the-shelf software and explore applications, such as desktop publishing, networks, and other business and personal uses for the 386.

HOW COMPATIBLE

IBM created a de facto standard for the PC, the XT and the AT. It was a standard that was easily copied and duplicated by clone manufacturers. Soon there was about $5 billion worth of hardware and about $6 billion worth of software for this PC/MS-DOS system.

The compatibles and clones were sold at much lower prices, and IBM lost a large share of the market. To recapture that market, IBM developed its PS/2 systems. The PS/2 systems are able to use most of the $6 billion of software that has been created in the past; however, the PS/2 systems cannot use any of the inexpensive boards and much of the $5 billion worth of hardware that has been developed for the IBM and compatible systems. The standard 386 system based on the earlier IBM architecture will have little or no problem using existing hardware. Since there are over 10 million of the older IBM compatible systems in existence, you can be sure that much more hardware will continue to be developed.

UPGRADING AN OLDER PC, XT, OR AT

I show how it is possible to upgrade and transform an older PC, XT, or AT machine into a potent 80386 by simply installing a new motherboard in it or by using one of the 80386 plug-in boards. Upgrading a system takes only a few minutes and is relatively inexpensive. Photographs and detailed instructions on these methods are included. This chapter alone could save you hundreds, even thousands of dollars. This simple operation prevents obsolescence and protects valuable investments.

CHAPTER SUMMARIES

This book is written in a language that should be easily understood by the novice, yet is technical enough to satisfy the experienced user. The subjects covered in each of the 17 chapters should be of interest to the beginner, as well as the old pro.

Chapter One describes the 80386 chip and gives reasons why a person should build his own compatibles. Chapter Two has descriptions of parts and components needed to assemble an 80386-based microcomputer. Chapter Three has photographs and instructions on how to assemble an 80386 system. Chapter Four describes how to assemble a baby 386 or upgrade a PC, XT or AT to a 386. Chapter Five describes operations of floppy disks. Chapter Six describes the operations of hard disks. Chapter Seven concerns the importance of backups. Chapter Eight goes into some detail about monitors. Chapter Nine describes the function and operation of memory. Chapter Ten covers keyboards and other methods of input to the computer. Chapter Eleven discusses some of the aspects of printers. Chapter Twelve discusses the importance of communications software and hardware, including modems, E-Mail and Fax. Chapter Thirteen briefly discusses Local Area Networks. Chapter Fourteen discusses one of the hottest new aspects of the computer revolution, desktop publishing. Chapter 15 briefly reviews some of the software that you will need. Chapter 16 lists a few sources for the materials you'll need. Chapter 17 contains a few tips on troubleshooting in the event something goes wrong. Hundreds of new words and acronyms have been developed during the computer revolution. The extensive glossary should help you hold your own in any computer setting.

Chapter 1

The Fantastic 80386

Computer technology is changing faster today than at any time in history. It is almost impossible to keep up with the latest advances. We are inundated with information about new technologies, new products, new research findings, and new developments. I subscribe to over 30 computer magazines. Every issue of every one of them has something new.

If you watch television commercials, then you know that the soap makers, new car manufacturers, and makers of other products continually improve their products. I'm not an expert on soap, but it seems to me that the new soap doesn't clean much better than the old. And the main difference in the new car models is that they add a little more chrome here and there. Basically the new, improved models still do about the same thing that the old products did. I suspect that many of those new improvements were made just to convince us that we should buy a new car even though our old one still gets us back and forth to work and around town.

At times it seems that the computer and software business is somewhat the same. If you have a system that is doing everything you need to do, it may not be worthwhile to invest in a shiny new "386" computer just because it may compute a few milliseconds faster than your old standby. And maybe you don't need new multitasking, multiusing, and very fast software packages if your old programs are doing the job.

If you decide that you do need a new computer system, this book can help you make an informed decision. In the old days it was relatively easy to make a choice as to which computer and peripherals to buy; there weren't many choices. Today there are so many choices that trying to determine which products to buy can be a dilemma. If you are faced with this problem, this book can help you.

There was an advertising campaign some time ago that said that no one had ever been fired for buying an IBM. Considering the high cost of IBM products compared to the clones, that statement may no longer be true. An IBM 386 Model 80, depending on the configuration, might cost from $9,000 up to $12,000. A clone system that will do everything the IBM will do can be assembled for less than half the price of an IBM system.

80386 VS. OTHER SYSTEMS

From the outside, an 80386 machine may look very much like an AT, XT or even a plain old PC. The main difference is that the heart of the 386 machine is an 80386 microprocessor chip. When enclosed in a ceramic package with all the leads and pins attached, the package is about 1½-inches-square. But inside the package is a small ½-inch-square of silicon that has over 275,000 transistors etched into it. (Figure 1-1 shows a 386 chip alongside a penny.) The 8088 microprocessor used in the PCs and XTs had about 29,000 transistors. The 80286 chip has about 130,000 transistors on a small ½-inch-square piece of silicon.

It is possible during manufacture for one or more of those 275,000 transistors on a 386 chip to be defective. The larger the number of transistors on a chip, the greater the odds of having defects. The chips are tested and those that are defective are rejected. Of course, the rejects reduce the yield. As a result, the 80386 is rather costly compared to other microprocessors. Another reason it is expensive is that Intel is the only manufacturer of the 80386.

Fig. 1-1. An 80386 chip alongside a penny.

The standard 80386 chip is designed to operate at 16 MHz and sells for about $300 each. Some of the chips are tested and certified to operate at 20 MHz. These chips sell for about $600 each. As a comparison, an 8088 chip can be bought for less than $10. But considering what the 386 will do, it is well worth the price.

Intel has no problem selling the chips at these prices. The company has built extra factories, but the demands and orders far exceed the number of chips Intel can manufacture. By the time you read this, almost 1 million 386 chips will have been sold and installed.

WHAT THE 80386 CAN DO

A minicomputer or a workstation can cost as much as $50,000. For some applications a 386 system that may cost between $3,000 to $10,000 can do an equivalent job. In many cases, the minicomputers and the workstations can only use special, very high priced custom software. There is over $6 billion worth of existing software that was developed for PCs, XTs and ATs. The 386 can use all of it. The 386 will be even more powerful and versatile as new software is developed to utilize more of its fantastic capabilities.

One of the more laudable features of the 386 is its speed. Computers use quartz crystal oscillators to mark very precise blocks of time in which to perform an operation. The standard 8088 processor operates at 4.77 MHz and processes two 8-bit chunks of data at a time. The standard 80386 processors operate at 16 MHz and can process 32-bit chunks of data at a time. Eventually the 20 MHz chip will be the standard. But Intel is already working on a 24 MHz 386 chip, and it will probably be available by the time you read this.

With an 8088 XT, a CAD program might take as long as 200 seconds to draw a complicated design on the screen of a monitor. A 386 can draw the same design in about 20 seconds or less. There are many other programs, such as large spreadsheets and databases, where the 386 can save a large amount of time. It can even save a considerable amount of time when doing word processing. I sometimes have to print out a single page in a large file. With an 8088, or even with an 80286, I had to wait several seconds for WordStar to find the page. The 386 can find the page almost instantaneously. The 386 is very fast when searching through files.

Waiting even a few seconds for a computer to perform an operation can seem like an eternity. Saving a few seconds may not seem like much, but if the computer is used for long periods of time, the savings can more than pay for the extra cost of the 80386.

REAL AND PROTECTED MODES

When the computer is reset, or booted up, it starts in the *real mode.* In the real mode, it acts like a very fast 8088 or 80286-based computer.

With the appropriate software or Operating System, the 386 can be switched to the *protected mode.* While operating in the protected mode, it can do multitasking, which allows the user to work on two or more tasks at the same time. It is possible to have a window on half of the screen with a WordStar file on one side and a dBASE III file on the other side. Data from either file could be transferred from one window to the other. It is possible to be running an MS-DOS application and a Unix operating system application at the same time.

In the protected mode, a type of barrier is imposed between programs that are being run concurrently so that neither one can interfere with the other. Running multiple tasks in the protected mode appears as if several 8086 machines were operating simultaneously and separately.

The early microcomputers could only address 64K of memory. The PC allowed only 640K. The 80286 can directly address 16 megabytes of memory and the 80386 can directly address 4 gigabytes. The 386 can also run in a *virtual mode* and switch large chunks of data in and out of memory. In this mode it can address up to 64 terabytes, or the data stored on 3.2 million 20M hard disks.

DO YOU NEED AN 80386?

The power and superb capabilities of the 386 make it well suited for business uses. If you use a computer just to do word processing and maybe a small spreadsheet once in a while, then you can get by with a PC, XT or 80286. The 80386-based computer doesn't cost much more than an 80286 to build. Even if you are just going to use it for a personal computer at home, you will be much happier if you spend a little more and get the best.

If you happen to be on a budget, you can buy a few parts at a time and gradually build it up. As I mentioned earlier, most of the components are the same as those used in the PCs, XTs and ATs, except for the motherboard.

If you are hesitant about building your own system from scratch, you can buy a barebones model that has just the basic components and then add to it. Though it is quite easy to assemble a system, it is possible to make a mistake or to get a component that is defective. The barebones systems have usually been checked out so they could save you some time and problems.

80386SX

Intel has also developed the 80386SX microprocessor. It is a 16-bit version of the 32-bit 80386 and is capable of doing just about everything the standard 80386 will do, although it is slower in some applications. Currently, not many motherboards can use the 80386SX; however,

Compaq and several other companies have already introduced microcomputer systems using the 80386SX. The 80386SX systems are priced as much as $1000 less than their standard 80386 systems, yet the main difference is that the 80386SX costs about $150, while the standard 80386 is about $300. In the near future, there are sure to be several motherboards and even more microcomputer systems that use the 80386SX.

SOURCES

I have been criticized by some for not naming more sources in my first two books. One reason I did not is because the computer business and technology are so volatile. Every day a few businesses fall by the wayside, but for every one that fails, a dozen more pop up. I could not possibly name them all. It is not fair to name one source and possibly overlook another one that is even better.

Another reason that I am reluctant to name extensive sources is because of the appearance that I might have some connection with the companies named. I assure you that I have no connection or business affiliation with any company named in this book.

The best source of microcomputer components would probably be a computer store near you that can give you support if something goes wrong. A second choice would be a computer swap where you can compare and maybe even haggle over prices a bit. A third choice would be mail order. If you look through any of the dozens of computer magazines, you will find hundreds of good bargains.

I will have more to say about sources and mail order later in Chapter 15.

Chapter 2

Components Needed

I am frequently asked what it costs to build a computer. That is like asking, ''What is the cost of a car?'' The cost will depend primarily on what kind of computer you want, what you want the computer to do, whether you assemble it yourself, where you buy it, and how much you want to spend. There are over $5 billion worth of hardware on the market. Using that hardware, you can build almost any kind of computer and configure it to do almost anything.

Another reason it is difficult to determine the cost of a system is that there is so much competition, so the prices change almost hourly. I list some approximate costs. You can get a better idea by looking at the advertisements in magazines and checking out the costs of the various components. I have included a list of magazines in the Appendix that will help keep you current with this ever-changing technology.

All of the systems—whether PCs, XTs, ATs, or 80386—use similar basic components. They are all plug compatible. You can even take a power supply, or a plug-in board out of a true blue IBM, (except for PS/2s), and plug it into a compatible, or vice versa, and it will work. The main difference among the systems is the motherboard.

The motherboard and case of the standard AT and 386 is larger than the XT. But there are ''baby'' motherboards for the AT and 386 that are the same size as the PC and XT motherboards and are directly interchangeable. The baby motherboards are usually a bit more expensive and may not have as many slots and options as the standard size boards.

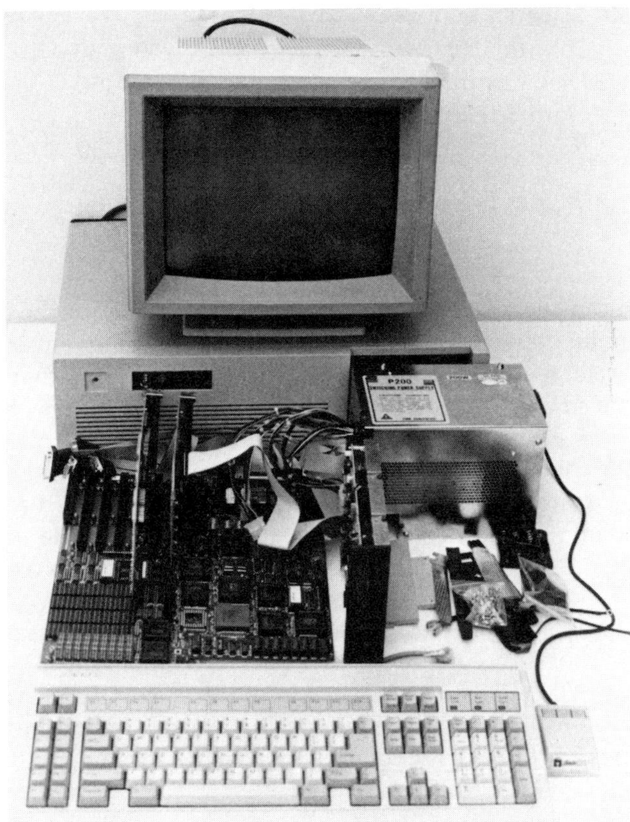

Fig. 2-1. Components needed to build an 80386-based machine.

80386 COMPONENTS

Here is a list of the basic parts and approximate cost to build an 80386 system.

ITEM	COST
Case	$ 65-100
Power Supply	70-135
Motherboard	1100-2000
Monitor	100-600
Monitor Board	40-400
Multifunction Board	50-200
Floppy Drive (1.44M, 3.5″)	125-250
Floppy Drive (1.2M)	75-150

Hard Disk Drives	
20M to 150M	250-1550
Disk Controller	75-150
Hard & Floppy	
Keyboard	50-150
TOTAL	$2000-5685

As you can see, there can be quite a large variation in the cost, depending on the particular components. There is also a large variation in cost from dealer to dealer. Some of the high volume dealers charge much less than the smaller ones, so it will pay you to shop around a bit and compare prices. These figures are only rough approximations. The market is so volatile that the prices can change overnight. If you are buying through the mail you might even call or check out the advertised prices before ordering. Often the advertisements have to be made up one or two months before the magazine is published, so the prices could have changed considerably.

I have listed several options that are not absolutely necessary for an operating barebones system. It is possible to buy a minimum 80386 system for less than $2000. If you are short of cash or if you don't need a lot of goodies at this time, you can buy such a system and add to it later. I will discuss each of the basic components briefly; they will be discussed in more detail in later chapters.

Case

The case usually comes with a chassis case and cover, a bag of hardware, a speaker, plastic standoffs, and guides. The case will usually have a switch panel that may or may not be assembled and mounted. The switch panel will usually have a set of keys and a lock that locks out the keyboard without shutting off the power. The panel may have several switches and LED indicators with wires that plug into the motherboard and other boards.

Power Supply

The original IBM PC had a power supply capable of only 65 watts. It was sufficient for one or two floppy drives. Since the PC only had five slots, the power supply could also provide enough power for five boards. But 65 watts is not nearly enough for the eight slots on present motherboards. I recommend that a 200 watt power supply be installed in all microcomputers. You may never need all that wattage, but the supply will run cooler if it has the greater capability.

Uninterruptible Power Supply

The power supply takes the 110 volts of alternating current from the wall socket and transforms it down to plus and minus 12 volts of direct current and plus and minus 5 volts of direct current. These are the voltages needed to drive the computer.

We don't usually have thunder and lightning in San Francisco and Los Angeles, so I have never worried too much about an uninterruptible power supply. But just recently I was working on one of the chapters of this book and a freak electrical storm came up. I had worked a couple of hours, polishing and redoing a whole chapter. Suddenly a large clap of thunder exploded directly over my house. The lights dimmed for just a fraction of a second, but my computer screen went blank. All of the work that I had done in the last two hours was gone. I don't have to tell you that I was just a bit unhappy.

I was mostly unhappy with myself. I should not have been working with my computer during a storm. But my deadline was fast approaching. So since I had to work, I should have followed the advice that I have preached for years: BACKUP, BACKUP, BACKUP. It is so easy to do. With WordStar, all I have to do is press the F9 key to save any work that is on the screen or in memory to the hard disk. Had I taken the fraction of a second that it takes to press F9, I could have saved hours of work.

Another alternative is to buy an uninterruptible power supply (UPS). Without a UPS, if there is a brief interruption of the 110 volt power, even for just a fraction of a second, any data in the computer's memory is lost. A UPS can take over during an interruption and continue to feed power to the computer until you can save your data to disk or complete whatever operation you are doing.

There are different types of UPS, varying in how much wattage they can supply and for how long. Some may be able to supply enough current for two or three computers for as long as two hours. Others may supply a single computer for 5 to 20 minutes only. Of course, they also have different prices that range from $300 to over $5000. If you live in an area where there are frequent electrical storms, or power outages, and your work is critical, you might consider buying one.

There are two types of systems: standby and on-line. The standby system uses a 12-volt battery and battery charger. The 12 volts is fed into an inverter that converts the 12 volts dc from the battery back to 110 volts ac. The standby usually has a sensor that can detect a power loss, and it immediately switches to supply 110 volts to the computer. There can be a delay of a few milliseconds before the standby can switch over.

The on-line types are in series with the 110 volts and provide power to the computer at all times. The 110 volts feeds a charger which keeps a 12-volt battery charged. The battery converts its 12 volts back into 110 volts and continuously feeds it into the computer. The advantage is that there is no delay in the event of a power outage. The 12-volt battery will continue to supply 110 volts to the computer until it becomes discharged.

Here is a short list of vendors and their telephone numbers. If you need a UPS, call them for their specifications and latest prices.

Applied Technology	(404) 951-9556
Clary Corporation	(818) 287-6111
Controlled Power	(800) 521-4792
Cuesta Systems	(805) 541-4160
Electronic Protection	(800) 343-1813
Electronic Specialists	(800) 225-4876
Elgar Corporation	(619) 450-0085
Kalglo Electronics	(800) 524-0400
Para Systems	(800) 238-7272
Perma Power	(800) 323-4255
PTI Industries	(408) 438-0946
Sola	(312) 253-1191
Staco Energy Products	(513) 253-1191

Motherboards

The standard size 386 motherboard has 8 slots. Some of the baby 386s may have one or two slots less. All of the slots have 62-pin connectors for the standard 8-bit PC bus. There are additional 36-pin connectors in front of some of the 62-pin connectors. These connectors are for the 16-bit data lines. The Intel type motherboard has two 62-pin connectors in front

Fig. 2-2. A comparison of some motherboards. Left to right, a 386, a 286 and an XT.

Fig. 2-3. Two different types of 386 motherboards. Intel's is on the left and a Compaq type is on the right.

of two of the standard 62-pin connectors. These connectors are for the 32-bit data lines for extended memory which can be up to 16 megabytes. The Compaq type of motherboard has a single 62-pin connector for the 32-bit data lines at the front of the motherboard. Some Intel type motherboards may have only one 62-pin connector; some may have three or more, and some do not provide connectors for the 32-bit lines at all. These boards usually come with up to two megabytes of memory on the motherboard.

It is also possible to get a backplane type of board. The backplane is just a row of connectors, usually connected in parallel. With this system, all of the main motherboard components are on a plug-in board that is similar to the standard plug-in boards. As you can see, there is no standard for the motherboard, one of the most critical parts in the 386.

You can use the older existing 8-bit type plug-in boards that were developed for the PC, XT and AT with the 62-pin edge connectors. They can be plugged into any of the 62-pin slots in the 386. The same is true for the 16-bit boards developed for the AT.

Currently, it is rather difficult to find 386 boards. Those that are available cost way too much. One of the cost factors is the amount of memory installed on the motherboard. The cost of one megabyte of DRAM

Fig. 2-4. A third type of motherboard, the V.I.P.C. The one that I bought.

Fig. 2-5. A baby 386 motherboard.

memory was less than $100 in October 1987. In May 1988, the cost was up to over $300 for the same chips.

More companies are developing motherboards, and several new companies are manufacturing DRAM memory chips. The prices are slowly coming down. By the time you read this book, you should be able to buy a good motherboard for less than $1100 with at least two megabytes of memory installed.

Monitor

It is possible to buy a monochrome monitor for less than $100, and I have seen them at swap meets for $65. They are perfectly good for ordinary usage, but I don't know why anyone would put a small monochrome monitor on a fantastic 386. I prefer color, even for word processing. I also prefer high resolution. If necessary, I would use the rent money and maybe skip a few meals in order to have color.

It is possible to get a high-resolution monitor for about $250. The better monitors will cost from $500 on up to several thousand, depending on size and resolution. I go into more detail on monitors in Chapter 7.

Monitor Board

The monitor must have a plug-in board to drive it. There are several on the market that cost from $40 up to over $400. A $40 *Monographics Graphics Adapter* (MGA) or a *Color Graphics Adapter* (CGA) is sufficient for a monocolor monitor (720 × 350). The CGA will drive a monocolor or a medium resolution color monitor (640 × 200).

For a high resolution color monitor you will need an *Enhanced Graphics Adapter* (EGA). At one time, the least expensive ones cost over $400. There are now several no-name brands that sell for around $100. The name brands will still cost over $300. A good *Video Graphics Adapter* (VGA) will cost about $400.

Some of the 386 motherboards have built-in EGA drivers, which saves you the expense of having to buy a board and also saves one of the precious slots for some other application board. Adapters are covered in more detail in Chapter 7.

Multifunction Boards

You will need a board to drive your printer. You will also need ports for a *modem*, an extra printer, or a *mouse*. There are several different kinds of multifunction boards. Most of them have utilities such as clocks, extra serial and parallel ports, extra memory, print spoolers, and RAM disks. Depending on the functions and utilities that are on the boards they will cost from $50 up to $200.

Floppy Drives

The 3.5-inch drive is the new standard. There are some very inexpensive 720K models, but I would strongly recommend that you buy the 1.44M models. They are only a few dollars more and will hold twice as much data. The better ones will read and write to the 720K format as well as the 1.44M format. They are available for between $125 and $250.

There are millions of 5.25-inch 360K diskettes in existence. Many software manufacturers are still using them to distribute their programs. Businesses have millions of man-hours invested in 360K systems. The 3.5-inch diskette has several advantages, but the 5.25-inch diskette will be with us for some time. Because of this, you should by all means have a drive that can read and write to the 360K format. Since the better 1.2M disk drives can do both, that is all you need.

Hard Disk

It is possible to assemble a 386 without a hard disk. But I can't imagine why anyone would do it. It is one of the essential elements that helps make the 386 so powerful.

There is literally a myriad of hard disks on the market. There are several types and grades of quality. It is such an important part of the microcomputer system that I have devoted all of Chapters 5 and 6 to disk drives.

Basically, you should select a well-known brand, with an access speed as fast as possible, and most important, with the largest capacity that you can afford. At one time ten megabytes was a large disk. Nowadays, that isn't enough to store more than one or two software packages. There seems to be an immutable law that says that data and files will increase on a hard disk to its full capacity.

Disk Controllers

The disks drives, both hard and floppy, must have a controller. The better controllers have both hard and floppy controllers on a single plug-in card. But there may be an occasion where you might want to buy a RLL or ADRT controller so that you could increase the capacity of your disk. Some of these controllers do not have floppy controllers on them. In this case you will have to buy a separate floppy controller. More about controllers in Chapters 5 and 6 on disk drives.

Keyboards

Data can be input to a computer in several different ways such as by modem, by scanners, by a mouse, and by voice. But the keyboard is, by far, the most often used and most important input device. There

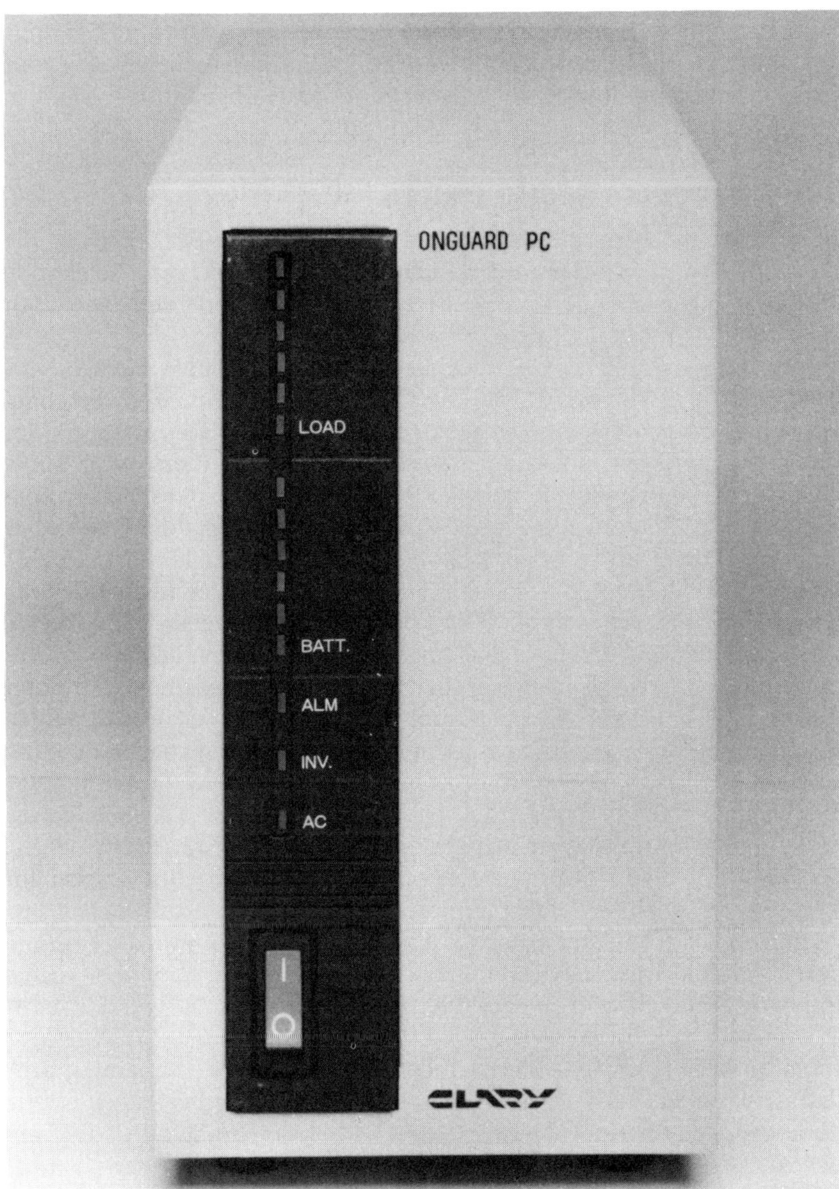

Fig. 2-6. An uninterruptible power supply (Photo courtesy Clary Corp.)

are several different types of keyboards. Some may cost as little as $50, and some as much as $250. Some of the lower priced ones that I have used seem to do as well as the high priced ones.

If at all possible, try out the keyboard before buying it. Some have very soft and sensitive keys. I have a heavy hand, and I have great difficulty using these types. Some of the better models have different springs that you can order and install under the keys to change them to suit your style. I have more to say about keyboards and other input devices in Chapter 9.

WHERE TO FIND THE PARTS

There are computer stores in most large cities. Check the advertisements in the daily and Sunday newspapers and in the telephone directory. Keep in mind that most retail computer stores sell items at or near the suggested list price.

If you live near a large city such as Los Angeles, San Francisco, New York, or Dallas, you probably know that there is a computer swap going on almost every weekend. This is one of the better places to shop. You can compare prices, look the parts over and even try them out in some cases. It is even possible to haggle a bit with the dealers, especially near closing time. Some will even sell the items at or near their cost rather than pack them up and cart them back to their main store.

Another alternative is to look through the mail order advertisements in the computer magazines. In the past, there have been some horror stories about a few unethical mail order companies. One person took out large full page advertisements in several computer magazines. Computer products were offered at unbelievably low prices. Thousands of people sent money and checks to the P.O. box number given. When the customers didn't receive the components they had ordered, they complained to the post office. The post office and the police investigated, but could not find the person who had rented the P.O. box.

Mail order and computer advertisements are the life's blood for computer magazines. A few phoney advertisements like the ones placed by the no good, low down piece of trash mentioned can ruin a magazine. Most magazines are very careful about who they accept advertisements from. The vast majority of the advertisers are honest and will deliver as promised.

If possible, look for advertisements from the same company in back issues of computer magazines. If a company has been in business for some time, then they are probably safe to deal with. Compare prices of different vendors. They should all be fairly close. If a vendor offers products at prices that seem too good to be true, then you should be a bit suspicious. More about mail order in Chapter 15.

In the next chapter we will have photos and instructions for putting all the parts together.

Chapter 3

80386 Assembly

In the previous chapter, I covered all the components needed to assemble an 80386-based microcomputer. Here is a list of the parts and what they cost me:

ITEM	COST
386 motherboard	$1825
NEC MultiSync monitor	560
Paradise VGA	349
Seagate 251-1 40M	399
Perstor PS180 Controller	245
3.5-inch floppy 1.44M	125
1.2M floppy	89
Floppy Controller	41
Northgate Keyboard	99
Power Supply	74
Case	62
TOTAL	$3868

There are several components above that I could have saved a bit of money on. For instance, I didn't need the NEC MultiSync. I could have bought a fairly good EGA monitor for about $250. The motherboard that I bought has an EGA adapter built in, so I didn't need to buy the Paradise VGA board. I looked at several motherboards; some were selling for as little as $1300. I finally found one that I liked at the V.I.P.C. Company, 384 Jackson, Suite #1, Hayward, CA, 94544, (800) 232-9090.

It was a bit more expensive than some of the others that I had looked at, but it has several extras that I was impressed with. It has a built-in EGA adapter that can give up to 640 × 480 resolution. It also has two *serial ports,* two *parallel ports,* and a *light pen* connector built into the board. It comes with a 16 Mhz 80386 chip that has been selected to run at 20 MHz. The clock speed can be switched by the keyboard down to 8 MHz for any programs that won't run at the 20 MHz speed. It came with one megabyte of 32-bit memory on-board in *Single In-line Memory* chips (SIMS). There are sockets for another megabyte of memory on-board, and a slot for a 32-bit memory board. It has a ROM setup on-board that allows you

Fig. 3-1. The V.I.P.C. motherboard.

to easily change the computer configuration. Just type <Ctrl-Alt-S> and a menu pops up that allows you to change the type of disk drives, the time and date, the CPU clock speed (which is also switchable at any time from the keyboard with <Ctrl-Alt-- +> or <Ctrl-Alt-- ->), and even select the *wait states*for the memory. You can select a 0 wait state for most applications, or interpose several if necessary. I am really quite happy with this board. Figure 3-1 shows the V.I.P.C motherboard I selected.

I have known Tony Cole, the owner of V.I.P.C., for some time. I was pretty sure that I would get good support if I ran into any problems. So far I have not had any problems.

I could have obtained a keyboard for about $50, but I really like the Northgate. Since I spend so much time at the keyboard, I figured I might as well get the best.

BENCHTOP ASSEMBLY

I first assembled the parts on a bench outside of the case to make sure that everything worked. I then turned the system on and ran it for five days to burn it in. Tony assured me that he had burned the board in for two days in his shop, but a little more doesn't hurt. This should take care of any infant mortality. If a semiconductor is going to fail, it will usually do so in the first 168 hours of use. Once we are sure that it works, then we will install it in the case.

Figure 3-2 shows the pins for the parallel and serial ports and the cables. The cable being installed is a serial port for COM2. The pins for COM1 are directly in front of it. The parallel port, LPT2, has a cable installed to the left. LPT1 is directly in front of it. The pins to the right of COM2 are the EGA output. To the right are the pins for the light pen.

Figure 3-3 shows the battery pack being connected. It plugs into pins near the keyboard connector. The battery holder is attached to the power supply by a two-inch square of double-sided foam tape. One problem that I had was that the motherboard has no designation as to which pin is positive and which negative. Plugging the battery pack in backwards could destroy the on-board CMOS ROM setup. I suspected that the positive would be the pin towards the front of the board. But I called Tony and he confirmed it. He also told me that I did not have to connect the battery. It doesn't hurt, but the motherboard has an on-board battery that should last about three years or so.

The CMOS setup for this board is controlled from the keyboard. On my old 286, any time that I wanted to reset the time or date, I had to out a floppy and run a routine. But the setup on this board pops up immediately to change: disk drives attached, amount of memory, memory wait states, time, and date. The clock speed is also switchable from this utility as well as from the keyboard.

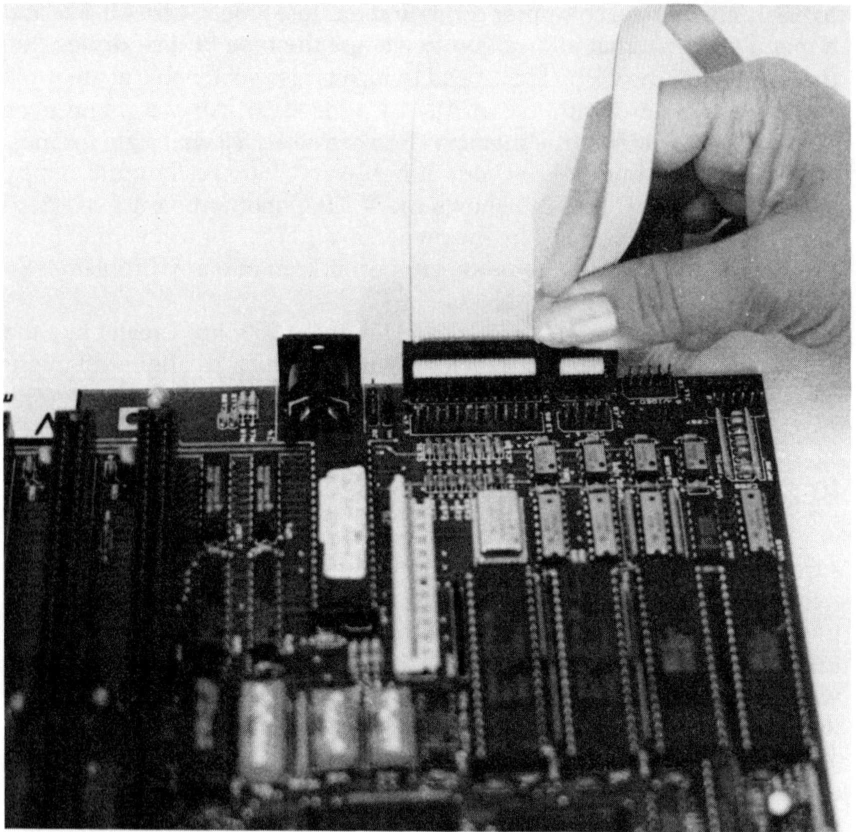

Fig. 3-2. Installing port cables.

Figure 3-4 shows the main power to the board being plugged in. Care should be taken here because it is possible to plug these two connectors in backwards. When installed properly, the four black leads are in the center.

Figure 3-5 shows my helpmate installing the Perstor hard disk controller. Figure 3-6 shows the controller cable for the hard disk being connected to the controller board. Be very careful because this connector can be plugged in backwards, possibly destroying the electronics on the hard disk and the controller board. This 34-wire ribbon cable has a colored wire on one side that indicates pin one. This cable may have a connector in the middle of it. If so it will be for a second hard disk drive if one is present.

Figure 3-7 shows the 20-wire data cable being connected. Note that it also can be plugged in backwards. It has a colored wire on one edge that indicates pin one. If only one hard disk is used, the row of pins

Fig. 3-3. Installing the battery cable.

nearest the 34-wire connector is used. If a second hard disk is installed, then there will be a second 20-wire cable to connect to the row of pins near the front of the controller board.

Figure 3-8 shows a 34-wire ribbon cable being connected to the floppy disk controller. Again, care must be exercised because it also can be plugged in backwards. It has a colored wire that indicates pin one which should go to pin one on the board.

Figure 3-9 shows the motherboard with the controller boards and cables installed.

Figure 3-10 shows the plastic slides that have to be installed on the disk drives. There are several holes in the slide so that it can fit almost any case. You should put in a single screw to hold one slide, then try it in the case to make sure you have the right holes before installing all of them. Figure 3-11 shows the installation of the slides.

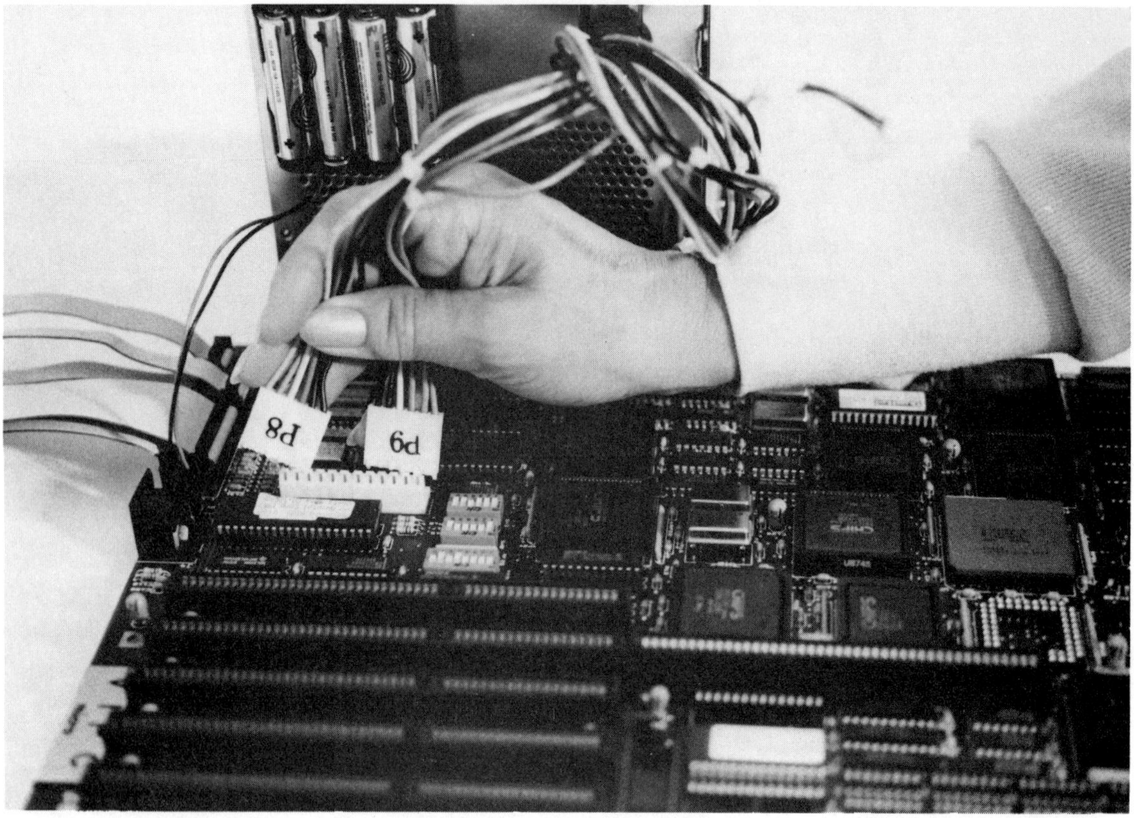

Fig. 3-4. Installing connectors for motherboard power. Note that four black wires are in center when properly connected.

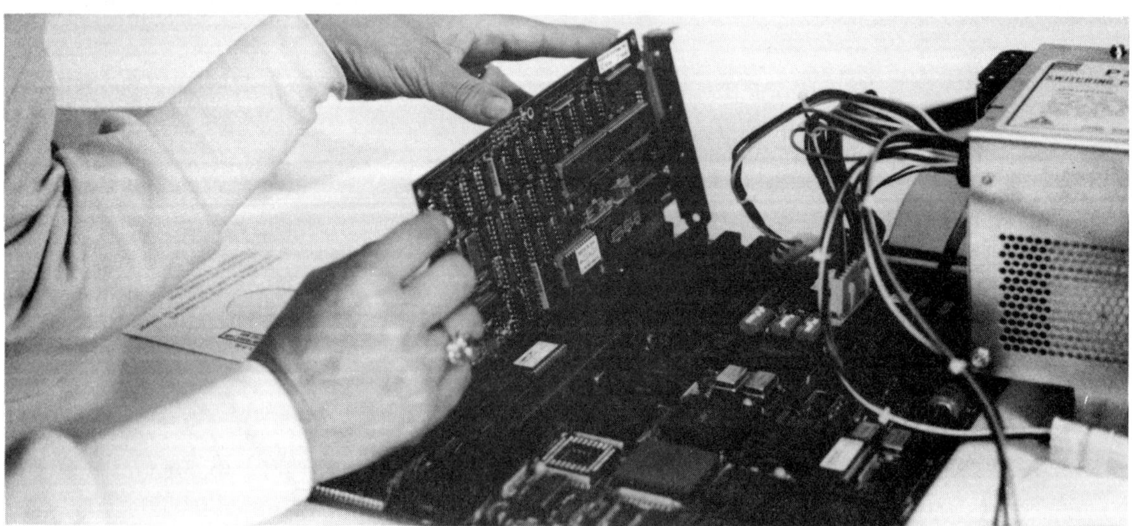

Fig. 3-5. Installing the Perstor hard disk controller card.

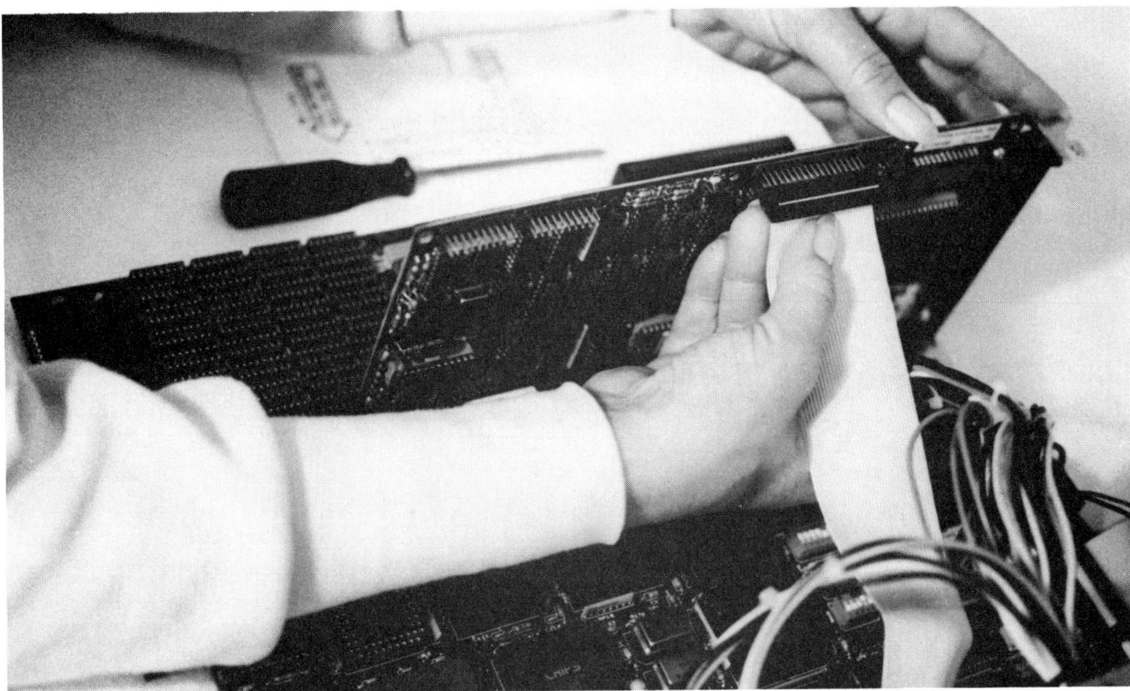

Fig. 3-6. Connecting the 34-wire ribbon cable to controller card. Make sure that the colored wire on the edge of cable goes to pin one on the board.

Fig. 3-7. Connecting the hard disk data cable to the controller card. Make sure that the colored wire goes to pin one.

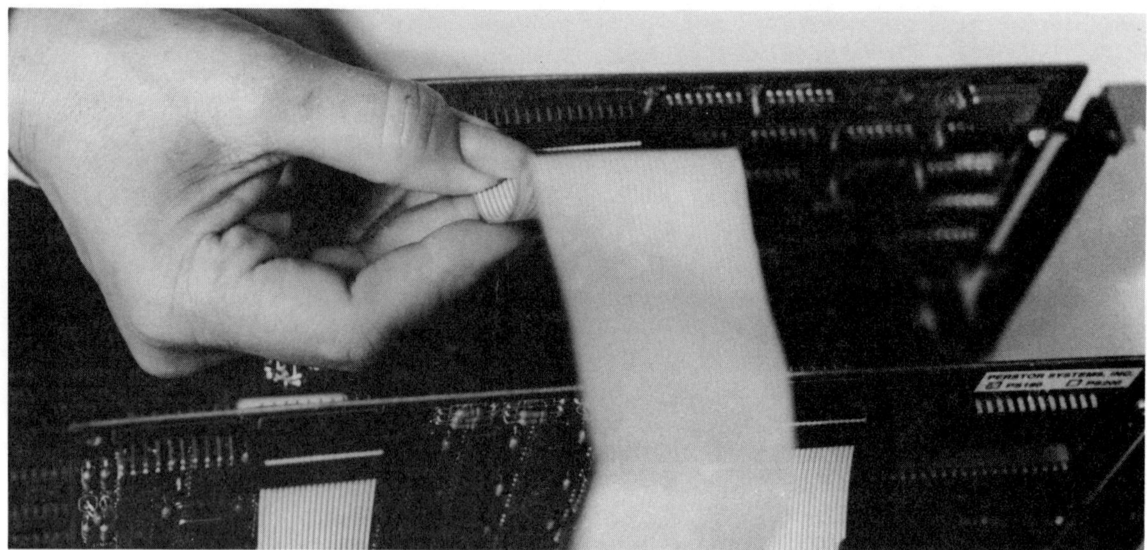

Fig. 3-8. Connecting the floppy disk controller cable. Make sure the colored wire goes to pin one.

Fig. 3-9. All controller cables are connected to the boards.

Fig. 3-10. Preparing to attach the plastic slide rails to the disk drives.

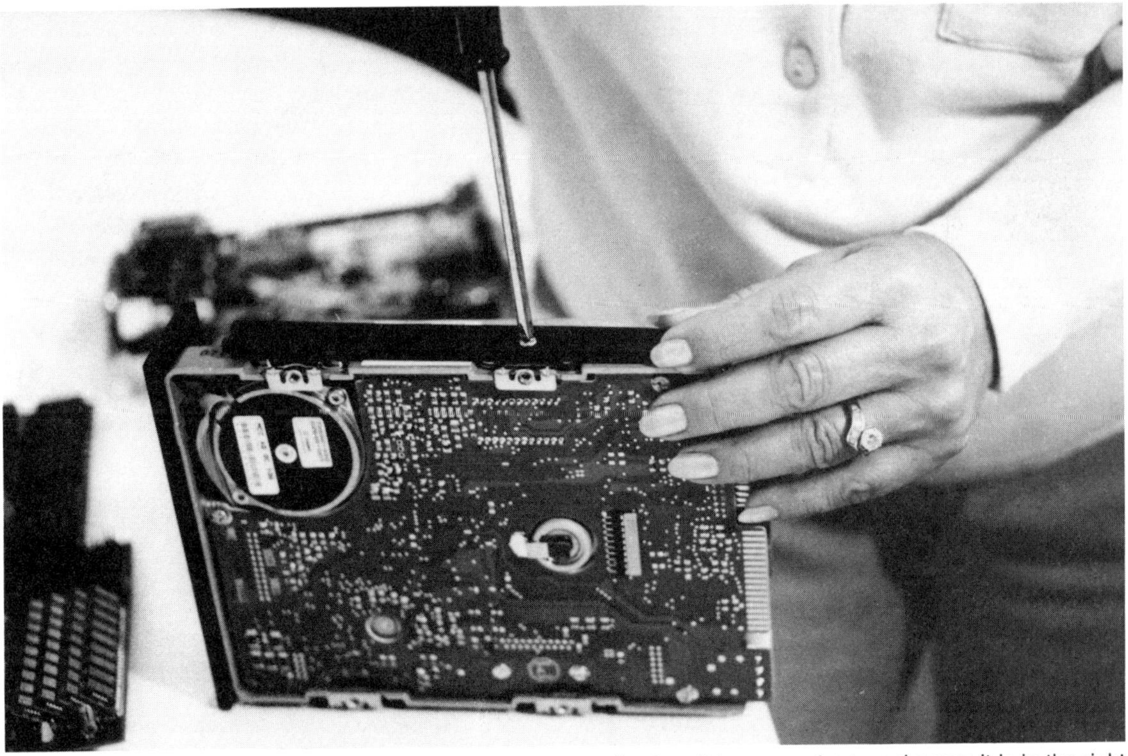

Fig. 3-11. Attaching the slide rails. Install one rail, then temporarily place it in a case slot to make sure it is in the right holes before installing all of them.

Figure 3-12 shows the connection of the controller cable to the hard disk. Again, it is possible to plug this connector in backwards. Look for the colored wire and an indication of pin one on the hard disk edge connector. Some cable connectors are keyed so that they can only be plugged in properly. The key consists of a bar installed in the face of the connector so that it slides into the cut slot in the edge connector.

Figure 3-13 shows the connection of the second controller cable to the hard disk. Again, it can be plugged in backwards. Take care that the colored wire goes to pin one on the edge connector.

Figure 3-14 shows the connection of power to the hard disk. The power supply has four cables for disk power. They are all identical and can only be plugged in properly.

Figure 3-15 shows the adapter cable adapter for the 3.5-inch floppy. Figure 3-16 shows the connection of the other end of the power cable adapter to the 3.5-inch floppy. It can only be connected properly.

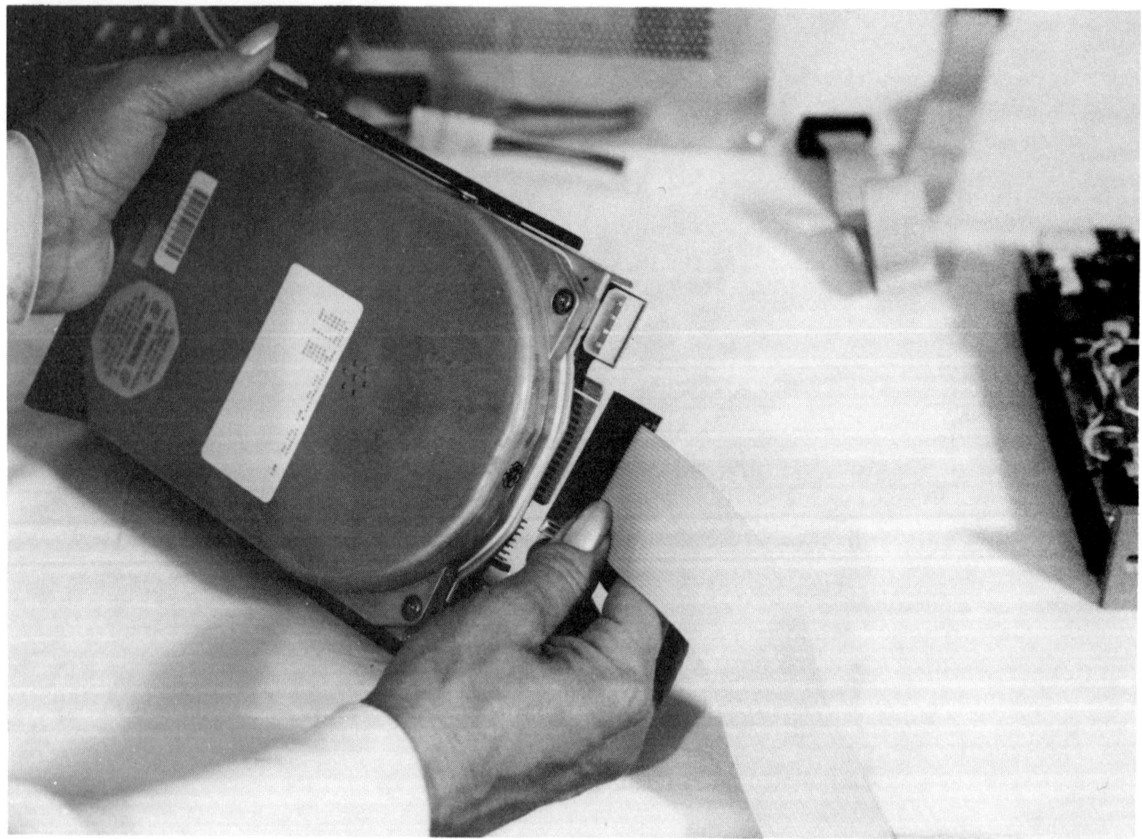

Fig. 3-12. Connecting the controller cable to the hard disk. The colored wire should go to pin one.

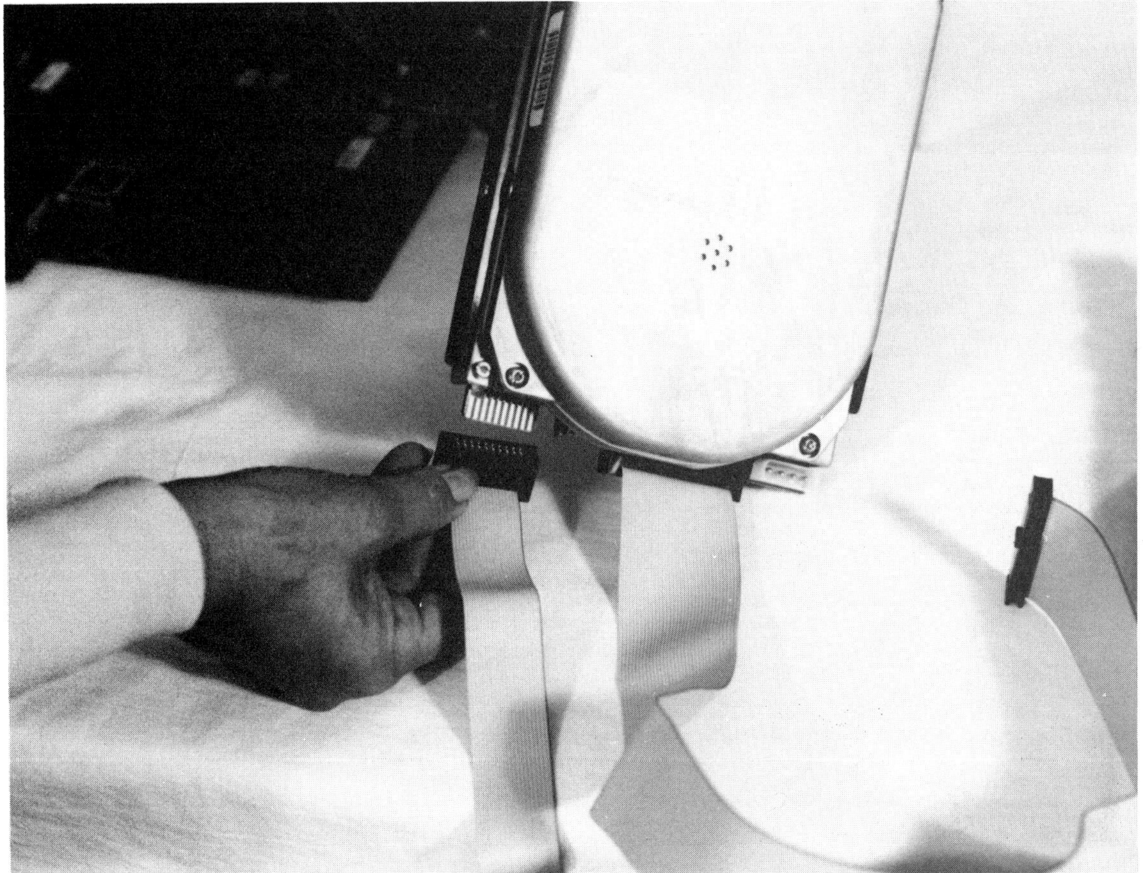

Fig. 3-13. Connecting the data cable to the hard drive. The colored wire should go to pin one.

floppy. It can be plugged in backwards. Match the colored wire with pin one on the edge connector. This floppy controller cable has three connectors, one on each end and one in the middle. Since the 3.5-inch floppy is going to be our B drive, it attaches to the connector in the middle.

Figure 3-18 shows the connection to the 1.2M floppy drive. This will be our A drive which is indicated by the split and twist in the cable. Once again, this connector can also be plugged in backwards. Look for pin one on the edge connector and make sure that the colored lead of the cable matches it.

Figures 3-19 through 3-23 detail further assembly steps. The system booted up immediately after assembly and ran. I installed several software packages on the hard drive and tried them out.

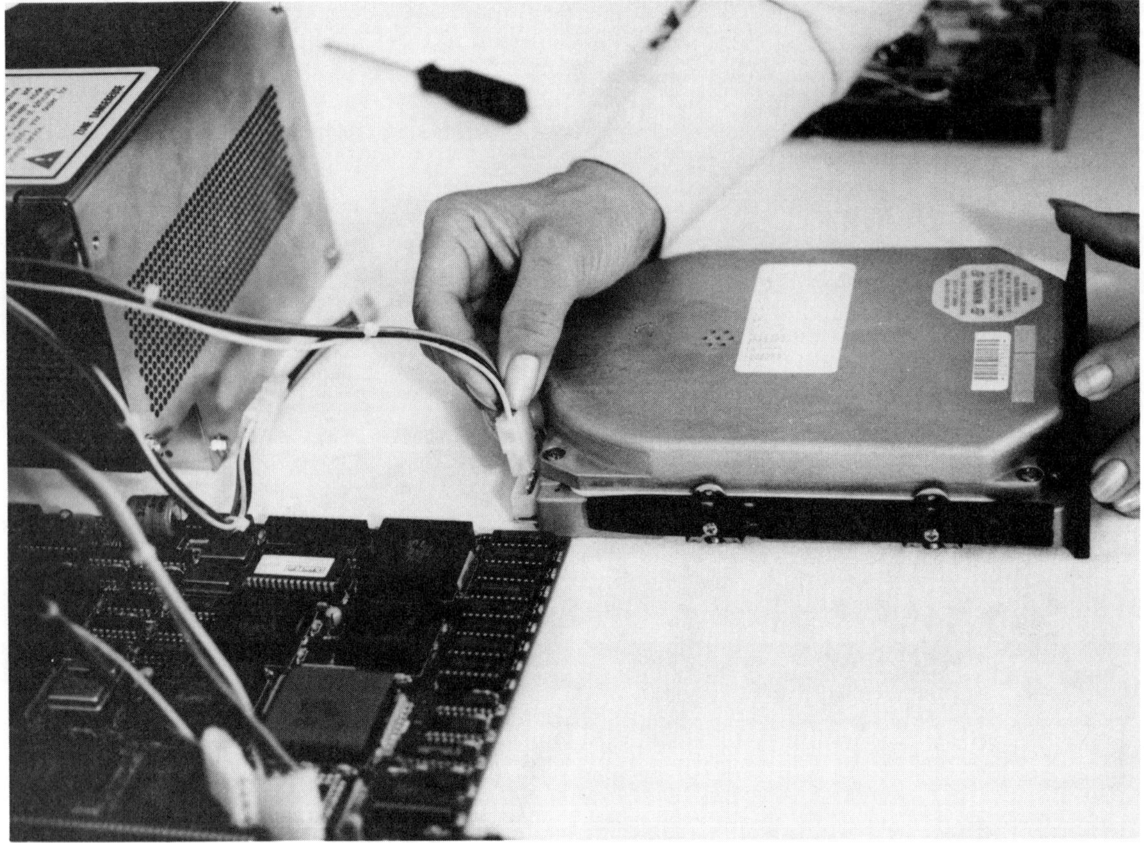

Fig. 3-14. Connecting the power cable to the hard disk.

PROBLEMS

I tried the 1.2M floppy by formatting a diskette for 1.2M. Since the configuration setup was set for 1.2M, the only command necessary was FORMAT A:. I could have used the command FORMAT A: /T:80 /N:15, which would have told it to format for 80 tracks with 15 sectors per track. I then formatted a 360K diskette by using the command FORMAT A: /4. I can write to this diskette with the 1.2M, then read it on a standard 360K drive.

I then tried my Toshiba 3.5-inch 1.44M floppy. I had a disk error, so I checked the meager manual that came with it. There is a recessed set of pins and jumpers on the back of the floppy that is hardly noticeable. I changed a couple of the jumpers. It could then read and write to 1.44M diskettes and could read and write to 720K, but it refused to format a 720K diskette unless I went back to my ROM setup and changed the setup for a 720K drive.

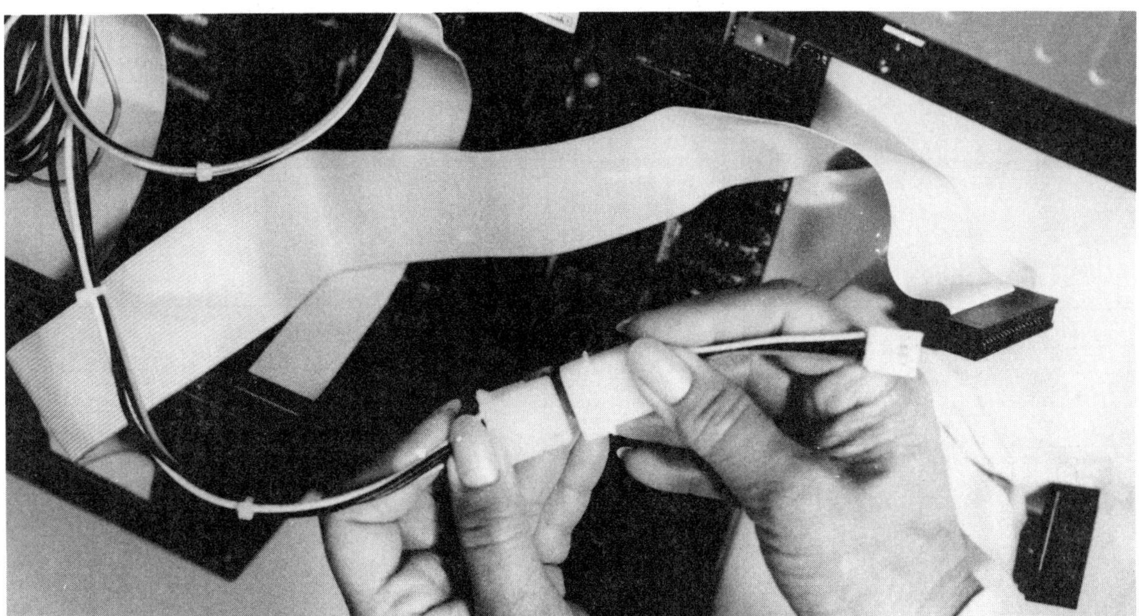

Fig. 3-15. Connecting a power cable adapter for the 3.5-inch floppy.

Fig. 3-16. Connecting the 3.5-inch power cable to the drive.

Fig. 3-17. Connecting the middle connector to the 3.5-inch drive. The colored wire goes to pin one.

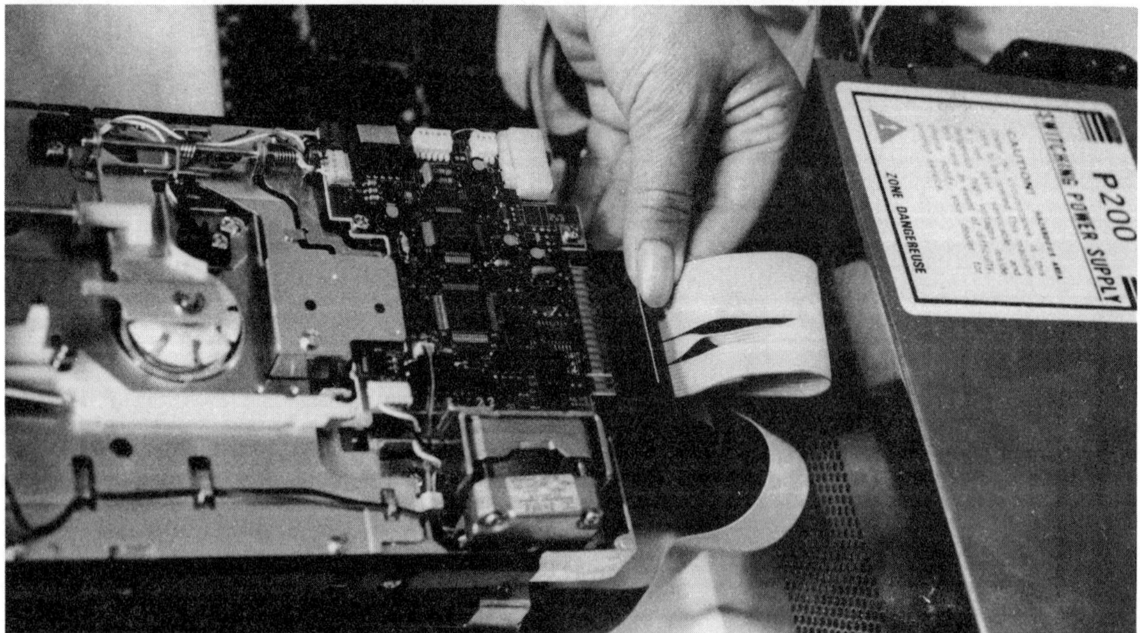

Fig. 3-18. Connecting the floppy controller cable to drive A. This is the end connector with the split and twist in the cable which indicates drive A. The colored wire goes to pin one.

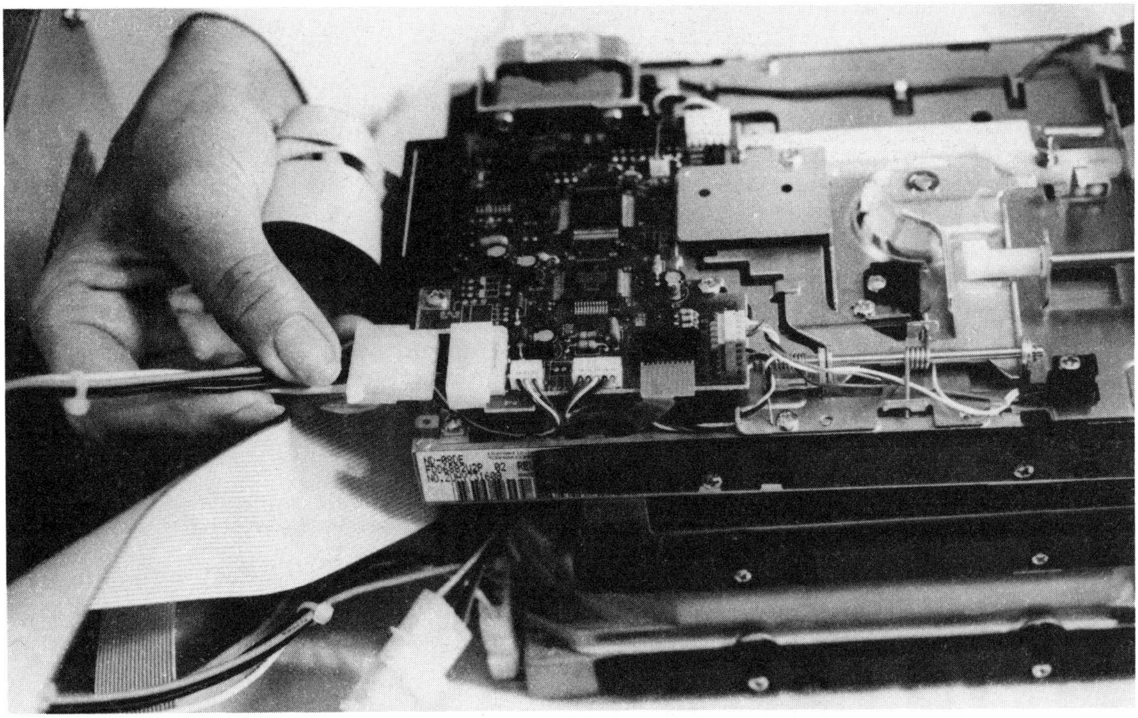

Fig. 3-19. Connecting a power cable to drive A.

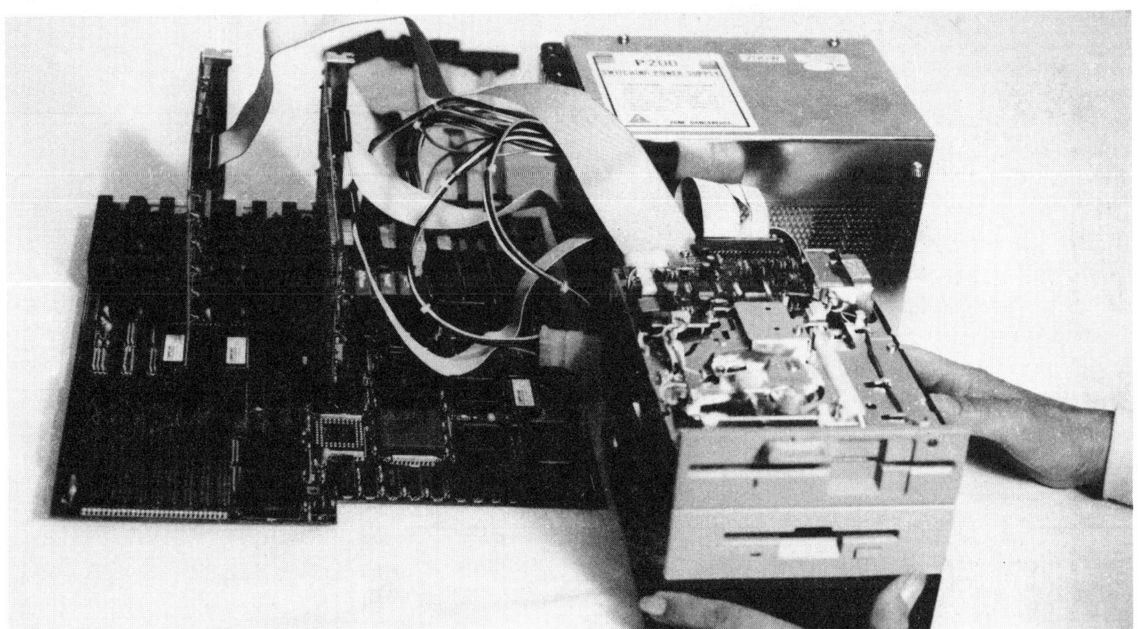

Fig. 3-20. All cables connected to the drives.

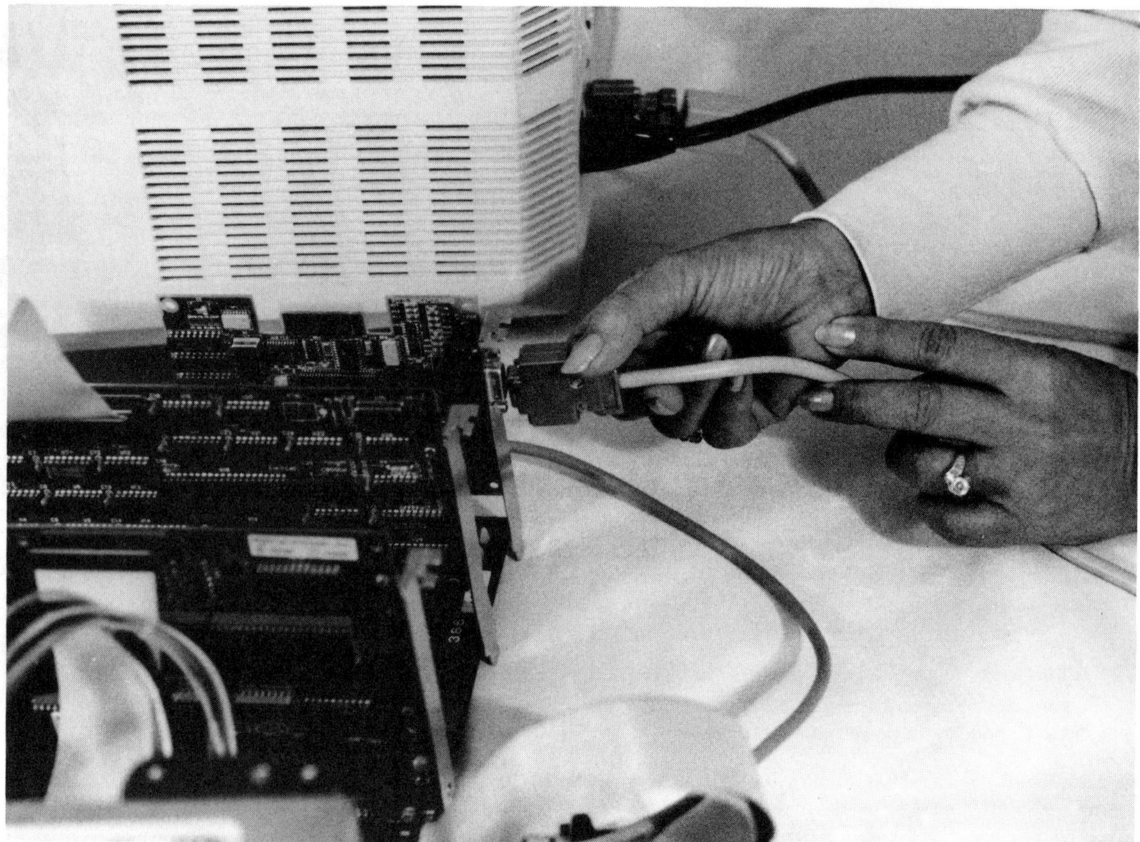

Fig. 3-21. Connecting the monitor cable.

I have a Sony 3.5-inch drive. It can read, write, and format to 1.44M or the 720K with no problem. There was something wrong with the Toshiba. I thought one of the jumpers was not set right. The Sony works fine. I bought the Toshiba drive from the Liuski Company, (818) 912-8313. They have a very good service department with lots of test equipment and experienced technicians. They changed the jumpers and the Toshiba now works fine.

I then noticed that my system wasn't keeping the proper time. I tried a new set of batteries, but it made no difference. I called Tony at V.I.P.C. None of his other customers ever had a similar problem. He gave me the name of the company who had designed the board for him. I called him, and he could not imagine what could cause my problem.

I only had two boards plugged in. I was using the on-board EGA to drive my monitor, so all I had was the Perstor hard disk controller card and the floppy disk controller card. I removed the floppy controller and

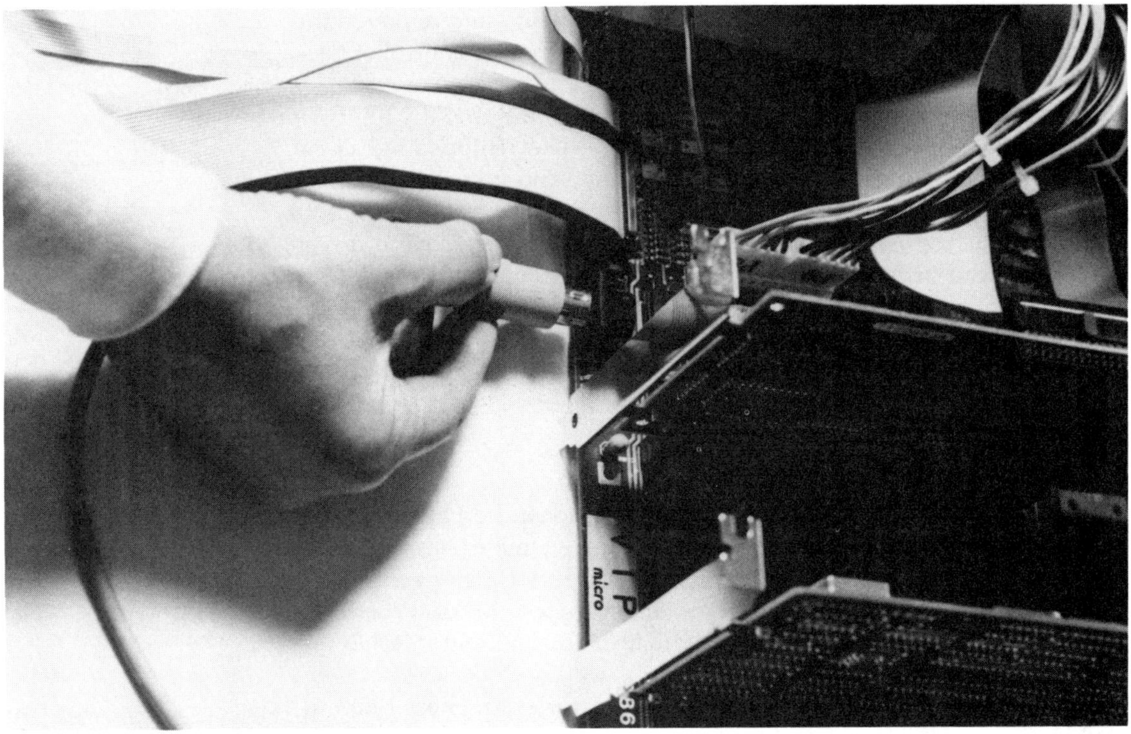

Fig. 3-22. Connecting the keyboard cable.

Fig. 3-23. All components connected; ready to apply power.

I still had time errors. I then replaced the floppy board and removed the Perstor board, and I got the correct time. I put the Perstor controller back in and the time errors returned.

I called Perstor, and they said that they had found that the BIOS on their card did not work with some clone BIOSs. They shipped me a new BIOS overnight. I installed the new BIOS chip, and it has kept perfect time since.

Then I started having problems with my floppy disks. The drives would not read or format at times. I could reboot and sometimes they would work, and other times they wouldn't. Finally, they quit altogether. It was the Mini-Micro floppy controller, of course. I had bought it at a swap meet. I returned it to the dealer who has a store nearby. He replaced it, and I have not had any further problems.

TEST.BAT

Once everything was working properly, I made a short batch file and used some of Norton's utilities for a test. Norton's Utilities has a Systems Information, or SI, test. It does a performance test as compared to the IBM XT, which is rated as one. It does a memory test, looks at the BIOS and its date, and several other very useful tests. My computer tested out at 20.7 on the performance test.

Here is my little batch test. I changed directories to where I had installed Norton Utilities, then typed:

```
C> COPY CON TEST.BAT
SI
DIR
TEST2.BAT
^Z
```

When I finished, I pressed <F6> to end the batch file. <Ctrl-Z> will do the same thing.

I then typed:

```
C> COPY CON TEST2.BAT
TEST
^Z
```

This set up a loop. It runs the SI command, then displays the directory, then calls TEST2.BAT which calls the TEST.BAT. This loop will run continuously. It can be stopped by pressing <Ctrl-C>. There are more elegant and sophisticated ways of testing. But this does a fairly good job, and it is simple.

INSTALLING THE COMPONENTS IN THE CASE

After running the system for five days on the bench with no problems, I installed it in the case. Figure 3-24 shows us preparing to mount the power supply. Note that there are two raised tongues in the floor of the case. There are two matching cutouts on the bottom of the power supply case. The power supply is placed over the raised tongues, then slid towards the back of the case. Figure 3-25 shows us installing four screws in the back of the case which secures the power supply.

Figure 3-26 shows the back side of the motherboard as we are preparing to slide it into place. The four white objects are plastic standoffs that slide into grooves in the raised channels on the floor of the case.

In Fig. 3-27, I have just run into an installation problem. There are three black plastic standoffs with a horizontal groove that accepts the right edge of the motherboard. As you can see from the photo, one of the standoffs is exactly where the light pen connector on the motherboard

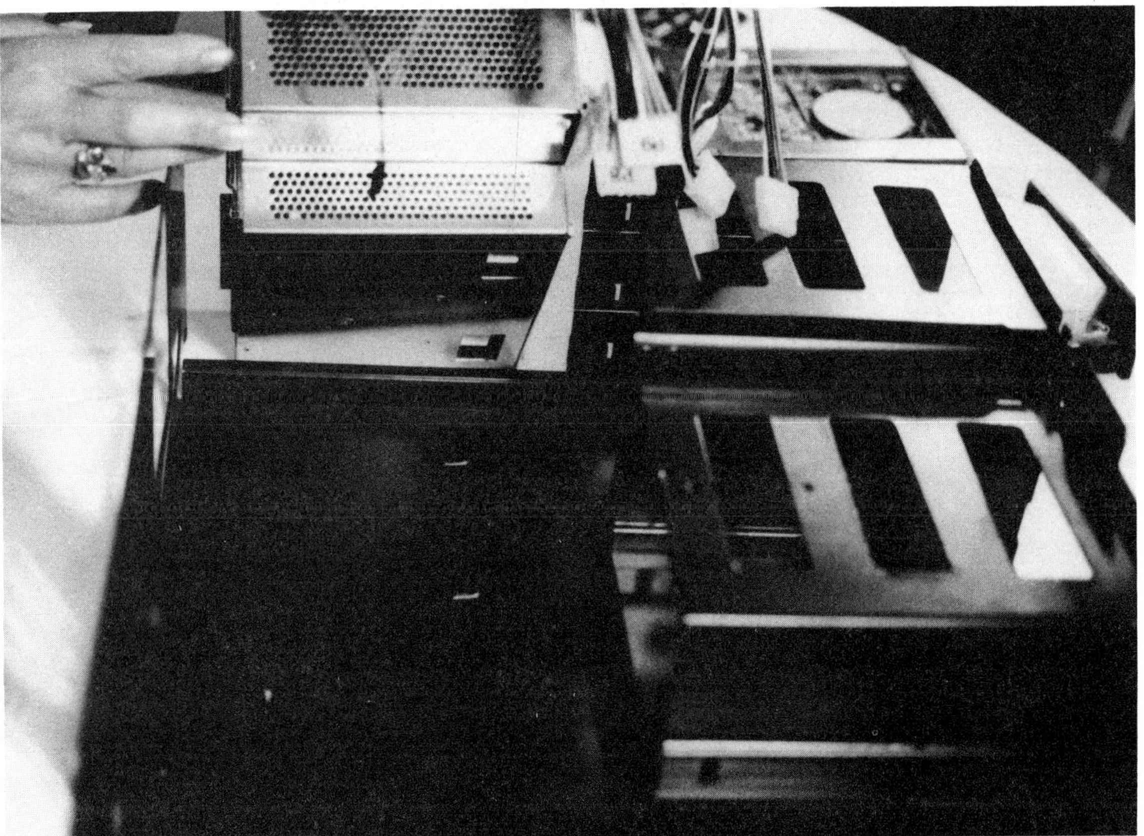

Fig. 3-24. Installing the power supply in the case. Note the raised tongues on the floor of the chassis and matching cutouts on the bottom of the power supply. These tongues hold the power supply down.

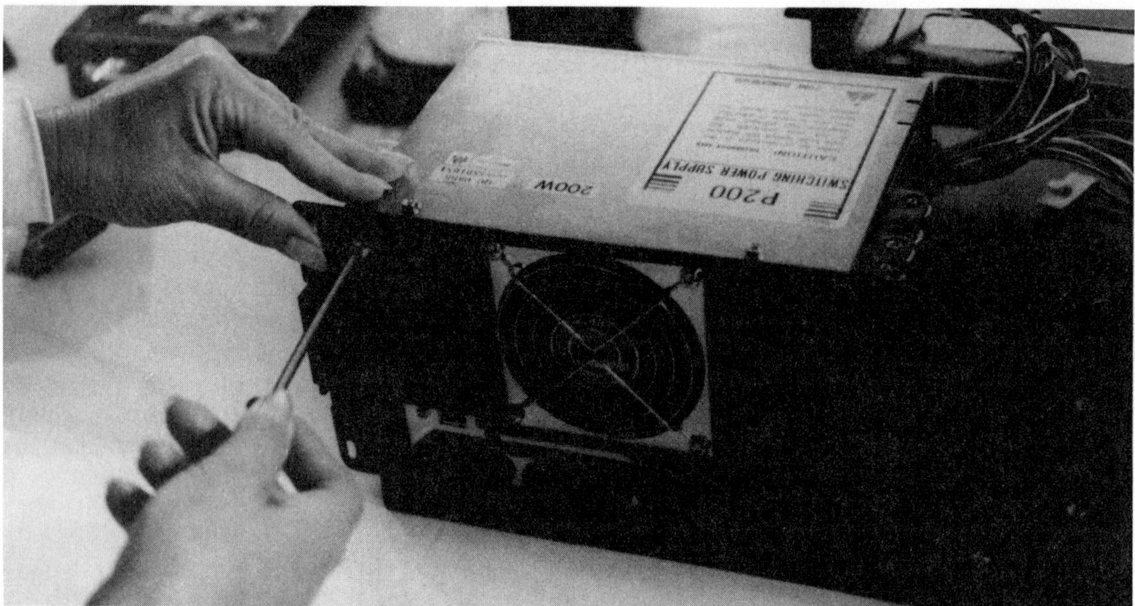

Fig. 3-25. Two screws in back of the chassis hold the power supply in place.

Fig. 3-26. Preparing to slide the motherboard into the case. The white objects are plastic standoffs that slide into grooves on raised channels in the case.

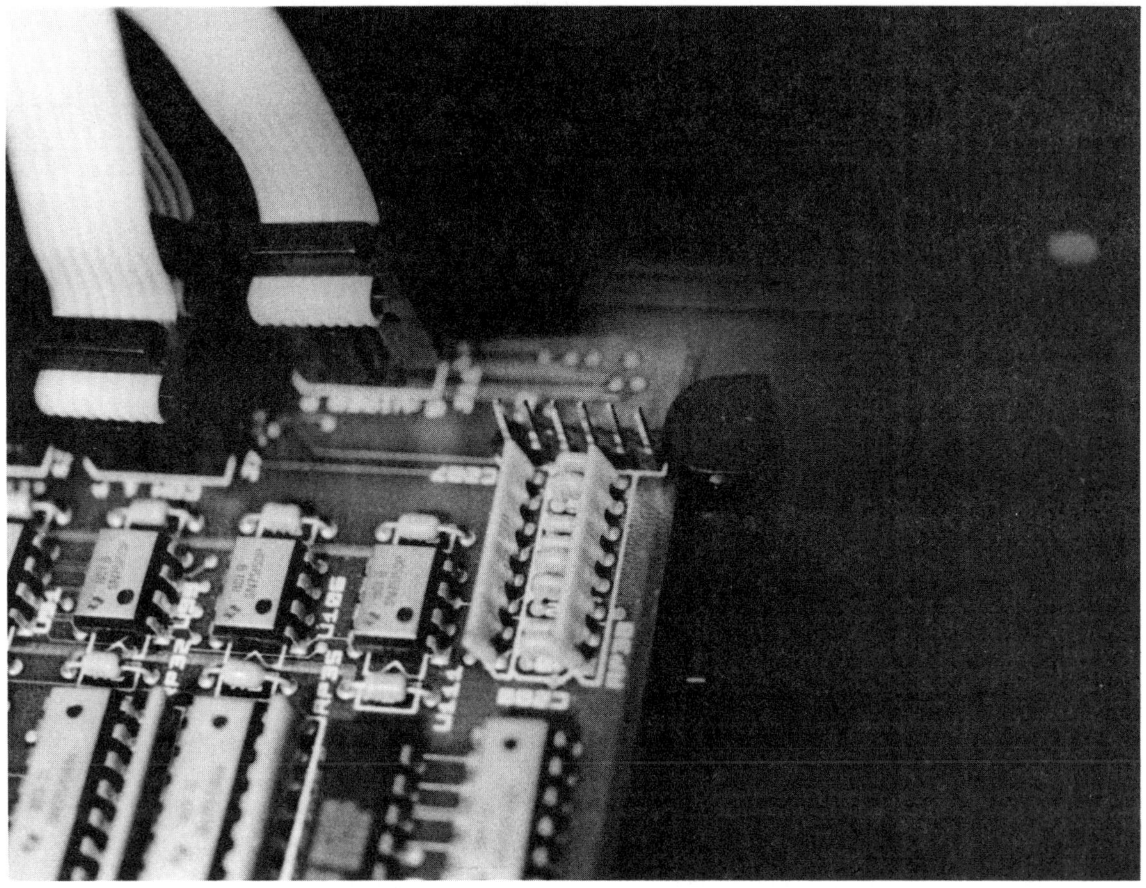

Fig. 3-27. A minor problem. A black plastic standoff is interfering with the connecting pins for the light pen.

is located. This is a slight design fault of the board. I need support for this edge of the board. I could drill a new hole and relocate the black standoff but, I found an easier solution. As shown in Fig. 3-28, I solved the problem by using a pair of cutters and cutting away some of the plastic standoff. The board now slips in easily.

Figure 3-29 shows us installing one of the two screws that are used to hold the board in place. The other screw is at the front of the board. Note that the power connection has the black wires in the center.

Also note that there are a lot of loose wires at the front of the case. These are the wires that came with the case. In some instances there may be 15 or 20 wires from the switches and LED indicators on the case switch panel. My case came with a keyboard lock, a turbo switch, a reset switch, a power-on indicator, a turbo mode indicator and a hard drive activity indicator.

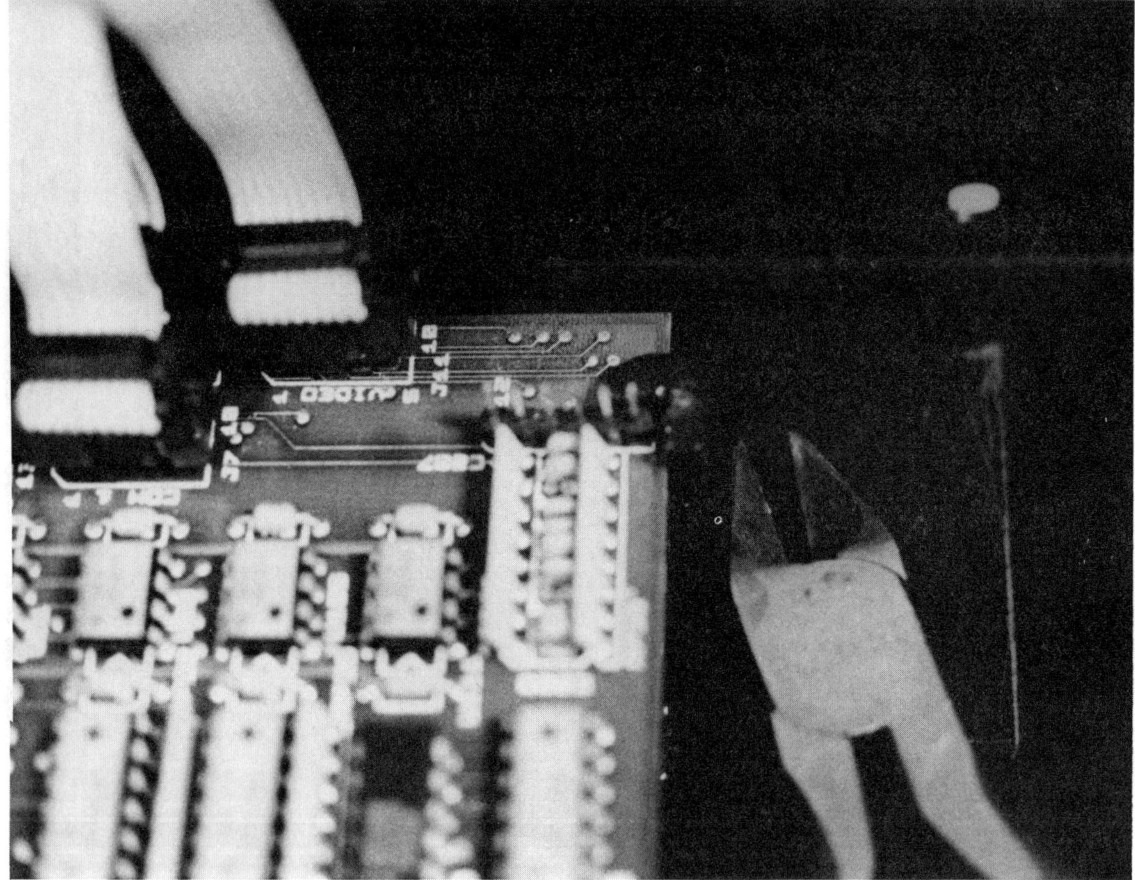

Fig. 3-28. Solution to the problem. I used a pair of sharp snips to cut away part of the top of the standoff.

Your motherboard and system may not use all of these wires and switches. You should get a manual with your motherboard that indicates where each of the wires should be connected. My motherboard does not have provisions to connect the turbo switch or the turbo indicator LED. Most hard drive controllers have a connection for the hard drive activity; however, the Perstor controller does not have one. Figure 3-30 shows all components installed, ready for the cover. In Fig. 3-31, the system is up and running.

SLOT COVERS

You may not use all of the available slots. But the openings at the back of the case should be covered. Usually the only noise you hear from your computer is the fan in the power supply. It is supposed to draw

Fig. 3-29. The motherboard is installed and power connected. A screw is being installed at the rear center of the board. One other screw will be installed in the front of the board to hold it down.

air in from the open grill in the front of the case, pull this cool air over all the boards and components, then exhaust it out of the opening at the back of the power supply. If there are several other openings at the front of the computer, air will be drawn from them and may not accomplish the cooling necessary. Heat is an enemy to semiconductors. Don't put anything in front of the computer that would cut off the circulation or put anything in back of it that would prevent the outflow of air. Your computer will last longer if you help to keep it cool.

Fig. 3-30. All components are installed in case, ready for the cover.

Fig. 3-31. Up and running.

Chapter 4

The Baby 386

If you are stuck with an old PC or XT, you may be perfectly happy if it does all you need to do. But you may feel like a person who is riding around in a Model T when everyone else is zipping around in new Cadillacs. You may have been dreaming of the luxury of the new 386s, so you want to get rid of your old clunker.

The trouble is that there isn't too much of a market for used PCs or XTs. If it has an IBM logo on it, you might have paid from $3000 up to $5000 for it a few years ago. You might be lucky to get $300 for it today. You could donate it to a charity, but the IRS probably won't let you deduct as much as you think it is worth from next year's taxes.

There is an easy way that you can salvage some of your investment. For about $1400 you can install a baby 386 motherboard. It's easy to do, only takes about 20 minutes, and will add about $2500 to its value.

Shortly after IBM released their 80286 AT in 1984, the Chips and Technology Company began designing *Very Large Scale Integration* (VLSI) chips that could integrate several of the AT motherboard functions. They were able to design a single chip that could replace as many as 30 chips on the standard sized motherboard. Using these chips, the standard sized AT motherboard was reduced to the size of the XT motherboard.

Chips and Technology has done the same thing with the large number of chips on the standard sized 386 motherboard. Several clone makers have used the Chips and Technology VLSI chips to design baby 386 boards that are the same size as the original PC and XT motherboards.

They are functionally equivalent to the standard sized boards. You can use one of these boards to replace the original motherboard in an IBM PC, XT, or a compatible and turn it into a more powerful 80386 machine.

COST TO CONVERT

This motherboard will be the most expensive component in your whole machine. You can buy XT motherboards for less than $100. The 386 motherboard will cost between $1200 and $1500. The rest of the components will be about the same as the cost of the XT components. In many cases, they are the same part.

You might have some case alignment problems in converting an original PC into a 386. The original IBM PC has only five slots. The XTs, 286s, and 386s usually have eight slots. So the openings on the back of the PC case that has only five slots will not line up with the eight slots of the 386. You could cut new holes or buy a new case for about $40. You should have no problems installing a baby 386 motherboard in an XT case. Everything should line up and fit.

The standard PC or XT case size is 19.6 inches wide by 16 inches deep by 5.5 inches high. The standard AT case that is also used for the 386 is 21 inches wide by 16 inches deep by 6.25 inches high. Several manufacturers are now also making special cases that have the same footprint as the XT but are an inch higher to accommodate some of the larger 16- and 32-bit boards. These cases have a keylock and, except for their smaller footprint, are very similar to the standard AT or 386 case.

One other problem that you may have in converting a PC or XT into a 386 is the power supply. Most of the original IBM PCs were sold with a 65 watt power supply. The XTs were sold with 135 or 150 watt supplies. For a 386, you will need to upgrade to about 200 watts. This will cost about $75.

Still another problem will be the keyboard. Most of the PC and XT keyboards will not work with an AT or 386. Both keyboards have the same type of connector, however, the keyboard itself is a small computer, and the scan frequency of the PCs and XTs is different than the 286s and 386s. Some of the clone keyboards have a switch that allows them to be used by both types. One of the best keyboards is made by Northgate. It sells for $99. I have seen some very good clones for as little as $45.

So if you have to replace the power supply, case, and keyboard, you probably won't have much left of your old computer except for the disk drives, a few plug-in boards, and your monitor. You might consider trying to sell your old PC or XT and starting from scratch or buying a barebones system.

Here is an example for the cost of a conversion. The total price for such a conversion will have a lot of variations of course, depending on what you already have and what you want in your new computer.

ITEM	COST
Baby 386 motherboard	$1300
Power supply	75
Keyboard	60
TOTAL	$1435

Even if you have to buy a new case for $60, it will still cost less than $1500 to convert to a marvelous 386. Your new board will have built in ports, a clock, and some may have other utilities. Of course, you may want to get a new EGA monitor and driver board. This could cost as much as $700 to $900 extra. And you might want to get a new 1.2M floppy for $90, a new 1.44M 3.5-inch drive for $125, and a new hard disk for $300 to $700. You could spend as much as $1500 on these extra goodies. But you would have an excellent and powerful machine, and it would still cost less than $3000.

UPGRADING AN IBM XT

Figure 4-1 shows us stripping down an IBM XT. Figure 4-2 shows the case with the motherboard removed. We left the original drives installed in the case. I know that these drives are good, so I am going to use some other drives to bench-test our motherboard and burn it in. Note

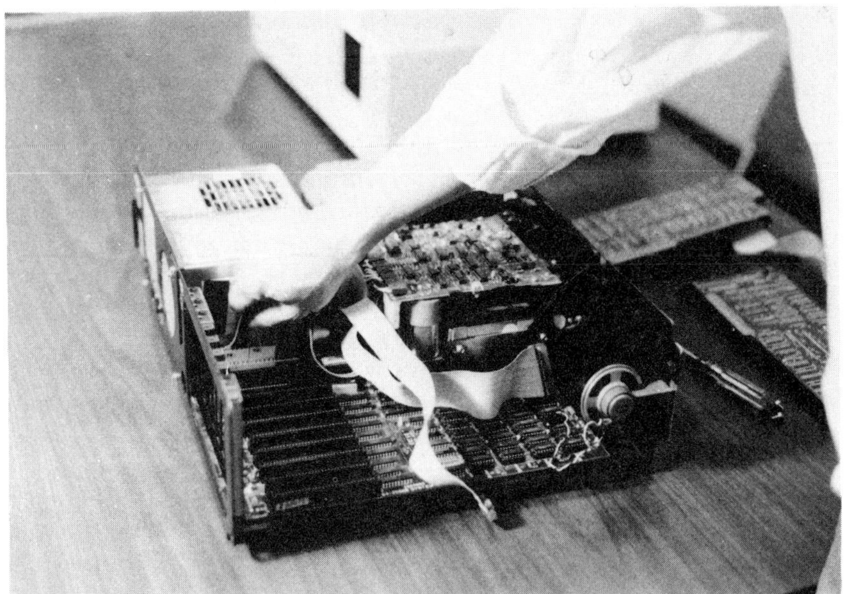

Fig. 4-1. Stripping down an IBM PC-XT in order to install a baby 386 motherboard.

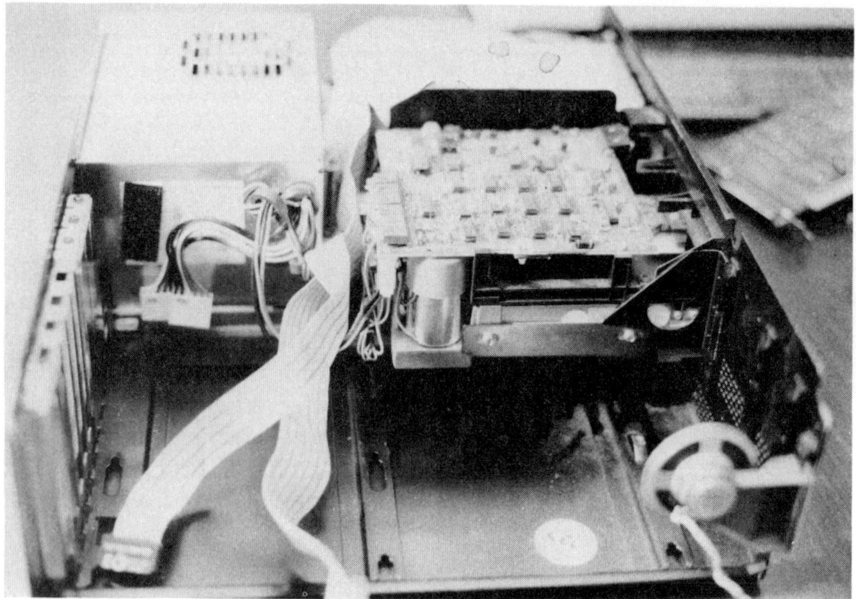

Fig. 4-2. Ready to install new motherboard. Note that it was not necessary to remove the disk drives and several other items.

that this is a fairly late model XT as evidenced by the raised channels that have slots for the plastic standoffs of the motherboard.

Figure 4-3 is our baby 386 motherboard. Note that there are eight large Chips and Technologies VLSI chips on the board. The large chip in the lower left corner is the 80386 CPU. Note that it does not have a second 62-pin slot for 32-bit memory. Also notice that it has two megabytes of 32-bit memory in the Single Inline Memory Modules (SIMMs) installed on board in the upper-left-hand corner. Any of several memory boards can be used in the 16-bit slots to add more memory.

Before I install the motherboard, I will connect all the components on the bench to make sure it works. The first thing to do is to connect the power supply as shown in Fig. 4-4. Note in Fig. 4-5 that the four black leads are in the center. Figure 4-6 shows a monitor adaptor board and a combination floppy and hard disk controller with cables installed on the board. All of the cables have a colored wire on one edge which indicates pin one. The floppy cable is plugged into the controller board on the row of pins nearest the back. Pin one is at the top of the board, so the connector is plugged in so that the colored wire is on top.

Figure 4-7 shows a 3.5-inch floppy being connected as drive B to the middle connector. The edge connector on the floppy disk board should have a 1 etched on one side and a 2 on the other side of the board. Or it may have a slit near the pin one end of the connector. Make sure that the colored wire on the connector goes to this end. Figure 4-8 shows the

Fig. 4-3. A baby 386 motherboard.

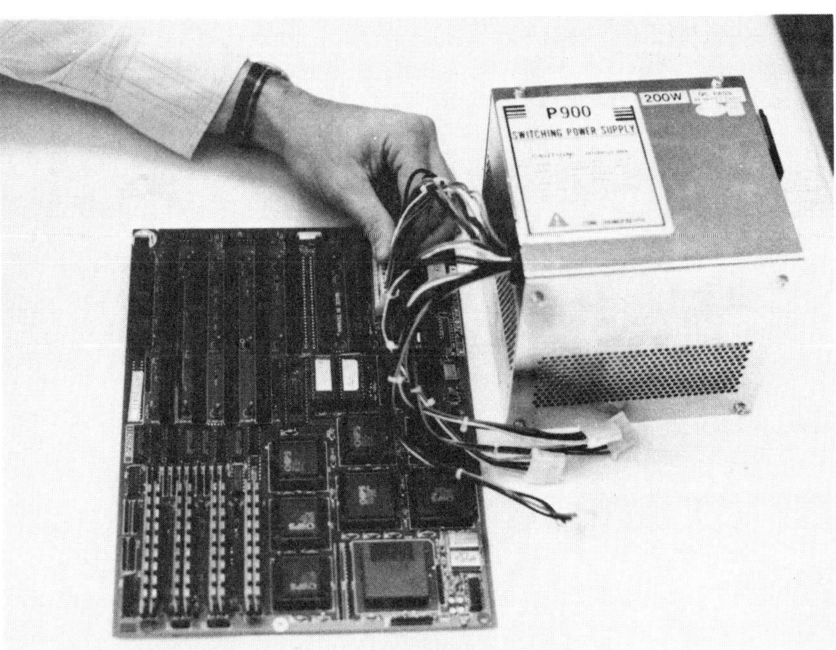

Fig. 4-4. Connecting the power supply to the motherboard for a bench-top test before installation in the case.

Fig. 4-5. Showing the correct installation of the power cables with the four black wires in the center.

Fig. 4-6. A combination hard and floppy drive controller card with all cables connected. On most boards, the floppy cable will be connected to the pins nearest the rear of the board.

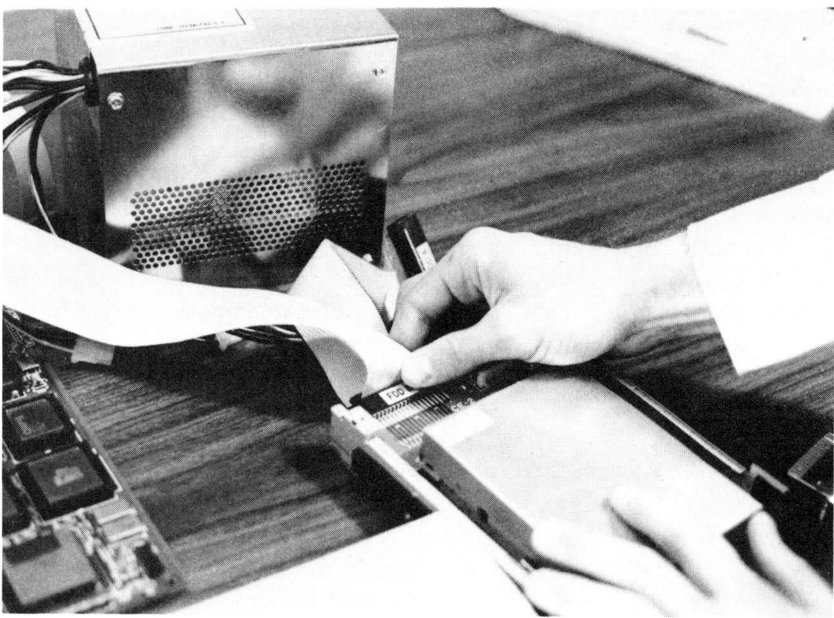

Fig. 4-7. Connecting a 3.5-inch, 1.44M drive to the board. It will be drive B, so it attaches to the connector in the middle of the cable. Make sure the colored wire on the cable goes to pin one.

Fig. 4-8. Connecting the power cable to floppy drive B.

power cable being connected to the 3.5-inch floppy. It can only be plugged in one way.

Figure 4-9 shows the ribbon cable for floppy drive A being connected. I know this connector goes to the A drive because it has the twist in the end of the cable. Make sure that the colored wire goes to the side of the edge connector marked 1 or 2. Figure 4-10 shows the connection of the power cable to the A drive.

Figure 4-11 shows the connections to a hard disk. It will have three cables, a 34-wire ribbon cable, a 20-wire cable, and the power cable. The 34-wire cable also has a colored wire that indicates pin one. Look for an etching of pin 1 or 2 on the hard disk controller board. If it is possible to add a second hard disk drive, there will be a second connector in the middle of the cable. The connector for the hard disk does not have a twist as with the connector for floppy drive A. Figure 4-12 shows the 20-wire ribbon data cable with the colored wire on the pin one side. Look for a 1 or 2 on the edge connector and plug the ribbon connector in to match it. If there is a second hard disk installed, it will be connected to the middle connector of the cable. The second hard disk will also have a separate 20-wire ribbon cable running from the row of pins nearest the front of the controller board. Figure 4-13 shows power connection to the hard disk. Figure 4-14 shows all the components connected and read, to fire up for a burn-in.

Fig. 4-9. Connecting a 1.2M floppy as drive A. Note that cable has the split and twist on this end connector. The colored lead should go to pin one.

Fig. 4-10. Connecting the power cable to the 1.2M floppy.

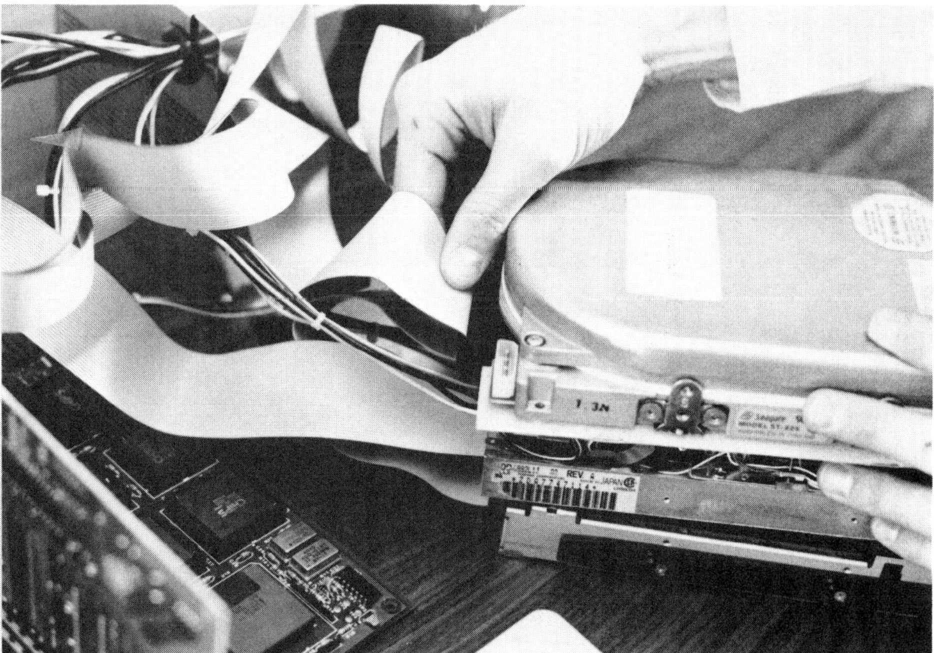

Fig. 4-11. Connecting the controller cable to the hard disk. The colored wire goes to pin one.

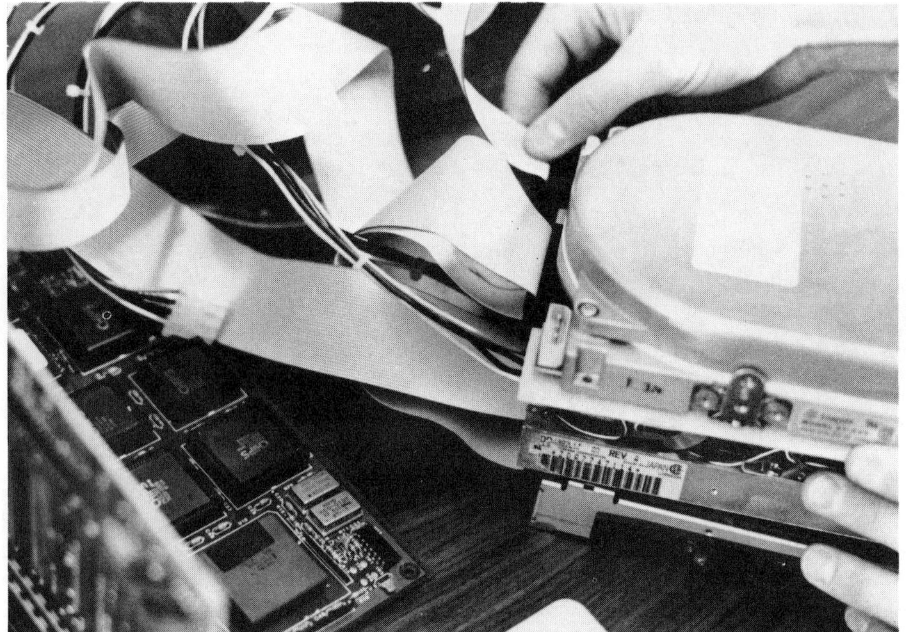

Fig. 4-12. Connecting the data cable to the hard drive. The colored wire should go to pin one.

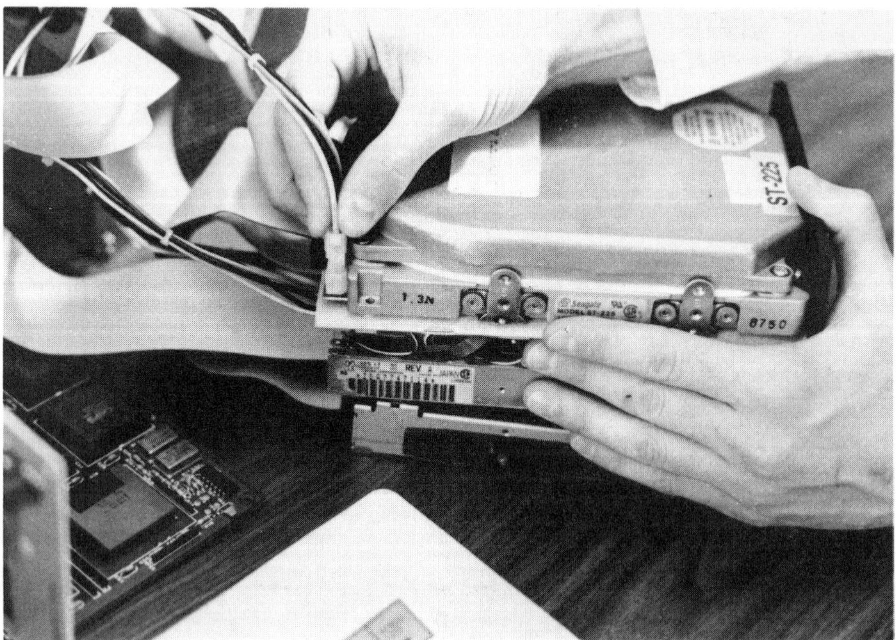

Fig. 4-13. Connecting the power cable to the hard drive.

Fig. 4-14. All components are connected, ready for burn-in.

The completed system worked like a charm, so I installed it back in the case as shown in Fig. 4-15. The owner had a good 20M hard disk and an original IBM full height 360K floppy drive. He decided to keep these drives, at least for the present.

Note that the IBM logo is also still in place. Although it is no longer an IBM, the owner wouldn't give up the logo. He works in a large office where there are several other IBM XTs. He didn't tell anyone about the update. On the outside, the microcomputer looked like all of the others, just a mild mannered XT, much like Clark Kent. But on the inside it was a ''supercomputer.'' Often people would come by to use his computer. He got an enormous kick out of watching their reactions when they first tried it. He said that the reactions alone were almost worth the price of the update.

In its previous form, as an IBM PC-XT, the computer operated at 4.77 MHz, was limited to 640K of RAM, and had all the other limitations of the older technology. But now it can process data four times faster, 32 bits at a time, can address up to 64 terabytes of memory, and can do multitasking and allow multiusers. The 386 boards have built-in clocks, and most of them have several built-in ports for printers, modems, and a mouse. This not only can save the cost of buying boards for these functions, it also saves having to use one of the precious slots. The 386 boards are capable of all the other outstanding things the 386 can do.

(The components for the assembly photos were furnished by Liuski International, (818) 912-8313).

Fig. 4-15. It may look like a mild mannered IBM XT on the outside, but inside it is a "super-computer".

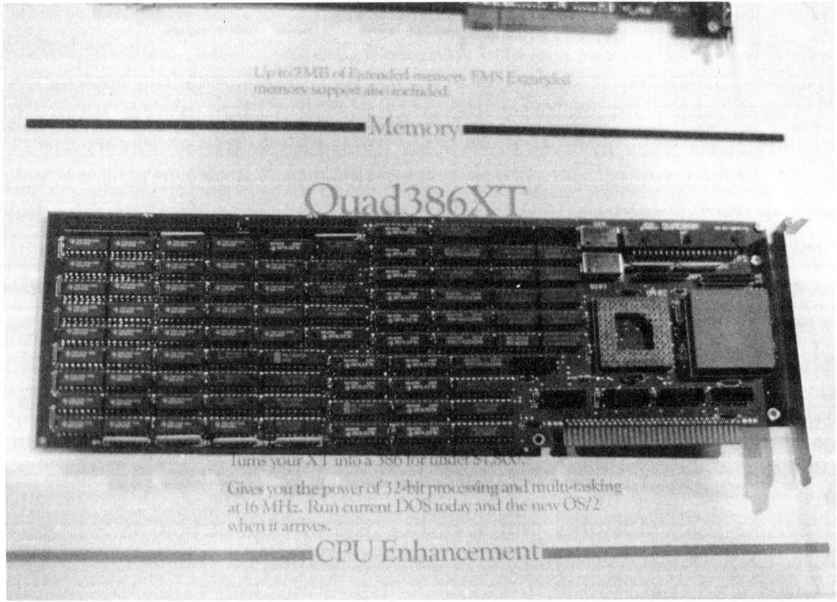

Fig. 4-16. Quad 386XT accelerator board. This is a fairly inexpensive way to realize many of the benefits of the 386.

BUILDING FROM SCRATCH

You might want to build one of these baby 386s from the beginning. They have the same performance characteristics of the larger standard size. In fact, they are better than their larger brother in several respects. They have a smaller footprint, so they take up less desk space. Because of the VLSI integration on board, there is less chance of individual chip failures. Again, the most expensive item will be the motherboard.

The other components such as the disk drives, plug-in boards, monitors, and other peripherals would be the same as for the standard size AT or the XT. Look at the advertisements in the magazines suggested in Chapter 16, and you will see that there is an abundance of components available at very reasonable prices.

There is a wide variation in the cost of the baby 386 motherboards. I have seen some advertised for as little as $1200 and some for as much as $1700. You may not get any memory with the advertised price of the motherboard. Many will list 0K in the specifications, indicating that they have zero K of memory.

During the summer of 1987, I bought one megabyte of 120-nanosecond memory on 256K chips. It takes nine 256K chips to make 256K of memory, so it takes 36 chips to make one megabyte. I paid $2.50 for each chip, so it cost me a total of $90. Those same DRAM chips today cost about $10 each at the lowest discount prices. That means that a megabyte of memory costs $360 today. Some have blamed the high cost on the tariffs placed on the overseas products. Others claim that IBM, Compaq, and some of the other large companies have bought up all the available stock and created a shortage. At one time the memory was free with the cost of the board. Now you may have to pay more for the memory than for the board.

ACCELERATOR BOARDS

There are several companies who are making plug-in boards that can essentially turn a PC or XT into a 386 machine. In some cases, this is the least expensive way to go. These boards cost from $995 up to $1995. Some of the boards replace the 8088 CPU in the XT by plugging a cable into the CPU socket. The 386 board then plugs into one of the XT slots. The XT then becomes a 386 for most applications.

One drawback to this approach is that the XT motherboard has only 8 bit memory slots. There are some add-on boards that have been developed for the 286 and the 386 that you will not be able to use. But you will be able to process large spreadsheets, CAD programs, and other CPU intensive programs at the speed of a standard 386.

The Intel Inboard 386/PC lists for $995. But I have seen advertisements from discount houses offering it for as little as $795. Intel also makes the

Table 4-1. Sources for Boards.

Company	Telephone No.	Board Name	Cost
PC AND XT BOARDS			
Applied Reasoning	(617) 492-0700	PC Elevator 386	$1995
Intel Corp.	(800) 538-3373	Inboard 386/PC	995
QuadRam	(404) 923-6666	Quad 386XT	995
AT ACCELERATOR BOARDS			
American Computer	(714) 545-2004	386 Turbo	$1199
Aox, Inc.	(617) 890-4402	Master386	1595
AST Research	(714) 863-1333	Prem. Fastbd.386	1995
Cheetah International	(800) 243-3824	CAT386	1495
Intel Corp.	(800) 538-3373	Inboard 386	1595
Orchid Tech.	(415) 683-0300	Jet 386	1299
PC Technologies	(800) 821-3086	386 Express	995
Seattle Telecom	(206) 820-1873	STD-386	1995

Inboard 386 board for the AT. It lists for $1595. According to a product comparison in the January 11, 1988 *InfoWorld*, the Inboard 386/PC outperformed the more expensive Inboard 386 for the AT in some tests. I called Intel and inquired about the big difference in price between the boards. An Intel spokesperson said that it was probably because the Inboard 386/PC was easier to build, so the savings were passed along to the consumer.

There are more boards available for the AT than there are for PCs and XTs. Strangely, almost all of the AT boards are much more expensive than the ones for the PCs and XTs. Considering the price of most of these boards and the limitations of an accelerator board, you could probably replace the motherboard in an AT for less money. This approach will also give you much more versatility and true 32-bit processing.

If you think an accelerator can satisfy your needs, you can call the companies listed in Table 4-1. No matter how you do it, if you move up to the 386 world you will find that the added speed, power and versatility of the 386 is well worth it.

Chapter 5

Floppy Disk Drives

Disk drives are among the most important components of your new system. You have probably heard the terms, PC-DOS or MS-DOS many times. DOS is an acronym for *Disk Operating System.* PC is a term adopted by IBM for Personal Computer. MS are the initials of the Microsoft Corporation who developed the disk operating system for IBM.

THE NEW STANDARD

IBM created a new 3.5-inch floppy disk standard with the introduction of the PS/2 systems. The 3.5-inch drives have several features that will hasten their acceptance. The 3.5-inch diskettes will store two to four times the data of conventional 5.25-inch diskettes in a smaller space. They have a hard plastic protective shell, so they are not easily damaged. They also have a spring loaded shutter that automatically covers the head opening when they are not in use.

Another feature is the write-protect system. A plastic slide can be moved to open or close a small square hole in the shell. When the slide covers the opening, the disk is write enabled, and when open, it is write protected. This method is opposite the 5.25-inch write protect system. If the square notch on the 5.25-inch system is left uncovered, a light can shine through, allowing the disk to be written to or erased. If the notch is covered, it can only be read. Most 3.5-inch diskettes come with a label that, when taped to the diskette, indicates which position allows write enable and write protect. The slide can best be moved with a ball point pen.

OLD STANDARD STILL ALIVE

There are about 15 million 5.25-inch disk drives installed in PCs, XTs, and ATs. There are about one million 386 machines that have 5.25-inch drives. There are many millions of 5.25-inch diskettes that are filled with programs and data. I have about 500 diskettes that are filled with data.

Considering this large base, many people are not overly anxious to adopt the new 3.5-inch standard. There are several reasons to stay with the old 5.25-inch standard. One reason is that the diskettes are very reasonably priced. The 3.5-inch 720K diskettes sell from $1 to $5 each. The 1.44M diskettes sell for $4.50 to $15 each. There are going to be some problems with the new standard. For one thing, most software vendors supply their programs on 5.25-inch diskettes. The larger companies offer both sizes, but it will be some time before all companies can do it.

The 5.25-inch disk drives are also inexpensive. I have bought new 360K drives for $50 each. Of course, some brand name drives still cost as much as $150, but I am not sure they are that much better than the low cost units.

THE BEST OF BOTH WORLDS

The best of both worlds is a 3.5-inch drive and a 1.2M drive. The 3.5-inch can read and write the 720K and 1.44M formats. Most of the 1.2M drives can also read and write to the 360K format. I have had no trouble with my Toshiba, but some drives have trouble formatting a diskette to 360K. If at all possible, it might be worthwhile to keep a $50 360K drive around. It could possibly be hooked up externally for formatting only. You could format a couple of hundred diskettes, then use them as needed.

FLOPPY CONTROLLERS

There are not too many stand-alone floppy controllers. Western Digital and Adaptec have combination controllers that work great with hard disks, 1.2M and 3.5-inch drives. But many of the RLL and ADRT controllers, such as the Perstor that I am using, do not have the floppy capability.

The older PC and XT controllers will work in a 286 or 386 to control 360K drives, but they cannot control 1.2M or 1.44M drives. The reason is that the older controllers had a transfer rate of only 250 kHz. The new controllers have a rate of 500 kHz.

The Micro Sense Company at (800) 544-4252, or (619) 589-1816 in California, has a controller that they claim is one of the most versatile on the market. I have not had a chance to personally evaluate it, but I

Fig. 5-1. A 5.25-inch drive with a 3.5-inch drive that has not had adapters installed.

have heard from people who have. It is supposed to work with PCs, XTs, ATs or 386s. It will support up to four floppy drives of any combination. It costs $150, which seems reasonable, considering its versatility. The Micro Sense Company also sells the Perstor controllers and several other controllers and floppy disks.

MOUNTING A 3.5-INCH DRIVE

Figure 5-1 shows a 3.5-inch floppy without extenders sitting in a drive opening below a 5.25-inch drive. Figure 5-2 shows the 3.5-inch drive with the extenders and adapters alongside the 5.25-inch floppy. There are special extender frames that fit around the 3.5-inch drives that allow them to be mounted in the standard 5.25-inch openings.

HOW FLOPPY DISK DRIVES OPERATE

The operation of the 3.5-inch and the 5.25-inch systems are basically the same. The floppy drive spins a diskette much like a record player. The floppy diskette is made from a type of plastic that is coated with a magnetic material very similar to the tape that is used in cassette tape recorders. It uses a head that records (writes) or plays back (reads) the

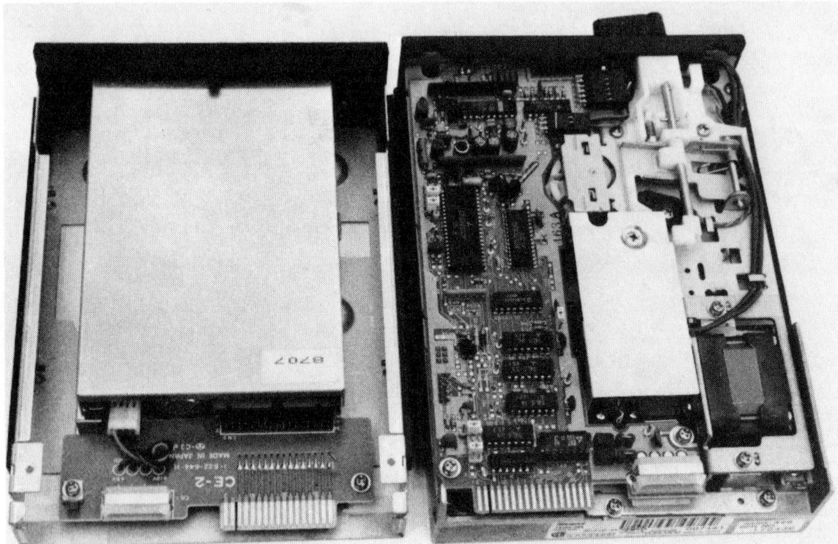

Fig. 5-2. A 3.5-inch floppy that has been mounted in the adapter kit alongside a 5.25-inch drive.

diskette much like the record/playback head in a cassette recorder. When the head writes or records on the magnetic surface, a pulse of electricity causes the head to magnetize that portion of track beneath the head. A spot on the track that is magnetized can represent a 1; if the next spot of the same track is not magnetized, it can represent a 0. So when the tracks are played back, or read, the head detects whether each portion of the track is magnetized or not and outputs a series of 1s and 0s accordingly.

A single 1 or a 0 is a *bit*. It takes eight bits to make one *byte*. It usually requires one byte to form a single character, letter of the alphabet, or a single number. Any letter, number, or symbol found on a keyboard can be formed with just 128 different eight-bit combinations of 1s and 0s. This is called the *American Standard Code for Information Interchange*, or ASCII. An extended system uses an additional 128 different eight-bit combinations for graphics and other special needs. If you have ever tried to look at a program in machine language, you may have seen some of these symbols, which include happy faces, playing cards, musical notes, and several other odd characters.

It is obvious that the speed of the disk drive and the length of time that a pulse is applied will be a factor in the amount of data that can be recorded. Most of the 5.25-inch floppy drives rotate at 300 RPM. The high-density 1.2M rotates at 360 RPM and the 3.5-inch drives operate at 600 RPM. Hard disks rotate at 3600 RPM. The speed is critical and should be regulated fairly close.

NEED FOR FORMATTING

Before a diskette or a hard disk can be used, it must be formatted. The format command partitions the diskette into *tracks* and *sectors.* The tracks on a floppy diskette are quite different than those on phonograph record. There is only one long continuous track on a phonograph record starting from the outer edge and ending at the center. But a formatted floppy diskette might have 40 or more individual concentric tracks on each side. A hard disk may have as many as 1000 or more individual tracks per inch (TPI).

During formatting, the tracks are numbered and divided into sectors, which are also numbered. With this system, a unique address can be assigned to any one of millions of bytes of data stored on the disk or diskette. This is similar to the layout of streets and house numbers in a city. Just as the postman can find any address in the city, the heads can quickly move to any track and sector on the diskette.

While formatting, the system checks for bad sectors or any faults in the thickness or deposition of the magnetic media. If it finds a bad sector, it will lock it out so that the diskette can still be used. Most diskettes will have no bad sectors. The hard disk surface is much more critical, and almost all of them have a few imperfections that are locked out.

The amount of data that can be placed on a diskette depends on the format, the number of tracks, the number of sectors on each track, and the *coercivity* of the magnetic media. The coercivity of the media is measured in *Oersteds* (OE). The higher density diskettes such as the 1.2M and the 1.44M have a bit of cobalt added to the media to raise the coercivity to 600 OE. The heads can usually detect the density of the diskette.

If you look at the head slot, you will see that there is only a little over one inch of usable space on a 5.25-inch diskette. On a 360K diskette, 40 tracks can be recorded on each side through the head slots. Each of the 40 tracks are divided into 9 sectors, and 512 bytes can be stored in each sector. (40 × 9 × 512 = 184320 bytes × 2 sides = 368640 bytes. Actually, only 362496 bytes are available. The other 6144 bytes are used by the disk for utilities.)

The 1.2M 5.25-inch high-density floppy diskette looks very much like the 360K floppy, but it has a different magnetic media that allows 80 tracks to be recorded on it with 15 sectors per track. The 3.5-inch diskette has an opening of less than one inch for the head slots, but it records 80 tracks on each side of the diskette. The format of the standard density 3.5-inch diskette divides each of the 80 tracks into 9 sectors with 512 bytes in each sector. Since it has twice the number of tracks that the 360K has, the amount of data that can be stored on this diskette is doubled to 720K. The high-density 3.5-inch diskettes will also format to 80 tracks on each

Table 5-1. Capacities of Various Drive Types

DRIVE TYPE	TRACKS PER SIDE	SECTORS/ TRACK	FORMATTED CAPACITY	SYSTEM USE	AVAILABLE TO USER	MAXIMUM DIRS.
360K	40	9	368640	6144	362496	112
1.2M	80	15	14898	1228800	1213952	224
3.5	80	9	12800	737280	724480	224
3.5	80	18	16896	1474560	1457664	224

side. But each track is divided into 18 sectors with 512 bytes in each sector. Doubling the number of sectors allows 1.44M to be stored on a single diskette. (Refer to Table 5-1.)

FORMATTING

Assuming that the 1.2M is the A drive, to format a 360K diskette with the 1.2M drive, type FORMAT A: /4. To format to 1.2M, you need the high-density diskettes. The drive will check the media and give an error message if you try to format a 360K disk at the higher density. If the system is configured and the controller allows it, you only have to type FORMAT A:.

To format a 720K diskette on a 1.44M, type FORMAT B: /T:80 /N:9. To format a 1.44M diskette, just type FORMAT B: or you might have to type FORMAT B: /T:80 /N:18. Again, the drive checks the media and will not format a low-density diskette to the high density.

FILE ALLOCATION TABLE

Notice that a certain amount of space is set aside for system use in Table 5-1. Part of this space is used for the *File Allocation Table* or FAT. The FAT is similar to the table of contents of a book. Anytime that a file is recorded, updated, or erased, the head first moves to the FAT and records the activity there.

Without the FAT, there would be no way for heads to find the data on the disk. It is so critical that a second section is set aside to back up the first section in case it becomes damaged or unreadable. Figure 5-3 shows four 3.5-inch diskettes. The upper two that are marked MFD2HD (Micro Floppy Diskette, the 2 means double sided, the HD is for High-Density) are high density. The two in the lower part of the photo are low-density diskettes. The one on the left is marked MFD-2DD (Micro Floppy Diskette, 2 sided, Double Density). Note that the one on the right has no markings at all. Note the arrows at the left top portion of the diskettes which indicate how they should be inserted into the drive. Because of

Fig. 5-3. 3.5-inch floppy diskettes. The two on the top are high-density 1.44M diskettes. The two lower ones are double density or 720K.

their design, they cannot be completely inserted into a drive upside down or backwards, so no damage can be done.

Figure 5-4 shows the reverse side of the diskettes. Note that the two on the left have the slide switch for the write protect/enable set to enable, and the two on the right to protect. In order to show the head openings on the two on the right, I have taped the spring loaded shutters so that they remain open.

Fig. 5-4. The back side of the diskettes. Note the metal hub. The diskettte on the top right has the cover pulled open to show the head opening. The diskettes on the right have the holes in the lower right corner open for write enable; the two on the left are open for write protect.

TRACKING ACCURACY

Though only 40 tracks are laid down on the 5.25-inch floppy, they are laid down at a rate of 48 tracks per inch (TPI). So the width of each track is one inch divided by 48, or .0208 inches. The 1.2M high-density 5.25-inch diskettes have 80 tracks laid down at a rate of 96 TPI. The width of each track is 1 divided by 96, or .0104 inches. The 3.5-inch diskettes have 80 tracks laid down at a rate of 135 TPI. The width of each of their tracks is 1 divided by 135, or .0074 inches.

When a 5.25-inch diskette is inserted into a drive, it is placed over a conical spindle. The center of the floppy has a reinforcing plastic hub ring, but the plastic does not allow for a very accurate placement of the diskette. It isn't too much of a problem because of the wider spacing of the tracks on the 5.25-inch diskettes. However, they may become worn or damaged with repeated use. In this case, the heads may not be able to read the diskette. If you are unable to read the diskette, it may help to remove it and reinsert it.

The heads can also become misaligned. They would have to be realigned by a service shop using very sophisticated equipment. Since service shops charge from $50 an hour, it might be less expensive to buy a new drive. Because of the closer tracks on the 3.5-inch diskettes, a tighter tolerance must be maintained. To accomplish this, a metal hub is bonded to the diskette. The spindle of the drive engages the small square hole and maintains a very accurate placement of the diskettes. The 5.25-inch diskettes have a hole near their center so that a light can shine through it to determine the beginning of the first sector. The 3.5-inch diskettes use the rectangular square hole in the metal hub for this purpose.

Many of the early disk drives had only a single head and recorded on one side of the diskette only. Most all of the drives today have two heads, one for each side of the floppy diskette. Both heads are controlled by a single positioner and move as a single unit. If track 1 is being read on the top side, the bottom head is over track 1 on the bottom side. The positioner moves the heads to whatever track or sector needs to be written to or read from.

CYLINDERS

If you could strip all the other tracks away from track 1 on the top and bottom of the diskette, the resulting shape could be likened to a cylinder. It is very easy and fast to electronically switch from the head on the top at track 1 to the head on the bottom at track 1. So, when a file is written, track 1 will be written on the top side. Rather than move the head, it is much faster to electronically switch to the bottom head, so the file will continue to be written on track 1 on the bottom side. DOS calls the top side 0, and the bottom side 1. The standard 360K diskette has

40 tracks on each side, so it has 40 cylinders. Of course the 3.5-inch 80 track diskettes have 80 cylinders.

CLUSTERS

Since 512 bytes is rather small, DOS treats two or more sectors on a track as a single unit called a cluster. For instance, if a 3K file is recorded on a floppy, 1024 bytes might be written in sectors 5 and 6 of track 1. If the next cluster on track 1 already has data in it, the system will check the FAT for the next empty cluster, which might be on track 20. The 1024 bytes will be written in it, and the locations of all the various parts of the file will be written in the File Allocation Table.

Since the FAT keeps track of where each part of every file is placed, we can add onto an existing file, modify it, or erase a portion of it. The data can be anywhere on the diskette and the head will still find it. Two different files or parts of two different files cannot be written in the same cluster. A 1K file will require one whole cluster of 1024 bytes. If a file had only two bytes, it would also require a whole cluster of 1024 bytes of its own. If a file has between 1025 bytes and 2048 bytes, it will require two clusters.

DIRECTORY LIMITATIONS

DOS sets aside only a certain amount of space for the number of files that can be held in a directory of a floppy (refer to Table 5-1). For a 360K diskette it is 112, for any of the 80 track diskettes, the maximum number is 224.

But it is possible to put many more files on a diskette than the listed number. I keep a copy of all my letters. Most of them are very short, only one page long. I have over 500 on my hard disk. When I tried to copy them to a 1.44M 3.5-inch diskette, I got a file creation error message after number 224 was recorded. When I did a disk check of the floppy, it showed that there was over 600K of empty space on the diskette. I erased all of the files, then created two separate directories on the diskette and was easily able to copy all 500 of my letters.

Multiple directories can be created on a diskette in the same manner as on a hard disk. At the B> prompt, I simply typed MD OLDLTRS. The MD is the command for Make Directory. I then made a second directory called NEWLTRS. I then used XTREE to sort my letters by date extension, tagged them, and copied them to the appropriate directory on the floppy.

VERY HIGH-DENSITY FLOPPY DRIVES

Kodak, Konica, 3M, and several Japanese companies are now manufacturing very high-density 5.25-inch drives. These drives can format a diskette with several densities from 3.3M up to 12M. Most of the drives can read the lower density formats of 1.2M and 360K.

Some of the Kodak drives use standard 5.25-inch 600 Oersted diskettes which are relatively inexpensive. The Kodak 12M floppy actually formats to 9.9M. The disk is encased in a hard shell and has a protective sliding door much like the shell of the 3.5-inch diskette. This diskette is fairly expensive, about $50 each. The prices of the Kodak high-density floppy disk drives range from $600 to $1200.

Konica

The Konica drive uses a 600 OE diskette that is similar to the type used on the 1.2M drives, but it formats to 480 tracks per inch and 10.9M of data can be stored on one diskette. A servo signal is embedded on each track of the diskette at the factory. This servo data is then used in a closed loop system to position the heads over the very narrow tracks. The diskettes will sell for about $18 each.

The drives rotate at 600 RPM rather than the 300 RPM of the standard 360K drives. The higher rotation contributes to the higher density recording. The drive has a built-in SCSI interface and controller. But an adapter card must be used on IBM and compatible computers. The drive will sell in large quantities for about $400. Of course, you, the end user, will have to pay a bit more. At least in the beginning.

This appears to be an excellent technology. Had it not been for the introduction of the IBM 3.5-inch 1.44M floppy, this 10M 5.25-inch drive might well have been the new standard. But even if it does not become a standard, it has many great advantages and will be quite useful to many individuals and companies.

The Bernoulli Box

The IOMEGA Company has a high-density floppy that can store up to 20M on a removable cartridge. On most floppy systems, the head directly contacts the diskette. The heads on the IOMEGA system hover microinches above the diskette similar to the heads on a hard disk. (Anyone who has ever taken a physics course is probably familiar with Bernoulli's Principle of aerodynamics. This principle explains how an airplane can fly.) The Bernoulli drives spin at 1820 RPM, approximately half the speed of a hard disk.

The IOMEGA company applied the Bernoulli principle to the heads in their box, thus the name. The Bernoulli Box is a good system, but it is rather expensive compared to other alternatives. I have seen advertisements from some companies who charge $1795 for a 20M Bernoulli system. They charge $84 for the removable cartridges.

Advantages

The high-density diskettes and removable cartridges have several advantages over hard disks. You always have to worry about a hard disk crashing and destroying all of your data and files. You may also have to be concerned about security if there is confidential or critical data that should have limited access.

In most large business offices, several people may use the same computer from time to time. It is very easy for someone to accidentally erase or alter an important file. Unauthorized copies of files and software may also be made. It is difficult to guarantee the security and integrity of data on a hard disk in a situation like this. But a high-capacity floppy or cartridge can be removed and locked up in a secure area.

It also makes the data more transportable. A program can be developed on one computer, then the diskette or cartridge can be moved to another computer in the same room or shipped across the country. Many software programs such as Lotus 1-2-3 are copy protected. The program allows only one installation on a hard disk. If you want to use it on another computer, it must be uninstalled back onto the original master diskette and then installed on another computer. Even if the software is not copy protected, most license agreements state that the software may be used on only one computer at any time. So, if there are three or four computers in an office area with hard disks, each one should have a separate copy of any software installed on it.

It isn't often that a person would be using all of the programs on a hard disk in one session. If a person is using a computer to do something like word processing, none of the other programs on the hard disk can be used by anyone else. Thus, expensive programs could be idle much of the time.

This could cost a considerable amount of money. Unless all of the computers were using the same software programs at the same time, it might be less expensive to install high-density drives on each computer. Then install each software program on a high-density diskette so that it can be used on any computer at any time.

It is also very important that a hard disk be backed up regularly. You can use standard 360K floppy diskettes to back up a hard disk. But it could require as many as 30 floppies just to back up 10 megabytes. This type of backup can also require a considerable amount of time. One or two very high-density diskettes or removable cartridges could do the job easily and quickly on one or two diskettes.

POWER AND CONTROLLERS

All of the 5.25-inch floppy disk drives use the standard four wire connector from the power supply. But some of the new 3.5-inch drives have miniature connectors for both power and controller lines. Adapter cables are available that can be used to connect the small drives. If you buy one of the RLL or ADRT controllers for a hard disk, they may not have the capability to control floppy drives. The Adaptec ACB-2372 controller has the capability to control two RLL, 1.2M, and 1.44M drives.

It is possible to use one of the older controllers in a 386 to control a 360K drive but they can't be used with the 1.2M or the 1.44M drives. The older PC and XT floppy controllers have a data transfer rate of 250 kHz. The 1.2M and the 1.44M drives have a transfer rate of 500 kHz.

CARE OF DISKETTES

The heads actually contact the diskette, so there is some wear each time a floppy is read from or written to. They can be used several hundred times before they wear out, but you should make backups of your master diskettes and others that have important data.

I mentioned the write protect notch systems earlier. When an unprotected 5.25-inch diskette is inserted into the drive slot, a light shines through the open slot and allows the diskette to be read, written to, altered, or erased. If this notch is covered, the diskette can be read, but it cannot be written on or erased. It is important that the notch be covered with an opaque tape so that no light can get through. Some people have used clear tape to cover the write protect notch and have ruined very valuable master programs.

When you get a new piece of software, or if you have any valuable data on a diskette, you should make sure it is write protected, then make a backup copy of it. This master should then be put away so that it is safe, and you should only use the backup copy. It is very easy to hit the wrong key and write over or erase some very important data or an expensive master diskette. If the copy becomes damaged, you can always make a new backup from the master.

It is very important that the diskettes be kept clean of dirt and foreign substances. You should be careful not to touch the diskette through the open slot. Oils from fingerprints can destroy data. You should also be careful not to allow any magnetic objects near your diskettes.

If you are traveling by air, do not allow any diskettes to be sent through the X-ray machines at the boarding gates. The X-rays will completely erase any data on your diskettes. You should remove any such diskettes from your carry-on luggage and pass them around the X-ray machine. Or, since most stowed luggage is not X-rayed, you could pack them in one of those bags.

SUMMARY

I would recommend that the 386 machine be equipped with a good 1.2M drive. It should be able to format, read, and write to both the 1.2M and 360K diskettes. I would also recommend that a 3.5-inch floppy drive be installed that can format, read, and write to both the 720K and the 1.44M diskettes. If the system is to be used in a business or large office, I would recommend that a 10M Konica floppy drive be installed.

SOURCES

As always, look for a computer store near you that can support you if anything goes wrong. Or try a computer swap if there are any in your area. In any case, you should be looking at the advertisements in some of the computer magazines listed in the Appendix so that you can get a good idea of what is available and the general price. If you cannot get the items locally, then mail ordering is the best choice.

Chapter 6

Hard Disks and Mass Storage

It is possible to buy a computer with just one or two floppy drives and without a hard disk. But I don't know why anyone would do such a thing. You may be able to save a few dollars by not buying a hard disk. But if your time is worth anything at all, and you do any serious computing, you will waste far more time than the cost of a hard disk. Besides, they are really not that expensive.

Incidentally, you may have seen the term *fixed disks* in IBM DOS manuals and other IBM literature. Almost everybody else in the computer world calls them hard disks. But since IBM was one of the pioneer developers of the hard disk, I suppose they can call them anything they want to.

WHY YOU NEED A HARD DISK

One of the main reasons to own a 386 is its fantastic ability to handle lots of memory. In its virtual mode it can address about 32,000 20M hard disks. If you are building a 386 for your own personal use at home, you probably won't ever need that capability. But for large businesses, companies, and factories, it is quite often necessary to be able to address large amounts of memory such as employee payroll files, customer lists, accounting, databases, spreadsheets, and maybe even the boss's golf scores.

Like the ever changing women's fashions and new car models, every day new software programs are introduced and old ones are improved. I suspect that many of the improvements are made for the same reason that soap is improved and women's fashions change so often. That is simply to sell more of their product.

Besides money, the cost of these improvements and ease of use is that the programs keep getting bigger and bigger. Many of today's user friendly software programs require more than 2 megabytes of disk space. When I got my first copy of WordStar, the entire program was on a 180K single sided diskette. WordStar Release 4 comes on six 360K diskettes. WordStar 2000 Plus, Release 3, comes on 21 diskettes.

WHAT SIZE DISK DO YOU NEED?

Just a few years ago, a 10 megabyte hard disk was sufficient. Now 20 megabytes is not enough. The more popular user friendly programs have lots of on-screen help and many menus. Some of the programs such as dBASE III Plus, WordStar 2000 Plus, Windows, and Excel, can use up the better part of 20 megabytes in a hurry. If you load in a few of these programs, you won't have much workspace left or room to install other goodies.

One of the main reasons to have a hard disk is for convenience. A few years ago, before I got my first hard disk, I often spent hours looking for a certain diskette. But with all of my files on my 78M hard disk, I can find and load any one of them in seconds with just a few keystrokes. They are no further away than the tips of my fingers.

There is an intoxicating feeling of power in knowing that you have several hundred programs at your fingertips that can pop up on your screen within milliseconds. Of course, you still need to keep the floppies as a backup just in case something happens to your hard disk. In many cases you may not ever have a need for a lot of the software that you accumulate. But there is some kind of immutable and inflexible law that decrees that if you throw something away you will almost certainly need it the next day.

There is another natural law that decrees that the requirements for disk storage will expand to fill whatever space is available. This is especially so if the computer is in an office where several people use it, or if it is used as a multiuser or server on a *Local Area Network* (LAN). I am the only one who uses my 78 megabytes of storage. But my hard disk is filling up so fast it almost seems as if those little bytes are getting together reproducing themselves.

We, the end users, are fortunate in that there is a lot of competition in the manufacturing of hard disks. Like most of the other computer components, the prices of hard disks continue to come down. You can now buy a fairly good 40 megabyte hard disk for about $350. A standard controller will cost less than $100. But if you can afford a little more, say $135 to $150 to buy a RLL controller, the 40M disk will store 60M. That is an extra 20 megabytes for about $50 more. This 60 megabytes for a total of $500 would have cost about $5000 just a few years ago. The RLL controller will control two hard disks. So you can install 120 megabytes for less than $1000. How sweet it is. More about RLL later.

HOW A HARD DISK OPERATES

Basically the hard disk is similar to the floppy. It is a spinning disk that is coated, or plated, with a magnetic media. The hard disks are also formatted similarly to the floppy. But the 360K floppy disk has only 40 tracks per inch (TPI); the hard disks may have from 300 to 2400 TPI. The 360K floppy has 9 sectors per track and uses two sectors per cluster. The hard disk may have 17 and up to 34 sectors per track and may use 4 to 16 or more sectors to form one cluster. Both floppy and hard disks store 512 bytes per sector. Another major difference is the speed of rotation. A floppy disk rotates at about 300 RPM. A hard disk rotates at 3600 RPM.

Everything that a computer does depends on precise timing. Crystals and oscillators are set up so that certain circuits perform a task at a specific time. These oscillating circuits are usually called clock circuits. The clock frequency for the standard *Modified Frequency Modulation* (MFM) method of reading and writing to a hard disk is 10 MHz per second. To write on the disk during one second, the voltage might go high for the first 1⁄10 of a second, then turn off for the next 1⁄10 of a second, then back on for a certain length of time. The track on the spinning disk is moving at a constant speed beneath the head. Blocks of data are written or read during the precise timing of the clock. Since the voltage must go plus or zero, in order to write 1s and 0s, the maximum data transfer rate is only 5 megabits per second, just half of the clock frequency. The *Run Length Limited* (RLL) system has a transfer rate 50% higher at 7.5 megabits per second. The *Enhanced Run Length Limited* (ERLL), *Small Computer Systems Interface* (SCSI), and *Enhanced Small Disk Interface* (ESDI) systems operate at 10 megabits per second.

You have probably seen representations of magnetic lines of force around a magnet. The magnetized spot on a disk track has similar lines of force. To read the data on the disk, the head is positioned over the track and the lines of force from each magnetized area cause a pulse of voltage to be induced in the head. During a precise block of time, an induced pulse of voltage can represent a 1, and the lack of a pulse can represent a 0.

The amount of magnetism that is induced on a diskette when it is recorded is very small. It must be small so that it will not affect other tracks on each side of it or affect the tracks on the other side of the thin diskette. Magnetic lines of force decrease as you move away from a magnet by the square of the distance. So the heads must be as close to the disk as possible.

The floppy disk heads actually contact the diskette. This causes some wear, but not very much because the rotation is fairly slow and the plastic diskettes have a special lubricant and are fairly slippery. But heads of the hard disk systems never touch the disk. The fragile heads and the disk would be severely damaged if they make contact at the fast speed of 3600 RPMs. The heads hover over the spinning disk, just microinches above it. The air must be filtered and pure because the smallest speck of dust or dirt can cause the head to crash.

The surface of the hard disk platters must be very smooth. Since the heads are only a few millionths of an inch away from the surface, any unevenness could cause a head crash. The hard disk platters are usually made from aluminum, which is non-magnetic, and lapped to a mirror finish. They are then coated or plated with a magnetic material.

The platters also must be very rigid so that the close distance between the head and the platter surface is maintained. You should avoid any sudden movement of the computer or any jarring while the disk is spinning because it could cause the head to crash onto the disk and damage it. Most of the newer hard disk systems automatically move the heads away from the read/write surface when the power is turned off.

Incidentally, another difference in the hard disk and the floppy is that the floppy comes on only when it is needed. Because of its mass the hard disk takes quite a while to get up to speed and to stabilize. So, it comes on whenever the computer is turned on and spins as long as the computer is on. This means that it is drawing power from the power supply all the time. This could possibly cause some problems if your system is fully loaded with boards and has a small power supply.

A hard disk system may have only 1 platter or up to as many as 10 or more. All of the platters, or disks, are stacked on a single shaft with just enough spacing between each one for the heads. Each disk has a head for the top surface and one for the bottom of each disk in the drive. All heads are controlled by the same positioner and they will all move as one. If head number one is over track one, sector one, then all the other heads will be over track one, sector one on each disk surface.

HEAD POSITIONERS

There are several different types of head positioners. Some use stepper motors to move the heads in discrete steps to position them over a certain track. Some use a worm gear or screw-type shaft that moves the heads in and out. The faster drive systems use voice coil technology similar to that used for loud speakers in Hi-Fi systems.

The voice coil of a loud speaker is made up of a coil of wire that is wound on a hollow tube which is attached to the material of the speaker cone. Permanent magnets are then placed inside the coil and around the outside. Whenever a voltage is passed through the coil of wire, it will cause magnetic lines of force to be built up around the coil. Depending on the polarity of the input voltage, these lines of magnetic flux will be either the same or opposite of the lines of force of the permanent magnets. If the polarity of the voltage, for instance a plus voltage, causes the lines of force to be the same as the permanent magnet, then they will repel each other, and the voice coil might move forward. If they are opposite, they will attract each other and the coil will move backwards. The voice coil system can move the heads quickly and smoothly to the desired track area. Most of the better and faster drives use this technology.

LOW-LEVEL FORMATTING A HARD DISK

When a hard disk comes from the factory it cannot be used until it has had an initialization, or *low-level format*, performed on it. After this procedure is done the DOS FDISK command is used to partition and high-level format the hard disk. The reason for this is that there are many options. For instance the factory wouldn't know whether the drive is to be used with a PC, a Macintosh, or a 386. Or what kind of controller the user will want. Or what interleave factor will be chosen and several other options.

The original IBM AT had a setup in ROM for hard disks. They recognized 15 different types at that time in 1984. Of course there are many more types today. Table 6-1 lists some of the types and their specifications.

The controller cards are usually designed so that they will operate with several different types of hard disks. Most have DIP switches or shorting blocks that must be set to configure it to your particular hard disk type. There is usually a manual or some sort of documentation that comes with the hard disk controller. But usually the manuals are rather difficult to understand, especially if you are a beginner.

Table 6-1. Types and Specifications for some Hard Disk Drives.

DRIVE TYPE:	1	2	3	4	5	6	7	8	9	10	11
No. Cylinders	306	615	615	940	940	615	462	733	900	820	855
No. Heads	4	4	6	8	6	4	8	5	15	3	5
Write Precomp	128	300	300	512	512	0	256	0	0	0	0
Landing Zone	305	615	615	940	940	615	511	733	901	820	855
Capacity M	10	21	32	65	49	21	32	32	117	21	37

Often the vendor who sells you the hard disk will also supply the controller. In this instance try to get him to do the low-level format for you. Or at least try to get a low-level software procedure on a diskette. I have gone through the computer books in several large book stores. Very few of the books, even those written specifically about hard disks, mention the fact that a new hard disk must be low-level formatted before it can be FDISK formatted and partitioned.

If you can't get your supplier to low-level format your drive, then you will have to use the DOS DEBUG for this procedure. Insert a diskette in Drive A: with the DEBUG command on it. At the A> prompt type DEBUG, then press the Enter key. A dash will come up. Immediately after the dash, type G=C800:5. Your screen should look like this:

```
A>DEBUG
-G=C800:5
This is a FORMAT routine. It will DESTROY any existing data on your disk!
Press <RET> if you wish to continue or <ESC> to abort . . .
```

If you press the Enter key, a list of menus will come up with the various options. One option is the interleave factor. Another is whether you want to input the bad sectors so they can be marked off. It is very difficult to manufacture a perfect hard disk. There are usually a few bad sectors and the vendor usually supplies a map of them. The formatting process will discover most of them, but it is a good idea to input them anyway. After this the low-level format will begin.

Depending on the capacity of the disk, it may take some time for it to complete. After the low-level format is done, you must then use the DOS command FDISK to partition the disk. After it has been partitioned, then a high-level format, or just plain format, must be done. With a copy of DOS in the A: drive, just type FORMAT C: /S. The /S will transfer the SYS.COMMAND or System, to C: so that it will be able to boot your computer. The SYS command occupies a special area of the disk. It is critical that you include the slash and S. If you do not, when you try to SYS C: after it has been formatted it will tell that there is insufficient space for it. You will then have to go back and reformat the disk.

If you upgrade from DOS 2.1 to 3.2 or 3.3, you will also have to reformat your disk. DOS 3.2 and 3.3 are much bigger than 2.1 so there is not enough space for SYS in the reserved area. DOS 3.3 can be installed over 3.2 with no problem.

INTERLEAVE

With the hard disk spinning at 3600 RPMs, data can be read much faster than the electronics can assemble, transmit, and process it. Suppose a request is sent out to read sectors one, two, and three of track 20. The head quickly moves to track 20 and reads sector one, sends the data through the interfaces, connectors, and cables and processes it. By the time sector one is read and digested, sector two has been passed over and the disk has already moved to where the head is over sector six. The disk must then complete the revolution so that the head can read sector two. By the time it has finished reading, sending, and processing the data from sector two, the disk has again passed over sector three and has spun around to where it is over sector seven. Again, the disk must make a complete revolution to get back to where it can read sector three. In this instance, the disk must make three revolutions just to read three small sectors.

One of the things that the low level format does is to set up an interleave system so that the consecutively numbered sectors on a track will be under the head when the computer is ready for the data. In a six to one interleave, sector one is formatted, then five sectors are skipped then sector two is formatted. Five more sectors are skipped before sector three is formatted. The formatting continues around the track, filling in every sixth sector. (See Fig. 6-1.) Note that the outer track in this drawing is set up for an interleave of 1 to 1. Each sector is numbered consecutively. The middle track is set up for 3 to 1 interleave. It begins with sector 1, then 7, then 13, then 2. The inner track is set for 4 to 1. It starts with sector 1, then 14, 10, 6 then sector 2.

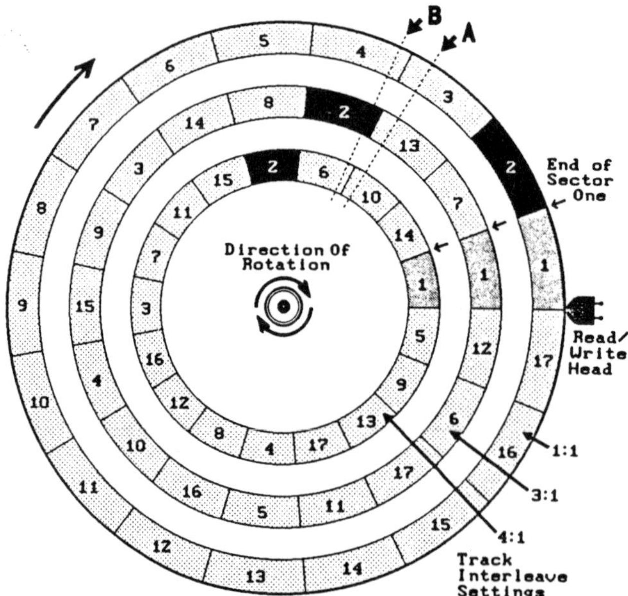

Fig. 6-1. Showing various interleave settings on a hard drive. (Drawing courtesy of Gibson Research).

The interleave factor can be as high as 6 to 1, or even higher in the early PCs and XTs. Some of the newer drives and controllers have made it possible to cut the interleave factor down to as little as 3 to 1. Some even achieve 1 to 1 or direct reading of the disk sectors. Of course the smaller interleave is an indication of a faster drive.

Steve Gibson, a columnist for the *InfoWorld* computer magazine, has developed a software program that will check the interleave factor on a hard disk. We usually don't know what the optimum interleave factor is. We can only go by the vendor's recommendation. But again, there are many options and what is ideal for one option might be only marginal for another. Because it is so difficult to change, once it is set during low-level format, it is seldom ever changed. If the interleave is set too high or too low, your disk will not operate at its fastest capability. Steve's SpinRite program will try various interleaves on a few tracks, then check and report the setting that yields the maximum transfer rate. This software is very valuable in selecting the optimum interleave factor during the original formatting.

Ordinarily, to change the interleave factor, the disk must be backed up, and the entire disk must be reformatted. But Steve's software reads a few tracks into memory, reformats those tracks, then moves the data back, and formats the next few.

During the original low-level format, the individual sector identification headers and sector regions are created. This information is written magnetically on the disk just as other magnetic data is written. The FDISK high-level format partitions the disk, builds directory structures, and storage allocation tables. Ordinarily, the low-level format is never rewritten unless a complete reformat is done.

Over a period of time, the information in the low-level format may become weakened and difficult to read. It may be due to residual magnetism of the heads, magnetization on nearby tracks, spurious electrical spikes in power sources and several other causes. This can cause disk read failures.

Steve's SpinRite has several other valuable utilities besides the low-level reformat. It is well worth the $59 that it costs. Contact Gibson Research, Box 6024, Irvine, CA 92716, (714) 830-2200.

OTHER DISK UTILITY SOFTWARE

Another software package that is valuable is the Disk Technician from Prime Solutions. It can check the entire disk and block out marginally bad sectors. If it locates one, it moves any data that happens to be in it to a safe sector. It also has several other very valuable utilities that help prevent failures and help to recover data after a failure. Contact Prime Solutions, 1940 Garnet Ave., San Diego, CA 92109, (619) 274-5000. List price is $99.

Mace Utilities is an excellent program for keeping an eye on your hard disk. Paul Mace was one of the pioneers in developing programs of this sort. Like the others, Mace Utilities can detect and mark out suspect sectors. It also has some very valuable utilities such as diagnose, UnFormat, UnDelete, UnFragment and several others. Contact Paul Mace Software, 400 Williamson Way, Ashland, OR 97520, (503) 488-0224. List price is $99.

Of course, no one should be without Norton's Utilities. Norton was one of the first to develop software to recover erased files. I am like a lot of other people. I have accidentally hit the wrong key and wiped out data that represented months of work. But with Norton's Utilities, I have been able to recover most of it. Again, the program has several very valuable utilities. Contact Peter Norton, 2210 Wilshire Blvd., #186, Santa Monica, CA 90403, (213) 826-8032.

THE 32 MEGABYTE HARD DISK LIMIT

DOS 3.2 and earlier versions have a limit of 32 megabytes that they can address on a hard disk. The 32 megabyte limit is due to the fact that DOS numbers each 512 byte sector sequentially and stores it as a 16-bit integer. Two taken to the 16th power (2^{16}) is 65,536, or 64K, of different 16-bit numbers. So DOS can only handle 65,536 sectors. If we multiply this number by the 512 bytes in each sector, it gives a total of 33,554,432 bytes or, rounded off, 32 megabytes.

DOS 3.3 allows you to use larger disks. After the low-level format is completed, the FDISK command must be invoked. A menu will come up like this:

```
IBM Personal Computer
Fixed Disk Setup Program Version 3.30
© Copyright IBM Corp. 1983, 1987

FDISK Options
Current Fixed Disk Drive: 1
Choose one of the following:
1. Create DOS partition
2. Change Active Partition
3. Delete DOS partition
4. Display Partition Information
Enter choice: [1]
Press ESC to return to DOS
```

When you choose option 1, a second menu comes up:

```
Create DOS Partition
```

Current Fixed Disk Drive: 1

1. Create Primary DOS partition
2. Create Extended DOS partition

You must first create the DOS primary partition that can have up to almost 33 megabytes or anything less. You can then go back and choose option 2 to create an Extended DOS partition of up to 32 megabytes. It keeps track of the amount of space on your disk and lets you know how much is left each time you create a logical partition. You can create as many extended logical disks as you want, or until you run out of letters of the alphabet. The Extended partitions are called logical drives because they are not actually physically separated from the first drive.

The Ontrack Computer Systems publishes a software package called Disk Manager. It provides the user with the ability to create a custom logical disk structure to meet their specific requirements. It will allow a hard disk to have as many as 16 partitions. It will permit a DOS boot partition of 32M and a non-bootable partition of as large as 512M. It is often more desirable to have a small C: bootable drive then a large single drive. It is much easier to access and run some programs if the data is all on one logical drive. I am using the Disk Manager on the Hitachi 42 megabyte hard disk on my 80286 computer. It has a RLL controller from Scientific Micro Systems to give me over 66,416,640 bytes. I have it divided up with only 3.8 megabytes on the C: drive and 62.5 megabytes on a single D: drive. Seagate supplies a copy of Ontrack software with the larger capacity drives that they sell. Contact Ontrack Computer Systems, 6222 Bury Dr., Eden Prairie, MN 55344, (800) 752-1333.

MFM AND RLL

Most standard hard disk systems use the *Modified Frequency Modulation* (MFM) method. With this system, each track on the disk surface is formatted into 17 sectors, and 512 bytes can be stored in each sector. So if we multiply 512 bytes times 17 sectors we can see that 8704 bytes can be stored on each track. A typical 10 megabyte hard disk has 306 tracks on each side of its two platters for a total of 1224 tracks. So 8704 bytes per track times 1224 equals 10,653,696 bytes. If you do a CHKDSK command on one of these disks, you may only see 10,592,256 bytes because 61,440 bytes have been used for the FAT, the directory, and other utilities.

The RLL system was developed by IBM some time ago for use on large mainframe hard disks. Adaptec Corporation of Milpitas first adapted the technology so that it can be used on PC hard disk controllers (Fig. 6-2). Since that time Scientific Micro Systems of Mt. View, Western Digital, and several other companies have developed similar controllers.

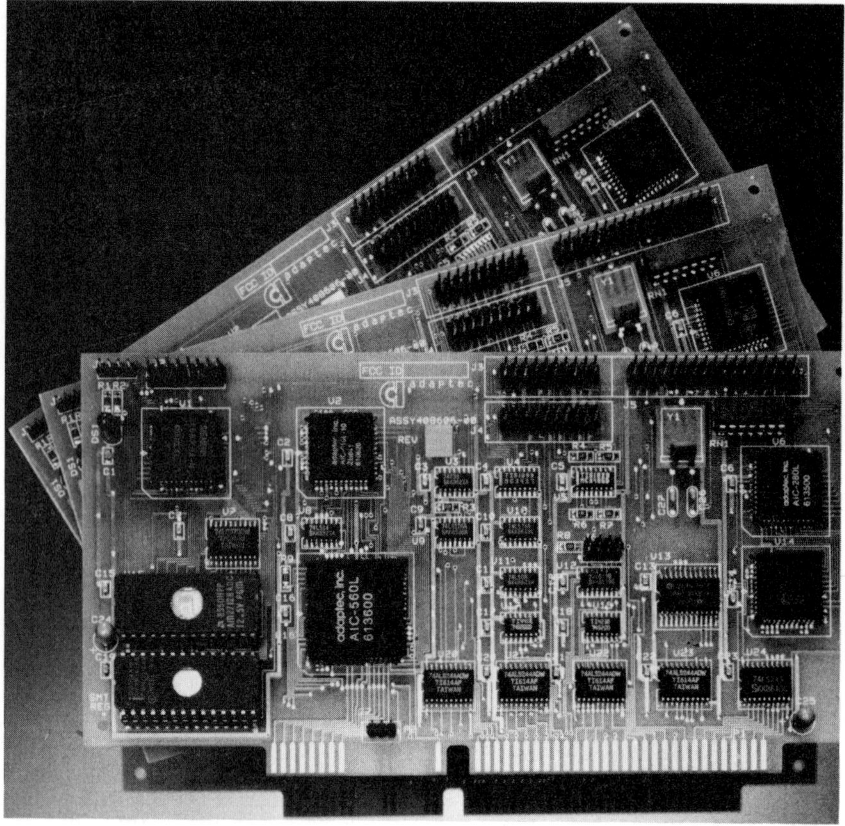

Fig. 6-2. Some of the controllers that are built by Adaptec. (Photo courtesy of Adaptec).

The main difference in the RLL and the MFM systems is that the RLL system manages to squeeze more sectors onto each track. Each sector still has only 512 bytes, but instead of the MFM's 17 sectors per track, the RLL controllers lay down 25 to 26 sectors per track. RLL is a fantastic and relatively inexpensive way to increase a hard disk's capacity. Most of the newer drives that use the thin film-plated and sputtered media will work with the RLL controllers. Many of the older drives that use oxide media and older electronics technology will not work.

The MFM encoding used on ST506/412 drives have a transfer rate of 5 megabits per second with a 100 nanosecond data window. The RLL controllers operate at a transfer rate of 7.5 megabits per second with a 66.6 nanosecond data window. In order to use the RLL controller, the disk drive and its electronics must be able to meet the higher and tighter specifications.

Fig. 6-3. The Perstor ADRT controller. Yields 78 megabytes when used with Seagate 40 megabyte hard disk.

ADVANCED DATA RECORDING TECHNOLOGY

Perstor Systems has developed controllers that will format each track of the hard disk to 33 or 34 sectors instead of the standard 17. This of course doubles the amount of data that can be stored. Perstor has tested several high capacity drives with their controller and claim that they work. They are continually testing drives to add to their list. Depending on the model and the quantity ordered, the controllers will cost from $160 to $245. If you need a lot of disk storage and don't have a lot of money, I would suggest that you investigate the RLL and ADRT controllers.

I bought a Seagate model 251-1 with 820 cylinders, 6 heads, 28 ms access time, and 40 megabytes for my 386. I bought a Perstor ADRT controller for it (Fig. 6-3). With this controller, using DOS 3.3, I have formatted the disk into two 32M disks and one 10M. Actually, I have a total of about 78 megabytes. The Perstor Company sent along an instruction booklet and software needed to do the low-level format.

The Perstor controller will control two hard disks. I paid $399 for the Seagate 40M drive which gave me 78M. So I could add a similar drive and have a total of 156 megabytes for about $1000. Most large disks with this much capacity will cost from $1500 to $4000.

I should warn you that Seagate and some of the other vendors are very conservative. They warn you that their warranty will be voided if you use one of their drives with an RLL or ADRT controller unless there is an R on the Model number, or some written notification, signifying

Table 6-2. Drives Tested by Perstor Systems (Courtesy of Perstor Systems).

MANUFACTURER	MODEL	CYLS	HEADS	ORIGINAL CAPACITY	CAPACITY W/PS180
MINISCRIBE	8425	615	4	21.4	39.0
	8438	615	4	21.4	39.0
	8425F	615	4	21.4	39.0
	8438F	615	4	21.4	39.0
	3650	809	6	42.2	77.0
	6032	1024	3	26.7	48.7
	6053	1024	5	44.6	81.0
	6079	1024	5	44.6	81.0
	6085	1024	8	71.3	130.0
	6128	1024	8	71.3	130.0
SEAGATE	*ST225	615	4	21.4	39.0
	ST238	615	4	21.4	39.0
	ST4026	615	4	21.4	39.0
	ST125	615	4	21.4	39.0
	ST251-1	820	6	42.8	78.0
	ST277	820	6	42.8	78.0
	ST4051	977	5	42.5	77.0
	ST4096	1024	9	80.2	146.0
NEWBURY DATA	NDR1065	918	7	55.9	101.0
	NDR1085	1024	8	71.3	130.0
	1140	1024	15	133.6	243.7
	2190	1224	15	159.8	291.4**
MAXTOR	1065	918	7	55.9	101.0
	1085	1024	8	71.3	130.0
	1140	1024	15	133.6	243.7
	2190	1224	15	159.8	291.4
CDC WREN 2	94155-19	697	3	18.2	33.1
	36	697	5	30.3	55.3
	38	733	5	31.9	58.1
	48	925	5	40.2	73.4
	51	989	5	43.0	78.4
	57	925	6	48.3	88.1
	67	925	7	56.3	102.7
	77	925	8	64.4	117.4
	86	925	9	72.5	132.1

NEC	D5126	615	4	21.4	39.0
	D5127	615	4	21.4	39.0
	D5146H	615	8	42.8	78.1
	D5147H	615	8	42.8	78.1
MICROSCIENCE	HH-1050	1024	5	44.6	81.0
RODIME	3055	872	6	45.0	83.0
	352	306	4	10.0	19.4
LAPINE	TITAN 20	615	4	21.4	39.0
PTI	PT225	615	4	21.4	39.0
	PT338	615	6	32.1	58.6
	PT238R	615	4	21.4	39.0
	PT357R	615	6	32.1	58.6
PRIAM	ID130	1224	15	159.8	291.0

*ONLY THE FOLLOWING SEAGATE ST255 DRIVES WORK WITH THE PS180:

- Those with revision #003 and a serial number above 1 million
- Those with revision #003B or above

** The quoted capacity is reached only when using the PS190T chip set, which is currently in beta testing. The formatted capacity when using the PS180 without the chip set is 243.7 megabytes (the chip set allows access to all 1224 cylinders of the drive).

that the drives are certified for the higher capacity. Of course they charge quite a lot more for the ones certified for RLL.

Perstor has done extensive testing on several drives. See Table 6-2 for a list of the drives they have tested up to the time of this writing. They claim that these drives operate with no problems with their controllers.

MFM controllers operate at 5 megabits per second. The standard RLL controllers operate at 7.5 megabits per second in all phases of operation. The faster data rate tends to overstress the disk drive media and electronics in some drives. The Perstor controllers operate at 5.5 megabits during the critical write phase and at 9 megabits during the read and data transfer phase. This makes it possible to use their ADRT controllers on many drives that cannot even use RLL.

Write or call them for the latest list of drives they have tested. Contact Perstor Systems, 7631 E. Greenway, Scottsdale, AZ 85260, (602) 991-5451.

ESDI AND SCSI

ESDI (Enhanced Small Disk Interface) is a standard that allows a data transfer rate of 10 megabits per second. At the present time it is usually found only on the high end, high-capacity, expensive hard disks. The ESDI interface can only be used with a controller that implements ESDI. Adaptec has developed several ESDI controllers.

SCSI (Small Computer System Interface) is a parallel hard disk interface standard. It also permits a data transfer rate of 10 megabits per second. It also needs a special interface controller. Adaptec has also developed several SCSI hard disk controllers.

Look for the fastest access time. Ask if stated capacity is with RLL or not. Some drives are advertised at the RLL capacity, not the standard MFM capacity.

HARD CARDS

There are several companies that make plug-in hard cards. Most of them are still only 20 to 30 megabytes. Rodime has developed a 45 megabyte card by using RLL on a 3½ 30 megabyte hard disk. I would expect that several other companies will soon be offering much larger hard disks on a plug-in card.

DIAGNOSTICS DISK

When you buy a 386 motherboard, you may get a diagnostic diskette and setup disk with it. This diskette will have the routines for checking out your machine and setting it up. It is also needed to set, or reset the clock on the motherboard. The diagnostic routine asks several questions, then configures the BIOS for that configuration. This part of the BIOS is in low-power CMOS semiconductors, and they are powered by a battery pack on the back panel of the computer. So the BIOS configuration is on all the time, even when the computer is turned off. If the batteries go too low to power the BIOS, there is a large capacitor that can power it for about 15 minutes, or the time it would take to replace the batteries.

Many of the newer 386 motherboards have the setup routine on-board in ROM. This makes it much more convenient. They also have on-board batteries, but many still allow an external battery pack to also be used.

CD-ROM

The *Compact Disc Read Only Memory* industry is one of the fastest growing of all the computer peripherals. Sony, Hitachi, Phillips, JVC, Amdek, Panasonic, and several others are manufacturing the drives. These drives are all compatible and can be interfaced to a 386 with a plug-in board.

Since that time when the first stone age man picked up a charred stick from his fire and drew a picture on the cave wall, man has been searching for newer and better ways to record data. There have been several noteworthy achievements—chiseled stone, writing on clay, then on papyrus, then Gutenberg with his press and the first printed Bible. (Incidentally, according to Gary Kildall, the inventor of CP/M, Gutenberg did not print the first Bible. He started it, but it was completed by his creditors who had foreclosed on him.)

Today we have mountains of printed matter. We also have a vast amount of data on magnetic disks and optical systems. We are almost inundated in a sea of information. Each day the haystacks become magnitudes larger, and it becomes more and more difficult to find the needle. The emerging CD-ROM technology makes it a lot easier to sift through the mountains of information to find what we are looking for.

These mountains of information are going to become even larger. There are about 200 off-the-shelf CD-ROM disks available today. By 1991, there will be over 10,000 off-the-shelf disks and over one million drive systems in use.

The off-the-shelf disks available cover a wide variety of subjects such as library and bookstore reference materials, general reference, literature, and art. There are disks on business, biology, medicine, physics, and most other branches of science and technology. There are disks on law, finances, geology, geography, government, and many others. In time, there will be disks on almost any subject that is found in a large library.

Fig. 6-4. A half height CD-ROM drive. (Photo courtesy Hitachi Company).

If you are interested in CD-ROM, turn to Chapter 16 and subscribe to the *CD-ROM Review* magazine listed there.

Several companies are now manufacturing half-height CD-ROM drives similar to the one shown in Fig. 6-4. This one is built by the Hitachi Corporation, (800) 262-1502.

The High Sierra Standard

One reason for the growth of the CD-ROM industry is that most of the larger companies have cooperated to form a standard. A group met at the High Sierra Hotel in Lake Tahoe, so the standard has been named the High Sierra. Of course there are some who have not adopted the standard, but almost all of the off-the-shelf disks will run on any of the several drives available.

Microsoft, the MS-DOS people, was one of the participants in creating the High Sierra Standard. They developed a MS-DOS Extension software package that is a part of the standard. It is possible to store over 600 megabytes on a CD-ROM disk. A floppy diskette stores only 360,000 bytes. If we divide 600,000,000 by 360,000, we find that we could store the contents of over 1,666 floppy disks on a single side of a CD-ROM.

One of the first CD-ROM disks published had the 21 volumes of Grolier's Encyclopedia on it. This 21 volumes takes up less than 20% of a single side of the 12 cm disk (4.72 inches). Any significant word, phrase, or subject can be found and displayed on the monitor almost instantaneously. Searches that might take hours in the printed volumes can be done in just seconds. Microsoft Bookshelf is a popular and useful disk. It includes Roget's Thesaurus, American Heritage Dictionary, and eight other books that are essential to anyone who does any writing. Another very popular disk is one that is published by the PC-SIG Company. This disk has over 700 public domain programs on it.

CD Creation Services

Many companies have rooms full of data. This data can include items such as catalogs, sales, financial data, policies and procedures, blueprints and drawings, schedules, archival records, employee records, and other large data bases. Much of it doesn't change very often.

Often this data is stored on reels of magnetic tape. This considerably reduces the amount of storage space that paper would require. But magnetic tape is rather fragile. For long term storage, it must be kept in a controlled environment. Even then it has a shelf life of only ten years or so. Tape is also subject to damage from stray magnetic fields, accidental erasure, or unauthorized alterations. Hundreds of reels of tape can be stored on a CD-ROM disk which has an indefinite shelf life and cannot be erased or altered.

Several companies are offering services to create CD-ROM disks with private data for companies. It may cost $20,000 to $50,000 for a company to develop and have a large data base published on a CD-ROM. This depends to a large extent on how complex the data base is and the amount of indexing and cross referencing that is needed.

ERASABLE OPTICAL MEDIA

Some have criticized the CD-ROMs because they cannot be changed or erased such as the media on a hard disk. But the CD-ROM is not meant to replace the hard disk. It is meant to be a valuable adjunct to it. Besides, there is a lot of data that should not ever be changed such as archival financial data, payroll records, and many other records. If it is necessary to update or change the data on a CD-ROM, a revision can be made in as little as 24 hours.

The Tandy Company has announced that they have developed an erasable CD-ROM. They claim that it can be as easily recorded and erased as a hard disk with no degradation. They have not made many details public, and it is not expected to be available to the public until 1990. But it will certainly be a fantastic tool if it does all that they claim that it can do.

WORMS

The *Write Once Read Many* (WORM) type of laser discs are similar to the CD-ROM except that CD-ROM is read only. The WORM lets you write data with a laser onto a disc. One gigabyte or more can be written on a single disc. The data can be arranged into the desired form with a computer, stored on a hard disk, then transferred to the WORM laser system. Many have complained that the problem with WORMs is that they cannot be erased and changed like a magnetic hard disk. But as stated above, there are certain records that should not ever be changed. Besides, there is enough space on these discs that an update can be written alongside the original. When a disc is filled, just start another. It is expected that the cost of the blank discs will eventually be less than $10 each. A WORM would make a great backup medium for all of your software and files.

Chapter 7

Backup

Everyone knows that the first thing they should do when they get a new software program is to write protect the original floppies, make copies of them, then store the originals away. Every major software package has at least one warning to the user advising this. Only the copy should be used thereafter. If a copy becomes lost, damaged, or erased, then a new copy can be made from the master.

It is fairly quick and easy to make a copy of a floppy by using DISKCOPY, so most people do it. They are even more inclined to do it if they have paid three or four hundred dollars for the software. But there are some people who use a hard disk that might have thousands of dollars worth of data on it and never back it up. They are the lucky few who have not yet lost a large amount of data. You can be sure that after any of the following disasters happen to them, they will be backing up their hard disks with more zeal than a born-again Christian.

A FEW REASONS WHY YOU SHOULD BACK UP

The technology of the hard disk systems has improved tremendously over the last couple of years. But they are still mechanical devices, and as such, you can be sure that eventually they will wear out, fail, or crash.

Most hard disks are now relatively bug free. Most manufacturers quote a figure of several thousand hours *mean time before failure* (MTBF). But this figure is only an average. There is no guarantee that it won't fail in the next few minutes. Hard disks are mechanical instruments, and I am sure that you have heard the old saying that sooner or later, anything that can break down, will break down. The MTBF figures quoted by manufacturers are similar to the average life span of the U.S. male, which is about 72 years. But some males die in their first year and some live to be 90 years old.

Head Crash. In the unhappy event of a crash, depending on its severity, it is possible that some of your data can be recovered, one way or another. There are some disk repair service companies who specialize in recovering and repairing failed disks. But a failure can be frustrating, time consuming and make you feel utterly helpless. But in many instances, data that may have taken hundreds of man-hours to create may be lost forever. It could be that it is irreplaceable.

General Failure. Outside of ordinary care, there is little one can do to prevent a general failure. It could be a component on the hard disk electronics or in the controller system. Or any one of a thousand other things. Even things such as a power failure during a read/write operation can cause data corruption.

Accidental Erasure or Formatting. Sometimes a person can be busy or be distracted and make an error. It is very easy to accidentally erase an important file or even an entire hard disk. Or even format the hard disk instead of a floppy disk.

Theft and Burglary. Computers are easy to sell so they are favorite targets for burglars. It would be bad enough to lose a computer, but many computers have hard disks that are filled with data that is even more valuable than the computer.

It might even be a good idea to store your backup files in an area away from your computer so that there would be less chance of losing them in a burglary, theft, or fire. The despair of these disasters can be alleviated to some extent if the hard disk has been backed up.

Archival. Another reason to back up is for archival purposes. No matter how large the hard disk is, it will eventually fill up with data. Quite often, there will be files that are no longer used or they may only be used once in a great while. Rather than erase the files, they can be backed up and stored.

Fragmentation. After a hard disk has been used for sometime, files begin to be fragmented. The data is recorded on concentric tracks in separate sectors. If part of a file is erased or changed, some of the data may be in a sector on track 20 and another part on track 40. There may be open sectors on several tracks because portions of data have been erased. Hunting all over the disk can slow the disk down. If the disk is backed up completely, then erased, the files can be restored so that they will again be recorded in contiguous sectors.

Data Transfer. Often it is necessary to transfer a large amount of data from one hard disk on a computer to another. It is quite easy and fast to use a good backup program to accomplish this. It is easy to make several copies which can be distributed to others in the company. This method could be used to distribute data, company policies and procedures, sales figures, and other information to several people in a large office or company. The data could also be easily shipped or mailed to branch offices, customers, or to others almost anywhere.

METHODS OF BACKUP

One of the least expensive methods of backup is to use the BACKUP.COM and RESTORE.COM that comes with MS-DOS. But there is a price to pay in that it is slow, time consuming, and rather difficult to use. But it will do the job if nothing else is available. The BACKUP and RESTORE commands in DOS 3.3 have been enhanced so that they are a little easier to use.

Tape. There are several backup systems on the market. Tape backup is no doubt the easiest method. But it can be relatively expensive, $600 to over $1500 for a drive unit and $10 to $30 for the tape cartridges. Most of them require the use of a controller that is similar to the disk controller.

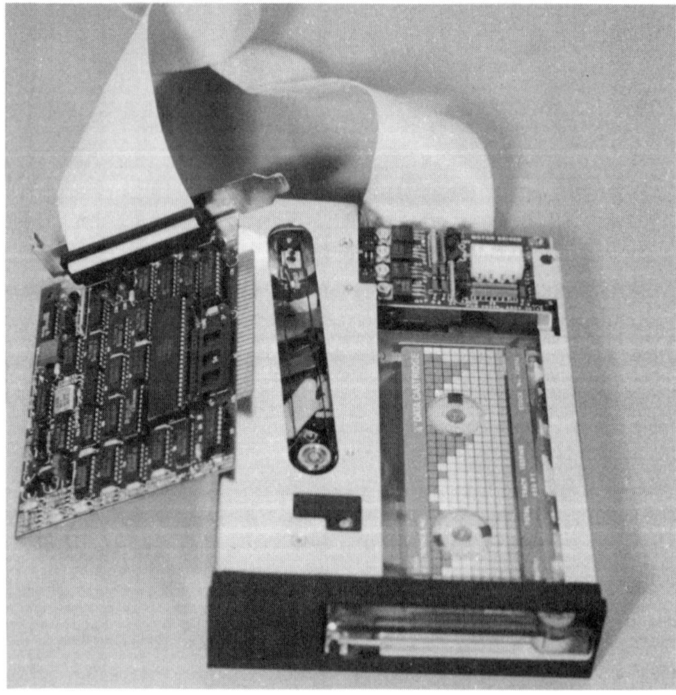

Fig. 7-1. A tape backup system.

So they will use one of your precious slots. Unless they are used externally, they will also require the use of one of the disk mounting areas. Since it is only used for backup, it will be idle most of the time. Figure 7-1 shows a backup tape and controller.

If you have several computers in an office that must be backed up every day, you could possibly install a controller in each machine with an external connector. Then one external tape drive could be used to back up each of the computers at the end of the day. With this system you would need a controller in each machine, but you would only have to buy one tape drive.

One of the biggest problems with tape is that no standards have been established for tape size, cartridges, reels, or format. Quite often a tape that is recorded on one tape machine, even from the same vendor, will not restore on another. The most common type drives use a quarter-inch tape that is similar to that used in audio cassettes. But the data from a hard disk is much more critical than the cacophony of a rock band. So the tapes are manufactured to very strict standards. Even so, it is possible that this tape will stretch and could cause the loss of data. There are also ½-inch drive systems for high end use. They will cost from $3000 to as much as $10,000.

Videotape. Another tape system, VIDEOTRAX, uses video tape and a standard home VCR to make backups. This system requires that an interface board be installed in the computer. From 60 to 120 megabytes of data can be stored on a standard videotape that costs from three to five dollars.

This type of system is ideal for the home user. Two leads from the interface easily connect to the VCR. After the backup is completed, the machine can be moved back to the living room for home entertainment. But this low cost system is also sophisticated enough to be used in large businesses and offices. The Alpha Micro VIDEOTRAX system has an option that will even do an automatic backup.

Besides being used for backup, these videotapes can be used to distribute large amounts of data. For instance, the contents of a hard disk could be copied and sent to another computer within the company across the room or across the country. This system could also be used by software publishers to distribute their programs. It is costly for a software store to stock the thousands of programs available, especially the public domain software. It would be very easy to download programs from videotape.

Alpha Micro has also demonstrated that it is possible to broadcast software over the TV channels. A VCR can record the software as easily as it does an old movie. The software can then be installed on any computer system that is equipped with an interface board. Two companies are foremost in this type of backup, the AUTOFAX and the Alpha Micro VIDEOTRAX. Their boards cost about $300 to $500. Contact:

AUTOFAX Corporation
4113-A Scotts Valley Dr.
Scotts Valley, CA 95066 (408) 438-6861

Alpha Micro Corporation
3501 Sunflower
Santa Ana, CA 92704-6944 (714) 641-6381

High-Density Disk Drive. A ten megabyte high-density floppy disk drive, such as the Konica, Kodak, or Bernoulli that were discussed in Chapter Six, would be much more useful as a backup. The tape drives can only be used for backup. They are usually only used once a day or maybe only once a week. The rest of the time they are idle and just take up space. A high-density floppy would have much more utility than the tape drive.

Hard Cards. It is now possible to buy a hard disk on a card for $300 to $600, depending on capacity and company. At this low price, it would be worthwhile to install a card in an empty slot and dedicate it to backup. If there are no empty slots, one might even consider just plugging in the card once a week or so to make a backup, then removing the card until needed again. This would entail removing the cover from the machine each time. I remove the cover to my computer so often that I only use one screw on it to provide grounding. I can remove and replace my cover in a very short time.

Software

There are several very good software programs on the market that let you use a 5.25-inch or 3.5-inch disk drive to back up your data. Ordinarily, you have backups of all your master software, so you shouldn't have to worry about backing up that software every day. Once you have made a full backup of your files, you need only back up those files that have changed since the last backup. Since DOS stamps each file with the date and time it was created, it is easy to back up only those files that were created after a certain date and time.

DOS also stores backup information about the file in the directory entry. One of the bits of information is the archive flag, either a 1 or 0. When the DOS BACKUP command has been used to back up the file, the flag is changed. Several commercial software packages such as FASTBACK make use of this flag so that only files that have not been backed up will be copied.

One of the most popular and fastest software programs is FASTBACK. Several thousand copies have been sold since it was first released in 1985. It has been upgraded and improved several times. The latest upgrade,

Fig. 7-2. FastBack software for backup.

FASTBACK PLUS, has recently been released. I was chosen to be one of their Beta testers for the new program.

I have used the original program since it was first introduced and was quite pleased with it. But the new version of FASTBACK PLUS is like moving up from a Chevy to a Cadillac. The new version has lots of plush goodies, utilities and pull down menus, and a well written manual.

The 120 page manual explains just about everything you need to know about backups such as the difference between an image backup and a file oriented backup. An image backup is an exact bit for bit copy of the hard disk copied as a continuous stream of data. This type of backup is rather inflexible and does not allow for a separate file backup or restoration. The file oriented type of backup identifies and indexes each file separately. A separate file or directory can be backed up and restored easily. It can be very time consuming to have to back up an entire 20 megabytes or more each day. But with a file oriented type system, once a full backup has been made, it is necessary only to make incremental backups of those files that have been changed or altered. The manual is written in plain language that should be easy for anyone to understand.

The program itself has lots of pull down menus with on screen help. The menus are layered and each selection will bring up another menu so that just about every option possible is offered. Once the files to be backed up and the options are selected the program can estimate how many diskettes will be needed and how long it will take to make the backup. FASTBACK PLUS uses a form of compression so that up to 70%

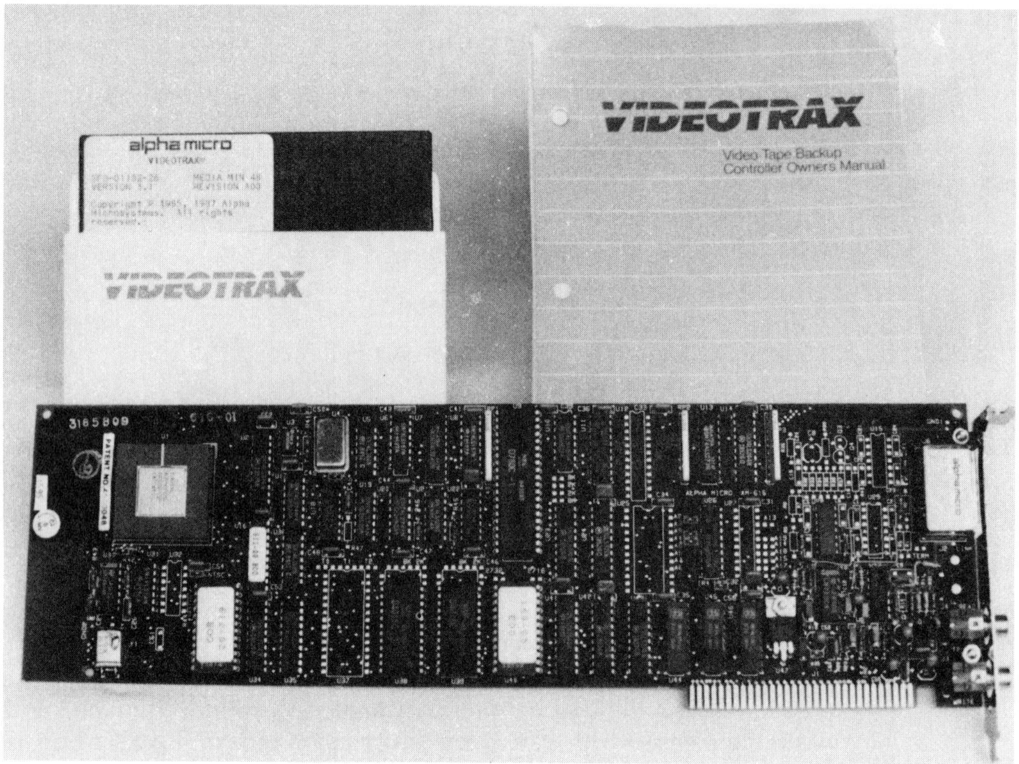

Fig. 7-3. Alpha Micro's Videotrax board for VCR backup.

more data can be stored on a given type of floppy diskette. Several different types of floppy drives can be used such as the 360K, the 1.2M, the 720K, and the 1.44M.

I have used several different types of backup. FASTBACK PLUS is one of the easiest and most versatile ways of doing it. The list price for FASTBACK PLUS is $189. Contact:

Fifth Generation Systems
11200 Industriplex Blvd.
Baton Rouge, LA 70809.

Another very good backup program is BACK-IT from Gazelle Systems, the people who developed the excellent disk management QDOS program. BACK-IT is very easy to use. A directory tree is presented and files can be tagged to be included or excluded. Wildcards can be used. The list price for BACK-IT is $79.95. Contact:

Gazelle Systems
42 North University Ave., Suite 10
Provo, Utah 84601 (800) 233-0383.

There are several more very good backup software packages available. Check through the computer magazines for their advertisements and for reviews. No matter what type of system or method is used, you should be using something to back up your data. You may be one of the lucky ones and never need it. But it is much better to be backed up than sorry.

Chapter 8

Monitors

One of the most difficult decisions you will have to make when you buy your system is what kind of monitor to buy. One reason it will be so difficult is because there are so many options. There are hundreds of different types and manufacturers of monitors. You have a very wide choice as to price, resolution, color, size, and shape. I have seen fairly good monochrome 12-inch monitors for as little as $65. I have seen super high resolution 19-inch color monitors that sell for as much as $10,000.

You will see many advertisements for low priced 386 barebones systems. In most cases, they will list a monochrome monitor as part of the system. I can't imagine why anyone would install an inexpensive monochrome monitor on a machine as fantastic as the 386. The time spent using a computer will be primarily spent looking at the monitor. Even if you do nothing but word processing, color makes the job a lot easier and more pleasant. Besides, color is not that expensive. More about prices later. Of course, what you plan to use your 386 for should determine what kind of monitor to buy.

MONITOR BASICS

Basically a monitor, or *display device* in IBM language, is similar to a television set. The face of a TV set or a monitor is the end of a *Cathode Ray Tube* (CRT). They are vacuum tubes and have many of the same elements that made up the old radio and electronic vacuum tubes that were used before the advent of the semiconductor age. The CRTs have a filament that boils off a stream of electrons. These electrons have a potential of about 25,000 volts. They are shot from an electron gun toward the front of the CRT where they slam into the phosphor on the back side of the face and cause it to light up.

This stream, or beam, of electrons must pass between a system of electromagnets before it reaches the back side of the CRT face. In a basic system, there would be an electromagnet on the left, one on the right, one at the top, and one at the bottom. Voltage through the electromagnets can be varied so that the beam of electrons are repulsed by one side and attracted by the other or pulled to the top or forced to the bottom. The CRT also has control grids, much like the old vacuum tubes, for controlling the input signal. The control grid, along with the electromagnetic system, causes the electron stream to emulate the input signal and write it on the screen.

Scanning Frequency

These electromagnets can manipulate the beam of electrons to start writing at the top left corner of the CRT, move all the way across to the top right corner, then move back to the left side and drop down one line and write another line across the screen. It does this very fast and soon fills the entire screen with lines in about $\frac{1}{60}$ second. This is the vertical scan rate. Some of the newer multiscan monitors can have variable vertical scan rates from $\frac{1}{40}$ up to $\frac{1}{100}$ second to paint the screen from top to bottom.

The horizontal scanning frequency of a standard TV set is 15.75 kHz. Many low resolution monitors use a similar frequency. The higher resolutions require higher frequencies. The multiscan monitors can vary from 15.5 kHz up to 45 kHz or more.

Resolution

A monochrome monitor has a single electron beam gun and a single color phosphor. It writes directly on the phosphor, and the resolution may be limited only to the bandwidth of the system. Color TVs and color monitors are much more complicated than monochrome systems. During the manufacture of the color monitors, three different phosphors, red, green and blue, are deposited on the back of the screen. Usually a very small dot of each color is placed in a triangular shape. Color monitors have three electron beam guns, one for each color. By lighting up the three different colored phosphors selectively, all the colors of the rainbow can be generated.

The guns must be very accurately aimed so that they will impinge only on their assigned color. To make sure that the guns hit their own color only, a metal shadow mask with very tiny holes is laid over the deposited phosphors. The more holes in the shadow mask and the closer together the color dots of phosphor, the higher the possible resolution of a monitor.

The distance between the holes, or perforations, in the shadow mask is called the *dot pitch*. The dots per inch determines the resolution. A high resolution monitor might have a dot pitch of .31 millimeter. (One mm. = .0394 inches; .31 mm. = .0122 inches). A typical medium-resolution monitor might have a dot pitch of .38 mm. One with very high resolution might have a dot pitch of .26 mm or even less. If you look closely at the characters or images on a low-resolution monitor you can see open spaces, similar to the printed characters from a low resolution 9-pin dot matrix printer. A good high resolution monitor will form solid, sharply defined characters and images.

Resolution is also determined by the number of *pixels* (picture elements) that can be displayed. The following figures relate primarily to text, but the graphics resolution will be similar to the text. A standard color graphics monitor can display 640 × 200 pixels. It can display 80 characters on one line with 25 lines from top to bottom. If we divide 640 by 80, we find that one character will be 8 pixels wide. There can be 25 lines of characters, so 200/25 = 8 pixels high. The entire screen will have 640 × 200, or 128,000, pixels. An enhanced graphics system can display 640 × 350, or 640/80 = 8 pixels wide and 350/25 = 14 pixels high. The screen can display 640 × 350, or 224,000, total pixels.

ADAPTER BASICS

It won't do you much good to buy a high resolution monitor unless you buy a good adapter to drive it. You can't just plug a monitor into your computer and expect it to function. Just as a hard disk needs a controller, a monitor needs an adapter to interface with the computer. And just as a hard disk can operate with several different types of controllers, most monitors can operate with several different types of adapters.

A combination Monochrome Graphics Adapter (MGA) and Color Graphics Adapter (CGA) for a monochrome monitor might sell for as little as $40. In the monochrome mode, this adapter can provide a very high resolution of 720 × 350. When used with a standard color graphics monitor, it will provide only 640 × 200 resolution.

An Enhanced Graphics Adapter (EGA) can drive a high resolution monitor to display 640 × 350 resolution. Most of the EGA boards are downward compatible so that they will also display older programs that developed for the CGA or MGA. A couple of years ago, EGA boards cost from $400 to $600. I have seen no-name brands at recent swap meets for less than $100. Just a couple of years ago, EGA monitors cost from $600 up to $800. I have seen some fairly good ones selling today for as little as $250.

ANALOG VS. DIGITAL

IBM introduced a new analog Video Graphics Array (VGA) display system with its PS/2 systems. It will eventually become the new standard. Up until the introduction of the PS/2, most displays used a digital system. But the digital system has some limitations. A CGA system can only display four colors at any one time out of a palette of 16. The EGA can display up to 16 out of a palette of 64; the VGA can display up to 256 colors out of a palette of 262,144. The EGA has a resolution of 640 × 350; the VGA has a resolution of 640 × 480.

Both the EGA and VGA are downward compatible and can run any of the older software programs. However, most of the older programs will not be able to take full advantage of the higher resolution unless special software drivers are supplied by the vendors.

Unlike the discrete digital signals, the analog signals that drive the color guns are continuously variable so that a very large number of colors and hues can be displayed. Enhanced EGA, or Super EGA, boards have been developed that can produce resolutions of 640 × 480 on an appropriate digital monitor. This is the same as the analog systems. But even with the higher resolution, the digital systems are still limited to 16 colors out of a palette of 64. At this time these boards are selling for $395 to $600 each.

Several manufacturers have developed compatible VGA monitors and boards that are equivalent to the IBM system. Many of the multiscan monitors can accept either digital TTL (Transistor to Transistor Logic) or analog RGB (red, green, and blue) signals. Of course they must have an appropriate adapter to drive them. The NEC MultiSync, and most of the other brands of multiscan monitors, will accept the analog signals of a VGA board. The multiscan monitors sell for $600 to as much as $3199 for the NEC 19-inch MultiSync XL. The VGA boards are selling for about the same price as the Enhanced or Super EGAs, $395 to $700.

An analog VGA monitor requires less circuitry and can be manufactured for less cost than a multiscan monitor. And since the VGA boards offer so much more for the same cost as the Enhanced or Super EGAs, it is expected that this market will dry up. It is sad news for the developers, but good news for us consumers. Eventually we will be able to buy the Super EGAs for about what the EGAs are selling for now, less than $100.

WHAT YOU SHOULD BUY

The primary determining factor for choosing a monitor should be what it is going to be used for and the amount of money you have to spend. If money is no object, buy a large 19-inch analog monitor with super high resolution and a good VGA board to drive it for about $3000. But for many applications, a low cost EGA board and a 13-inch EGA monitor, both for about $350, will be more than sufficient.

If you expect to do any kind of graphics, such as CAD/CAM design work, you will definitely need a good large screen color monitor with very high resolution. A large screen is almost essential for some types of design drawings so that as much of the drawing as possible can be viewed on the screen. You will also need a high resolution monitor for close tolerance designs.

For desktop publishing, some very high resolution monochrome monitors have been developed. Many of these monitors are designed to sit on their side so that they look a bit like an 8.5-by-11-inch sheet of paper. Instead of 25 lines, most have 66 lines, which is the standard for an 11-inch sheet of paper. They also have a phosphor that will let you have black text on a white background so that the screen looks very much like the finished text. Many of these monitors are WYSIWYG, or What You See Is What You Get. Many of the newer color monitors have a mode that will let you switch to a pure white background with black type. For accounting and spreadsheets or word processing, a monochrome monitor will probably be sufficient, but not nearly as pleasant as with color.

SELECTING A MONITOR

My first choice would be to look for an analog monitor, or a good multiscan that can accept both digital and analog signals. If possible, go to several stores and compare various models. Turn the brightness up and check the center of the screen and the outer edges. Is the intensity the same in the center and the outer edges? Check the focus, brightness, and contrast with text and graphics. There can be vast differences even in the same models from the same manufacturer. I have seen monitors that displayed demonstration graphics programs beautifully, but were not worth a damn when displaying text in various colors.

Ask the vendor for a copy of the specs. Check the dot pitch. For good high resolution it should be .31 mm or less. The analog models will have a single horizontal frequency. But the digitals should have a horizontal frequency from about 15.5 kHz up to 35 kHz or more. The vertical scan rate should be about 45 Hz up to 75 Hz.

You might also check for available buttons or knobs to control and adjust the brightness, contrast, and vertical/horizontal lines. Some manufacturers place the controls on the back or some other difficult area

Fig. 8-1. A Paradise VGA monitor board.

to get at. It is much better if they are accessible from the front so that you can see what the effect is as you adjust them.

If the monitor will accept analog signals, I would by all means look for a VGA board to drive it. There is a lot of difference in VGA boards. Most of the VGA boards can operate in 17 different modes that go all the way back to the Monochrome Display Adapter (MDA) for text only, the MGA, the CGA, EGA and VGA at various text and graphics resolutions. The VGA even improves on CGA programs that were designed to run at 640 × 200. Because it only has one frequency, it runs the CGA programs at 640 × 400.

DRIVERS

Most of the new software being developed today has built-in hooks that allow it to take advantage of the new EGA and VGA standards. Since the older software programs were written before EGA and VGA were developed, many of them cannot normally take advantage of the higher resolution and extended graphics. Some manufacturers have written software drivers that will allow many of the older programs to utilize the advantages of the new adapters.

Vendors have written drivers for older programs such as Windows, Lotus, AutoCAD, GEM, Ventura, WordStar, and others. Some vendors supply as many as two or three diskettes full of drivers. Some vendors, such as IBM and Compaq, don't supply any at all with their VGA boards. Depending on what software you intend to use, the drivers supplied with the adapter you purchase should be an important consideration.

SHADOW MASK

I mentioned the shadow mask earlier. It is a metal mask with thousands of small perforations that allow each specific colored beam to strike only its assigned color. Ordinarily, the metal in these masks heat up and becomes distorted. This distortion can affect the resolution of the monitor.

After several years of research, Zenith has developed a flat-screen monitor with a unique shadow mask. They install the shadow mask under high tension so that it cannot change to any degree. The flat screen also cuts down on the glare of reflected light so that it is much easier on the eyes, and the resolution is very good.

Compared to some of the other monitors, the Zenith ZCM-1490 is rather expensive, $999 plus $599 for their Z-499 video board to drive it. But those who have used it claim that it is well worth it.

SWIVEL BASE

It may not seem important, but if at all possible, get a monitor with a swivel and tilt base. It can be very disturbing if there are lights in the area that reflect off the screen. If it can be tilted, you can usually eliminate this problem. You should also be able to adjust, or tilt, it to where it is most comfortable for you to view. If several other people use the computer, chances are that they will not all be the same size, so it is nice to be able to adjust the screen for each individual.

There are tilt and swivel stands that can be purchased for those monitors that do not come with one. Even if you can afford a flat-screen Zenith that is not affected by light reflections, it is a good idea to have a swivel for it.

Several companies offer a plastic light polarizing filter that can be glued onto the screen to cut down on glare. They cost about $15 each. You will be looking at your monitor almost all of the time that you spend working with your computer. I would suggest that you spend as much as you can afford to get one of the better ones.

MONITOR AND ADAPTER SOURCES

I have only bought about a half-dozen monitors in my lifetime. So, I have not personally had a chance to evaluate the following products.

But, I subscribe to *PC Clones, Computer Shopper, PC Magazine, PC Week, Byte, Personal Computing, InfoWorld, PC World,* and several other magazines. Most of these magazines have test labs and do extensive reviews of products. Since I can't personally test all of these products, I rely heavily on their reviews.

I can't possibly list all of the vendors. I suggest that you subscribe to the magazines listed above and in the Appendix. Check the reviews and advertisements for other vendors. Note that the prices below are list prices. In many cases, the products can actually be purchased for less. Besides, in this volatile market, the prices change almost daily. Call first, even if ordering from a magazine advertisement.

Multiscan Monitors (13 inch, unless noted):

CTX Model 1435 (14 inch) $435
CTX International
260 Paseo Tesoro
Walnut, CA 91789
(714) 595-6146

Conrac Model 7250, (19 inch) $2995
Conrac Corp.
1724 South Mountain Ave.
Duarte, CA 91010
(818) 303-0095

Intecolor MegaTrend/2 (19 inch) $1995
Intecolor
225 Scientific Dr.
Norcross, GA 30092
(404) 449-5961

Logitech Autosync TE5155 $699
Logitech Inc.
6505 Kaiser Dr.
Fremont, CA 94555
(425) 795-8500

Magnavox Multimode Model 8CM873 $899
Magnavox
P.O. Box 14810
Knoxville, TN 37914
(615) 521-4316

Microvitec Model 1019 (19 inch) $2195
Microvitec Inc.
1943 Providence Ct.
Airport Perimeter Business Center
College Park, GA 30337
(404) 991-2246

Nanao Flexscan 8060S $919
Nanao USA Corp.
23510 Telo Ave., Suite 5
Torrance, CA 90505
(213) 325-5202

NEC MultiSync Plus (14 inch) $1395
NEC MultiSync XL (19 inch) $3195
NEC Home Electronics
1255 Michael Dr.
Wood Dale, IL 60191
(312) 860-9500

Princeton Ultrasync $795
Princeton Graphics Systems
601 Ewing St., Bldg. A
Princeton, NJ 08540
(609) 683-1660

Taxan Multivision 770 Plus $915
Taxan USA Corp.
18005 Cortney Ct.
City of Industry, CA 91748
(818) 810-1291

Thompson Ultrascan 4375M (14 inch) $895
Thompson Consumer Products
5731 West Slauson Ave. Suite 111
Culver City, CA 90230
(800) 325-0464

Zenith ZCM-1490 (14 inch) $999
Zenith Data Systems
100 Milwaukee Ave.
Glenview, IL 60025
(312) 699-4839

Enhanced EGA Boards:

American Mitac SEGA $199
American Mitac Corp.
410 East Plumeria Dr.
San Jose, CA 95134
(408) 432-1160

Boca Research MultiEGA $299
Boca Research
6401 Congress Ave.
Boca Raton, FL 22487
(305) 997-6227

Genoa Systems SuperEGA $489
Genoa Systems
73 East Trimble Rd.
San Jose, CA 95131
(408) 432-9090

IGC EGAcard $450
Intelligent Graphics Corp.
4800 Great America Pkwy. Suite 200
Santa Clara, CA 95054
(408) 986-8373

NSI Smart EGA $499
NSI Logic
Cedar Hill Business Park
257B Cedar Hill Rd.
Marlborough, MA 01752
(617) 460-0717

Paradise Autoswitch $349
Paradise Systems
99 South Hill Dr.
Brisbane, CA 94005
(415) 468-7300

Quadram ProSync! $395
Quadram
One Quad Way
Norcross, GA 30093
(404) 923-6666

SMT Pro-EGA $249
SMT Corp.
1145 Linda Vista Dr.
San Marcos, CA 92069
(619) 744-3590

Tecmar EGA Master $595
Tecmar Corp.
6225 Cochran Rd.
Cleveland, OH 44139
(216) 349-0600

Tseng EVA 480 $595
Tseng Labs
10 Pheasant Run
Newtown, PA 18940
(215) 968-0502

VGA Boards:

ATI VIP VGA $449
ATI Technologies
3761 Victoria Park Ave.
Toronto, Ontario
Canada M1W 3S2
(416) 756-0711

Compaq VGC $599
Compaq Computer Corp.
20555 FM 149
Houston, TX 77070
(713) 370-0670

IBM PS/2 Adapter $595
IBM Corp.
900 King St.
1A515 Rye Brook, NY 10573
(914) 934-4793

SigmaVGA $499
Sigma Designs
46501 Landing Pkwy.
Fremont, CA 94538
(415) 770-0100

STB VGA Extra $395
STB Systems Inc.
1651 North Glenville
Richardson, TX 75081
(214) 234-8750

Tatung Platinum Card $445
Tatung Co. of America
2850 El Presidio Dr.
Long Beach, CA 90810
(213) 979-7055

VEGA VGA $499
Video Seven
46355 Landing Pkwy.
Fremont, CA 94538
(415) 656-7800

Zenith Z449 $499
Zenith Data Systems
100 Milwaukee Ave.
Glenview, IL 60025
(312) 699-4839

Chapter 9

Memory

Memory is one of the most critical elements of the computer. When we work with a software program, it is placed in RAM. Here we can manipulate the data, do calculations, enter more data, edit, search data bases, or do any of the thousands of things that software programs allow us to do. Since it is in RAM, we can access the data very quickly.

Random Access Memory (RAM) is somewhat like an electronic blackboard. But unlike an ordinary blackboard, RAM is easily erased. If the computer is turned off, or if it loses power and the data in RAM has not been saved to disk, it is gone forever. *Read Only Memory* (ROM) is another kind of memory. We can write to or read RAM memory. But ROM is firmware that can only be read, usually only by the computer. It usually contains instructions and rules, such as those contained in the BIOS ROM, that controls the operation of the computer.

One of the reasons to move up to the 386 is so that we can have much, much more memory. When you are limited to 640K, some software programs, such as a large spreadsheet, may not be able to fit entirely in RAM. You will get an error message saying that the program is too big to fit in memory. You will not be able to proceed.

But we should be able to go out and buy a couple megabytes of memory and be able to address all that RAM, right? Wrong. Simply adding memory, even to a 386, will not allow you to use more than 640K if you are using DOS.

At one time, it was determined that one megabyte of RAM would be more than sufficient for any eventuality. So DOS was designed for that limit. The 8088 CPUs found in all PCs and XTs can access one megabyte of RAM. But only 640K is available for applications, the other 384K is reserved for internal use of the BIOS, the display, and other functions.

THE PC BUS

The 8088 accepts two parallel 8-bit chunks of data, then internally adds 4 bits and sends them out over a 20-line bus. With the 20 lines, it is possible to address any individual byte in one megabyte, that is 2^{20} or 1048576 bytes. Most motherboards will have from five to eight 62-pin connectors for 8-bit hardware.

The 80286 accepts 16-bit chunks of data, then internally adds 8 bits and sends them out over 24 lines which allows them to address 16 megabytes or (2^{24} = 16,777,216 bytes). The 80286 motherboard also has all of the standard 8-bit slots plus two or more 16-bit slots with 36-pin connectors.

The 80386 accepts data 32 bits at a time and sends it out over 32 lines. It can address four gigabytes (2^{32} = 4,294,967,296 bytes). A gigabyte is also the same as a billion bytes. In its virtual mode, the 80386 can address 64 terabytes, or 64 trillion bytes. This is the amount of data that could be stored on 3.2 million 20M hard disks.

Most of the 80386 motherboards have all of the 8-bit slots, one or two 16-bit slots and connectors for one or two 32-bit boards. Some developers have designed boards without 32-bit slots. Instead, they make provisions for up to 2 or more megabytes to be installed on the motherboard. Extra memory can be installed in 16-bit slots.

TYPES OF MEMORY

There are four main types of memory, *real* or *conventional, extended, native 386,* and *expanded.* Real or conventional memory is the one megabyte of memory that the 8088 and 8086 systems are able to directly address. Each one of those million bytes have a unique address, much like the individual addresses of streets and houses in a city. The CPU can go to any one of those addresses in the lower 640K and read the data that might be there or write data to that address.

Extended Memory

Extended memory is the 15 megabytes of memory that can be installed above one megabyte. If it weren't for the DOS 640K limitation, it would be a seamless continuation of memory. OS/2, Xenix, and Unix regard it as such and will let you address it. But since the 8088 and 8086 have only 20 address lines, they are not physically able to address more than one megabyte.

Native 386

The 80386 can address up to 4 gigabytes of RAM or ROM. It can address up to 64 terabytes of virtual memory. In the *virtual 86* mode it can behave as if it were several independent 8086 machines, each with one megabyte of address space and up to 640K of real or conventional memory. Chances are that you will probably not ever install the maximum amount of memory possible in your 386. Especially if you are using it at home.

Expanded Memory

Some large spreadsheets require an enormous amount of memory. A couple of years ago, in a rare instance of cooperation among corporations, Lotus, Intel, and Microsoft got together and devised a system and standard that would allow a computer, even a PC or XT, to address up to 8 megabytes of memory. They called it the LIM/EMS for Lotus-Intel-Microsoft Expanded Memory Specification.

With this system, up to 8 megabytes of memory can be installed on boards and plugged into the computer's expansion slots. Memory on the boards is divided into pages of 16K each. Expanded memory finds a 64K window above 784K of the one megabyte memory. Hardware circuits on the boards and software programs can switch the pages in and out of the expanded memory into this window.

The AST, Quadram, and Ashton-Tate Corporations decided that the LIM EMS system could be improved. They cooperated to develop the AST-Quadram-Ashton-Tate Enhanced Expanded Memory Specification (AQA EEMS). This specification had a bit more versatility than the LIM

Fig. 9-1. The Attention memory board from Newer Technology for 2 to 5 megabytes. (Photo courtesy Newer Technology.)

Fig. 9-2. The Concentration memory board from Newer Technology for up to 32 megabytes. (Photo courtesy Newer Technology.)

Table 9-1. Memory Hierarchy.

Address	Memory	
4 Gb	NATIVE 386 MEMORY Up to 4 gigabytes of RAM or ROM	
16M	EXTENDED MEMORY Up to 15 megabytes in Protected Mode.	
1024K	CONVENTIONAL OR REAL MEMORY ROM BIOS 256 K reserved space	EXPANDED MEMORY Up to 32 megabytes
784K	VIDEO 128K reserved Space	
640K 0K	RAM for DOS and applications programs	

EMS. In 1987, all of the above corporations got together and revised the specification and made several improvements. It is now called LIM EMS Version 4.

This new version allows several of the OS/2 functions to be run with DOS. LIM EMS 4 can now address 32 megabytes instead of the original 8 megabytes. It is now possible to load *Terminate and Stay Resident* (TSR) programs, such as Side Kick, WordFinder, and others, in memory outside of our precious 640K. It also includes functions to allow multitasking so that several programs can be run simultaneously. Many of the 80386 systems are being shipped with up to 2 megabytes of memory installed on the motherboard. Of course, DOS will not let you use more than 640K of that extended memory except for *RAM disks* or *print spoolers*. But LIM EMS 4 will allow the extended memory be used as expanded memory with the proper software and drivers. See Table 9-1 for a diagram of the PC's memory map.

OS/2 VS. DOS PLUS EXPANDED MEMORY

DOS 3.3 lists for $125. OS/2 costs $325. When the Presentation Manager portion is released, it will cost over $700. (Incidentally, OS/2 1.0 requires about 2.5 to 3M of hard disk space. It is expected that the Presentation Manager will add considerably to that amount of required disk space. DOS 3.3 requires about 500K.)

You probably know DOS fairly well already. You may not need all of the multitasking and other exotic functions on OS/2. Depending on

Fig. 9-3. Two megabytes of memory in single inline memory modules (SIMMs) on a baby 386 motherboard.

what you need to do with your 386, you might be able to get by with a LIM EMS board and the DesqView software package. You will probably need to buy memory cards no matter which system you choose. The expanded memory cards cost about the same as other memory. The main difference is that they are sold with utility software.

MEMORY BOARDS

There are several companies in the United States and overseas who are manufacturing boards with large amounts of memory on them. Memory boards are still expensive, from $500 to over $5000.Some boards may advertise a 2-megabyte board for a fairly low price. But if you look closely at the ad, this may be with 0K memory. This does not mean that the memory is OKAY. It means that there is zero K, or no memory installed for the price advertised.

Since these are fairly high cost items, it may be worthwhile to have the vendor demonstrate the board on a large file. If it is a clone, or a lesser known brand, you might have him compare it with a well known brand, such as Intel's Above Board or AST's RAMpage. This is not meant to condemn all clones. There are some that are very good and sell for about half of the cost of the major brand names.

Since we didn't have IBM to set a standard for the 386, most motherboards are different. Compaq has one slot devoted to 32-bit memory. But it went against tradition and put that particular slot at the front of the board. A few manufacturers have followed the Compaq design, but a larger number have followed the Intel design that uses one or more 62-pin connectors in line with the original 8-bit 62-pin connector.

Some manufacturers do not provide a slot at all for 32-bit memory. Instead they provide for installation of 2 megabytes or more of 32-bit memory directly on the motherboard. If you need more memory, then you will have to install it in one of the 16-bit slots. Accessing this memory at 16 bits per chunk cuts down somewhat on the speed of the 32-bit system.

Each type of board requires a different type of plug-in memory board. Since there is no standard and there are several kinds of motherboards, there are not too many memory boards that are available. Those that are available are rather expensive. But there will soon be over one million 386 machines in operation. If the industry can be satisfied with the few present 386 motherboard models then the memory board designers can settle on just a few designs. If this happens, we will be able to buy our memory at a more reasonable price.

DRAMS

Almost all of the memory used on microcomputers is Dynamic Random Access Memory (DRAM) chips. Each memory cell in these chips is like a small capacitor. A capacitor is similar to a rechargeable battery. It can be charged up, and it will remain charged for a while. So if a DRAM cell is charged up with a jolt of electricity, it can represent a 1, a cell that is not charged up can represent a 0. But a DRAM memory cell can only hold a charge for a few millionths of a second before it starts leaking off. In order to keep it charged up, the computer interrupts its activities and recharges, or refreshes, all of them. A computer spends about 7 percent of its time refreshing DRAM cells.

DRAMs are rated in nanoseconds (ns). A nanosecond is one billionth of a second. There are some DRAMs that can operate at a higher frequency than others. If the CPU is operating at the original PC and XT speed of 4.77 MHz, then a fairly slow DRAM that is rated at 200ns will be fine. But for 8 MHz or higher frequencies we must have DRAMs rated at 150ns or less.

Most of the DRAM chips will be marked with two digits, 20 will indicate 200ns, 15 is 150ns, and 12 is 120ns. The smaller the number, the higher the frequency with which it can be used. The 16 MHz 386 will work best if the chips are at least 100ns. For 20 MHz, they should be about 80ns or less. But of course, the higher frequency chips are more difficult to manufacture and cost much more.

In early 1987, discount stores were selling 120ns 256K chips for as little as $2.50 each. It takes nine 256K chips to make 256K of memory. One megabyte of memory requires four banks or rows of chips, with nine chips in each bank, for a total of 36 chips. At $2.50 each, the one megabyte of memory would cost $90. That same one megabyte of 120ns memory today costs about $350 at discount houses to over $500 at some of the brand name stores. The 80ns and 100ns 256K DRAMs cost more. And the one megabyte DRAM chips are even more expensive.

The Japanese and other Far East companies were flooding the market with low cost DRAM chips. The few American companies who were still making DRAMs complained that the Japanese were dumping the chips in this country, selling them below cost and competing unfairly. Tariffs and limitations were placed on imported memory chips, and we are now paying two to three times more for the same chips. Several American companies have gone back to manufacturing DRAMs. But it will probably be a long time before we see low cost memory again. And just when we really need it for the newer computers and software.

WAIT STATE

As you know, the computer works in very precise blocks of time. If it is not designed for optimum speed or it has slow DRAMs, the CPU may operate faster than it can be supplied with data. It cannot slow down its speed of operation. So if a process such as refreshing the DRAM cannot be accomplished in a specified cycle or number of cycles, it will sit idle and wait for the process to complete.

A billionth of a second may not seem like a long time to have to wait. But a few billionths here and a few billionths there and pretty soon we are talking about real time. The wait states can be very apparent and time consuming in some applications such as large spreadsheets and databases. Compared to a zero wait state system, a system with one or two wait states may take from 25 to 50 percent longer to run the same software program.

INTERLEAVE

It can take about twice as long to refresh a DRAM cell as it does to access it and read its state. Some systems have been devised so that the memory is split into two banks. The first bank can be refreshed while data is being accessed from the second bank. Then the process is reversed, and the second bank is refreshed while data is processed from the first bank.

This process works great if every other call for data goes to the opposite bank. But quite often two access calls in a row will ask for data in the same bank. In that instance, a wait state may be imposed on the CPU. But the interleave does help to reduce the number of wait states.

STATIC RAM

Static RAM is made from transistor circuits. The individual transistors can be switched on or off. They will remain in whatever state they are placed in until they are changed or the power is turned off. They do not have to be refreshed. Static RAM is very fast and can operate at very high frequencies. But it is bulky and requires much more space than the DRAMs. Static RAM is much more expensive to manufacture also.

Some manufacturers install a small amount of static RAM which is used as a fast cache. Many programs access the same data over and over. If the last used data, from a hard disk or a DRAM section of memory, is in a very fast cache area, it can be accessed very quickly. A good cache system can considerably improve the overall performance of a system.

MEMORY BOARD VENDORS

The following is a partial list of vendors who manufacture memory boards. Contact them for your particular needs.

AST Research	(714) 863-1333
Boca Research	(305) 997-6227
IDEAssociates	(800) 257-5027
Intel Corp.	(503) 629-7354
Newer Technology	(316) 685-4904
Orchid Technology	(415) 490-8586
Quadram Corp.	(404) 564-5566
STB Systems	(214) 234-8750
Tecmar Inc.	(800) 624-8560

Chapter 10

Input Devices

Before you can do anything with a computer you must input data to it. There are several ways to input data such as from a disk, by modem, by a mouse, by FAX, or on-line from a mainframe or a network. But by far the most common way to get data into the computer is by way of the keyboard. For most common applications, it is impossible to operate the computer without a keyboard.

I am not a very good typist, but I do a lot of writing. The main reason I bought a computer several years ago was so that I could throw my old typewriter away and use word processing software. Typewriter keyboards are fairly standard. But I have had several computers over the last few years and every one of them has had a different keyboard. The main typewriter characters aren't changed or moved very often, but some of the very important control keys like the Esc, the Ctrl, the Prtsc, the \, the function keys and several others are moved all over the keyboard.

Very few of the early microcomputers had identical keyboards. But IBM came along and established a layout that everyone thought would be a standard. It was an excellent keyboard, built like a Sherman tank and had very good tactile feel. There were some minor gripes because it did not indicate whether you were in the Caps or Num lock mode. It also had a small Return key. But the clone makers soon fixed that by adding LEDs to indicate when the Caps and Num locks were on and a larger Return key.

About a year later, IBM came out with a keyboard that also had LED indicators and a large Return or Enter key, but for some unknown reason, they rearranged and moved several of the very important keys. The Esc, the \, Prtsc, and several others were moved. These are very important keys and are used constantly. I have not been able to find anyone who can give me any reason why they were moved. Just when I thought for sure that the 84-key keyboard would be the standard, IBM released their new PS/2 line with a new keyboard layout.

The lower keyboard in Fig. 10-1 has 84 keys. The upper keyboard has 17 extra keys for a total of 101. Except for F11, F12, and Pause, the other 14 extra keys are duplicates of keys that were already on the keyboard. They separated the numeric keypad with four keys with the up, down, right, and left arrow keys that perform the same function as those arrows on the numeric keypad. They also installed six separate keys above the arrow keys for Insert, Home, Page Up, Delete, End, and Page Down. Again, these keys perform the same function as those on the numeric keypad. They also added an extra Enter on the numeric keypad. And they now have Ctrl and Alt keys in line with, and on each end of, the shortened space bar.

A lot of people and many large companies use their computers for spreadsheet and accounting programs that require intensive numeric input. The separate numeric keypad makes the entry of data and numbers much easier which can increase productivity.

The original IBM keyboard had the very important and often used Esc key just to the left of the 1 key in the numeric row. The 84-key keyboard moved the Esc key over to the top row of the keypad. The tilde

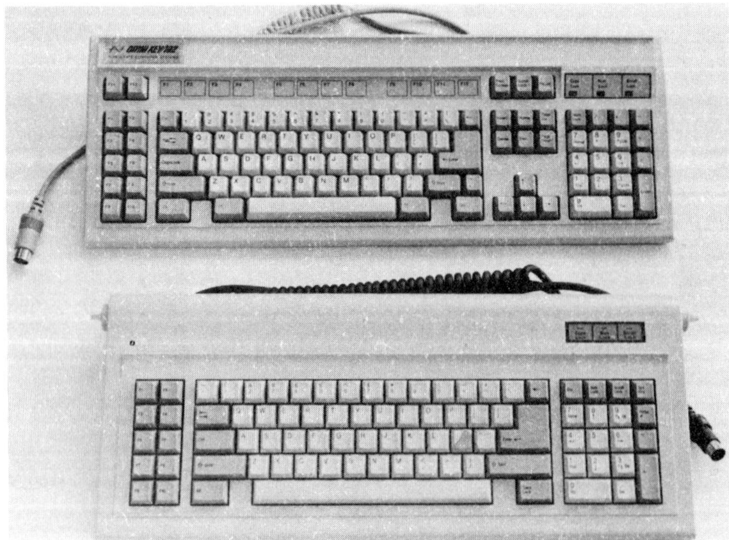

Fig. 10-1. The Northgate 101-key keyboard on the top and a clone 84-key keyboard on the bottom.

(~) and grave ( ) key was moved to the original Esc position to the left side of the 1. The new 101-key keyboard moves the Esc back to its original position.

Another very important and often used key is the Control or Ctrl key. The 101-key keyboard added an extra Ctrl key. I don't mind having an extra Ctrl key, but they moved it from its original position alongside the A down to where the Alt key was on the 84-key keyboard. They put the other Ctrl key in the position that the CapsLock occupied on the 84-key keyboard and moved the CapsLock over to where the Ctrl key had been for years.

The only good thing that I can say about this new arrangement is that it is now possible to do a warm boot with one hand. Once the computer is on, you can reset it by pressing the Ctrl, the Alt, and Del keys all at the same time. With the old layout you had to use both hands. It is now possible to press the Alt and Ctrl at the right end of the space bar with two fingers and still be able to reach up with another finger and press the newly added Del key.

For some unknown reason, IBM also decided to move the function keys to the top of the keyboard above the numeric keys. Many people have purchased programs like Framework that uses the function keys intensively. Anyone who buys a copy of Framework gets a cutout plastic overlay that describes the commands associated with each function key. Many other companies have made plastic overlays that fit over the keyboards for programs like dBASE III, WordStar, MultiMate, and many others. These overlays are great for learning, and even a novice can become productive in a short time. These overlays will not fit on the new keyboards.

When I sit down to write an article or a letter, my time is not too critical. I can afford to stop and look for the right key. But there are some large businesses where the operators don't have this luxury. The companies must input billions of bits of data to their computers daily. In many of these offices there are hardware devices, or software programs, that count each keystroke that the operator makes during the 8 hour shift. If the operator's number of keystrokes falls below a certain level, he or she can be fired.

The constant strain by a person to maintain the average number of keystrokes can be as bad as the tension and stress suffered by airport controllers. Can you imagine the problems these computer operators have if they must learn a new keyboard layout every so often? It is bound to slow down productivity. It must cost many business offices, including the large offices of IBM, millions of dollars for their employees to have to relearn a new keyboard every so often.

Except for special orders for PCs and XTs, IBM will no longer supply the older 84-key keyboards. But the keyboards are available from several clone makers at much less than what IBM would charge. The clone makers have also developed keyboards that are similar to IBM's 101 key layout. But many of them have moved some of the keys back to their old positions.

Many of the Far East clone keyboards have a very soft feel with little or no tactile feedback. My first clone had such a keyboard. I finally went to a computer swap and tried out several keyboards until I found one that I liked. I will never buy another keyboard unless I can try it out first.

Northgate Computer Systems has received a lot of very good reviews on their keyboard. I ordered one on the condition that I could return it if I didn't like it. I am writing this on one of their OMNI KEY/102 keyboards. It has an excellent tactile feel and has several other good features. The Northgate is a bit more expensive than many of the clones. I have seen some very good clones for as little as $45. The Northgate sells for $99. I am convinced that it is well worth the extra money.

As an optional feature, some of the Northgate models have the function keys back in their original position on the left hand side of the keyboard. They also offer another excellent option. I mentioned earlier that the IBM configuration placed the CapsLock key in the position where the Ctrl key was for years. Northgate provides a hardware switch on the back of some of their keyboard models that lets you switch the Ctrl key back to where it is supposed to be. You can set this switch on, and it will change the functions of the CapsLock and Ctrl keys. It is a simple matter to pry off the key caps and replace them with the new key caps provided.

Datadesk International's Turbo-101 also offers the capability of switching the CapsLock and Ctrl positions. They give a 30 day money back guarantee. They also include Borland's Turbo Lightning software with the keyboard, both for only $149.95. Turbo Lightning is a memory resident word spelling program that gives instant access to the Random House 80,000 word dictionary and 60,000 word Thesaurus. Turbo Lightning works with Sidekick, Lotus 1-2-3, most word processors, and other software. It sells separately for $99.

The KeyTronic Corporation also makes an excellent keyboard. They were the first to improve on the original IBM design by adding LEDs and a larger Enter key. The keyboard became very popular so the Far East clone makers quickly made copies of it and sold them for about half of what KeyTronic was selling them for. Some of the clone keyboards are almost as good as the KeyTronic in look and feel.

KeyTronic offers kits with various tension springs that can be installed on their keyboards. If you don't like the tension and feel of your keyboard, you can easily change it to suit you. Honeywell also manufactures a good keyboard. Honeywell conducted a human factors study to find out what typists wanted. They then developed a keyboard that is very similar to the feel of a good typewriter.

SPECIAL KEY FUNCTIONS

A computer is great for number crunching. Several of the keys on the keyboard have two or more purposes.

*—The asterisk is used as the multiplication symbol. It is also used as a wildcard in DOS. For instance if you want a listing of all the programs that have a .COM extension such as COMMAND.COM you could type in DIR *.COM.

\—The backslash is used by DOS to denote a subdirectory. To change from one subdirectory to another you must type CD\ then the directory name. If no name is given, you will be returned to the root directory. The backslash should not be confused with the slash. If you use the slash where the backslash should be used, you will get an error message, or if it is part of a program, the program will not work.

/—The slash is also called the *virgule,* the shilling, and the solidus. In calculations it is used as the division symbol.

<—Means less than.

>—Means greater than.

^—The caret is the symbol for exponents.

Plus +, minus – and equal = do those normal functions.

FUNCTION KEYS

The 12 function keys are multi-purpose keys. What they do is usually dependent on the software you are using at the time. Many software programs use the function keys to accomplish a goal with a minimum of keystrokes. Quite often the function of the keys will be displayed somewhere on the screen.

Certain functions are available from DOS:

F1—If you have entered a DOS command, pressing F1 will redisplay the command a character by character each time the key is pressed.

F2—If you have entered a DOS command and you want to change part of it, you can enter a letter of the command and all of the command up to that letter will be displayed. You can then change the command from that point onward. This can save a few keystrokes.

F3—Will redisplay the entire command that was previously entered. For instance you can enter the command COPY A: B: and when it has finished, if you want to make a second copy, just press F3 and the command will come up. All you have to do then is press Enter.

F4—If a command has been entered and you want to reuse the last portion of it, just press a letter of the command and the portion from that letter to the end of the command will be displayed.

The arrow keys move the cursor one line up or down and one character right or left. The page down and page up will move a whole page up or down. The Home key will send the cursor to the top left corner of the screen. The end key will send it to the end of the current line.

With the Ins (Insert) key on, it will push the characters to the right and insert anything typed. With the insert off, anything typed will overwrite other characters that happen to be on the same line.

MODEL SWITCH

I should note that the PC, XT, AT, 80286, 80386, and the PS/2 keyboards all have the same connectors. Any keyboard will plug into any one of those machines, but the PC and XT keyboards have different electronics and scan frequencies. An older PC or XT keyboard can be plugged into an 80286 or 80386 machine, but they will not operate. Most of the clone makers install a small switch beneath their keyboards that allows them to be switched so that they can be used on a PC or XT or on the 80286 or 80386.

SOURCES

Datadesk International 7650 Haskell Ave. Van Nuys, CA 91406 (800) 826-5398	Model Turbo-101	$149.95
Honeywell Keyboard Div. 4171 North Mesa, Bldg. D El Paso, TX 79902 (915) 544-5511	Model 101RX	$168
KeyTronic P.O. Box 14687 Spokane, WA 99214 (800) 262-6006	Model KB 101-1	$139
Northgate Computer Systems 2905 Northwest Blvd., Suite 250 Plymouth, MN 55441 (612) 553-0111	Model OMNI KEY/102	$99

MOUSE SYSTEMS

It is possible for a person to use an Apple Macintosh without knowing much about computers. Use a mouse with pull down menus and icons and all you have to do is point and click. There is no question about it. The Macintosh is easy to use. The MS-DOS world finally realized this and we now have several good software programs with Macintosh-like menus. Unfortunately, as of May of 1988, Apple has sued to stop development of these types of software. Apple's suit against Microsoft and Hewlett-Packard says that their software is too similar to their Macintosh screens. Apple has asked the court to declare that all windows type software is in violation of Apple's copyrights. They have asked that all such software be confiscated and destroyed and that Apple be paid damages.

Many people think that Apple has no chance of winning the suit, but it has served to put a damper on the development of software that takes advantage of icons and the mouse. Microsoft has countersued demanding that Apple pay them an unspecified amount of damages because their suit is hurting Microsoft's business. The suit could drag through the courts for years. Either way, Apple wins because there will be a slowdown in the development of Macintosh-like software for the MS-DOS world. We the consumers are the losers.

It is rather ironic that Apple did not develop the technology that they are trying to keep all to themselves. The icon and mouse concept was first investigated and used by the Xerox Palo Alto Research Corporation (PARC) in the late 1970s. Xerox dropped the idea of further development and Apple picked it up.

Lack of Standards

There are dozens of companies who are manufacturing mouses. There are several software programs that are virtually worthless without a mouse, such as Windows, CAD programs, paint and graphics programs, and many others. One of the problems for mouse systems is that there are no standards for software or for mouse operating systems. You can't just plug in a mouse and start using it. The software, whether Windows, WordStar, or a CAD program, must recognize and interface with the mouse.

Most mouse companies develop software drivers that allow the mouse to operate with various programs. The drivers are usually supplied on a diskette. Ordinarily they are installed in the CONFIG.SYS file of a system. The Microsoft Mouse is the closest to a standard so most other companies emulate the Microsoft driver.

Mechanical vs. Optical

There is also no standardization of the types of mouses. Some use optics with an LED that shines on a reflective grid. As the mouse is moved across the grid the reflected light is picked up by a detector and sent to the computer to move the cursor. For a design that demands very close tolerances the spacings of the grid for an optical mouse might not provide sufficient resolution. You might be better off in this case with a mouse that utilizes a ball that provides a smooth and continuous movement of the cursor. You don't need a grid for the ball type mouses, but you do need about a square foot of clear desk space to move the mouse about. The ball picks up dirt so it should be cleaned often. Some of the less expensive mouses have a resolution capability of only 100 to 200 dots per inch (DPI). Logitech has developed a HiREZ mouse that has a resolution of 320 DPI.

Number of Buttons

The Macintosh mouse has only one button. That doesn't give you much choice except to point and click. Almost all of the PC mice have at least two buttons which gives the user three choices: click the left button, click the right button, and click both buttons at the same time. Some of the mice have three control buttons. With three buttons the user has a possible seven choices: click left, click middle, click right, click left and middle, click middle and right, click left and right, and click all three. Despite all these choices, most software requires that only two of them be used, one at a time.

Interfaces

Most of the mouses require a voltage. Some come with a small plug-in transformer that should be plugged into your power strip. Some of the mouses require the use of one of your serial ports for their input to the computer. This may cause a problem if, for example, you already have a serial printer using COM1 and a modem on COM2. Some of the motherboards have ports built into the board so that you don't have to use a slot and install a board for a port. But you will still need a cable from the on-board COM ports to the outside world.

Microsoft, Logitech, and several other mouse companies have developed a bus mouse. It interfaces directly with the bus and does not require the use of one of your COM ports. But the systems come with a board that requires the use of one of your slots. The Numonics Corporation has developed the Manager Mouse Cordless. This cordless mouse uses infrared beams that work on the same principle as the television remote controls.

The Manager Mouse Cordless can operate as far as six feet away from the computer. Its beam must be aimed at a small receiver that is attached to the case of the computer with velcro. Care must be taken that no obstruction is placed between the receiver and the mouse that would block

Fig. 10-2. A CalComp pen plotter. (Photo courtesy of CalComp).

the beam. Its list price is $199. The Manager Mouse is a serial device so it must be plugged into one of your serial ports.

Security

A letter in a recent PC Magazine from a Mr. Ronny Richardson pointed out the fact that he could use the lock on his computer and walk away and no one could use his keyboard. But locking the keyboard out does not prevent anyone from using a mouse that might happen to be connected to the computer. In many cases, the mouse can access data files and do almost everything that can be done from the keyboard. It is suggested that if you are working with sensitive data, that you should turn off the computer and lock up the mouse.

Sources

It is best to call the listed companies for their latest price list and spec sheets.

IMSI Economouse	(415) 454-7101
Logitech Inc.	(415) 795-8500
Microsoft Mouse	(206) 882-8088
Mouse Systems Corp.	(408) 988-0211
Numonics Cordless Mouse	(800) 654-5449
Summagraphics Corp.	(203) 384-1344

TRACKBALLS

Trackballs usually do not require as much desk space as the ordinary mouse. If your desk is as cluttered as mine, then they may be what you are looking for. The Honeywell Disc Instruments Company has developed a couple of trackball cursor devices that look much like the ball on some video games. The microLYNX trackball has a connector that plugs in series with your keyboard connector. This device derives its needed voltage from the same line that feeds your keyboard. The comLYNX is an identical trackball except that it plugs into a serial port. They both have three buttons and come with a pop-up menu software program and several drivers. They are integral units 8.5 × 3 inches. Cost is $169 for either one.

Fulcrum Computers has also developed a trackball that has six buttons. The six buttons can be used for certain emulations and control. The Fulcrum is unlike the LYNX in that it uses an optical system. It is a serial device that must be plugged into a port. The cost is $95.

The MicroSpeed PC-Trac has a trackball that is in the serial or bus versions. It is compatible with Microsoft Mouse programs and comes with several drivers. The serial version is $119 and the bus is $139. Another device that is somewhat similar in operation to the trackballs is the Felix PC200. It is 5.5 inches square with a single slide button. It is a serial device and must be plugged into a serial port. It also must have power from a small five volt plug-in transformer. The cost is $199.

For more information, contact the respective companies:

Felix PC200	(415) 653-8500
Fulcrum Computer	(707) 433-0202
Honeywell LYNX	(800) 224-3522
MicroSpeed PC-Trac	(415) 490-1403

DIGITIZERS AND GRAPHICS TABLETS

Graphics tablets and digitizers are similar to a flat drawing pad or drafting table. Most of them use some sort of pointing device that can translate movement into digitized output to the computer. Some are rather small, while some might be as large as a standard drafting table. Some cost as little as $150, others over $1500.

Some of the tablets have programmable overlays and function keys. Some will work with mouse-like devices, a pen light, or a pencil-like stylus. The tablets can be used for designing circuits, for CAD programs, for graphics designs, freehand drawing, and even for text and data input. The most common use is with CAD type software. Most of the tablets are serial devices but some of them require their own interface board.

Here is a list of companies that sell digitizers and graphics tablets. Contact them for more information.

CalComp	(714) 821-2142
GTCO Corp.	(301) 381-6688
Koala Pad	(408) 438-0946
Kurta Corp.	(602) 276-5533
Pencept Inc.	(617) 893-6390
Summagraphics Corp	(203) 384-1344

SCANNERS AND OPTICAL CHARACTER READERS

Most large companies have mountains of memos, manuals, documents, and files that must be maintained, revised, and updated periodically. If a manual or document is in a loose leaf form, then only those pages that have changed will need to be retyped. But quite often a whole manual or document will have to be retyped and reissued.

Several companies now manufacture *Optical Character Readers* (OCR) that can scan a line of printed type, recognize each character, and input that character into a computer just as if it were typed in from a keyboard. Once the data is in the computer, a word processor can be used to revise or change the data, then print it out again. Or the data can be entered into a computer and stored on floppies or a hard disk. If it is a huge amount of data it could be stored on a Write Once Read Many (WORM) optical disk or on a CD-ROM so that it takes less space to store.

If copies of the printed matter are also stored in a computer, they can be searched very quickly for any item. Many times I have spent hours going through printed manuals looking for certain items. If the data had been in a computer, I could have found the information in just minutes.

Optical character readers have been around for several years. When they first came out they cost from $6,000 to more than $15,000. They were very limited in the character fonts that they could recognize and were not able to handle graphics at all. But vast improvements have been made in the last few years. Many are now fairly inexpensive, starting at about $900. Some handheld ones that are very limited are as low as $200. And there are some very sophisticated commercial models such as the Palantir and Kurzweil that can cost as much as $40,000. The more expensive models usually have the ability to recognize a large number of fonts and graphics.

The Houston Instruments Company specializes in manufacturing plotters. They have developed a scanning head for one of their plotters that can scan a large drawing, digitize the lines and symbols, then input them to a computer. The drawing can then be changed and replotted very easily.

For more information on commercial scanners, contact the following companies.

AST Research	(714) 863-1480
Canon U.S.A.	(516) 488-6800
CompuScan	(201) 575-0500
Datacopy Corp.	(415) 965-7900
Dest Corp.	(408) 946-7100
Houston Instrument	(512) 835-0900
Howtek	(603) 882-5200
Microtek Lab	(213) 321-2121
Saba	(800) 654-5274
Shape	(800) 247-1724
Transimage 1000	(408) 733-4111

BAR CODES

Bar codes are a system of black and white lines that are arranged in a system much like the Morse code of dots and dashes. By using combinations of wide and narrow bars and wide and narrow spaces, any numeral or letter of the alphabet can be represented. Bar codes were first adopted by the grocery industry. They set up a central office that assigned a unique number, a Universal Product Code (UPC) for just about every manufactured and pre-packaged product sold in a grocery store. Different sizes of the same product have a different and unique number assigned to them. The same type products from different manufacturers will also have different and unique assigned numbers. Most large grocery stores sell everything from automobile parts and accessories to drugs and medicines. Each item has its own unique bar code number.

When the clerk runs an item across the scanner, the dark bars absorb light and the white bars reflect the light. The scanner decodes this number and sends it to the main computer. The computer then matches the input number to the unique number stored on its hard disk which has the price of the item, the description, the amount in inventory, and several other pieces of information about the item. The computer sends back the price and the description of the part to the cash register where it is printed out. The computer then deducts that item from the overall inventory and adds the price to the overall cash received for the day.

At the end of the day the manager can look at the computer output and know exactly such things like how much business was done, what inventories need to be replenished and what items were the biggest sellers. With the push of a button on the computer, he or she can change any or all of the prices of the items in the store.

In the middle 1970s the Department of Defense (DOD) started looking for a better way of keeping track of its huge inventories of military items. They set up a committee and in 1982 they decreed that all military materials sold to the government would have a bar code label on it. Many of the suppliers screamed and cried because it added to their cost. But it was passed on to the government, so it wasn't too much of a burden.

It wasn't long before many of the people who had complained about having to use the bar codes found that they could make good use of them in many other ways to increase productivity, keep track of their inventory and a thousand other benefits. There are very few businesses, large or small, that cannot benefit from the use of bar codes.

There are several different types of bar code readers or scanners. Some are actually small portable computers that can store data to later be downloaded into a PC, XT, 286, or 386. Some systems have their own interface card which must be plugged into one of your slots. Some companies have devised systems that can be inserted in series with the keyboard so that no slot or other interface is needed. KeyTronic has a keyboard with a bar code reader as an integral part of the keyboard.

There are special printers that have been designed for printing some types of bar codes. But for many applications, they can be printed on dot matrix and laser printers. There are also several companies who specialize in printing up labels to your specifications.

A bar code scanner can read data into a computer at about 1700 characters per minute. And do it with absolute accuracy. Know anyone who can type that fast? Whole books have been written about the bar code, and other means of identification. There are hundreds of vendors and companies who offer service in this area. If you are interested in the bar code and automatic identification technology, there is a free magazine that you should be subscribing to called *ID Systems.* Almost anyone who has any business connections can qualify. ID Systems also publishes a very comprehensive directory of all the companies who offer bar code and automatic identification hardware, software, services and supplies.

COMPUTER VISION

Many companies have set up video cameras on their production lines to monitor the production process. For example, to inspect the items as they came off the assembly line. For instance, an image of a circuit board that is perfect concerning component placement and appearance is digitized and stored in the computer. Each time a circuit board comes off the assembly line, the camera focuses on it and the computer compares it to the stored image. If the two images match, the board is sent on to be further assembled or electronically tested. A computer can check a circuit board much faster than a human and do it better and more consistently.

COMPUTERIZED VOICE OUTPUT

Computer synthesized voice systems have been developed to do hundreds of tasks. Sensors can be set up so that when a beam is broken a signal is sent to a computer to alert a person of danger. The Atlanta airport has an underground shuttle to move people to the various airline gates. It has several sensors that feed into a computer. If a person is standing in the doorway, it will ask the person to move, and the train will not move until it is safe to do so.

Many automated banking systems will allow you to dial a number over the telephone into a computer. A computerized voice asks questions and lets you pay your bills, move money from one account to another, and do almost all of your banking by telephone. The telephone system has computerized voices for the time and for giving out numbers when you dial 411. Many more uses are being developed every day.

VOICE DATA INPUT

Another way to input data into a computer is to talk to it with a microphone. Of course you need electronics that can take the signal created by the microphone, detect the spoken words, and turn them into a form of digital information that the computer can use. The early voice data input systems were very expensive and limited. One reason was that the voice technology requires lots of memory. But the cost of memory has dropped considerably in the last few years, and the technology has improved in many other ways.

Voice technology involves training a computer to recognize a word spoken by a person. When you speak into a microphone, the sound waves cause a diaphragm, or some other device, to move back and forth in a magnetic field, creating a voltage that is analogous to the sound wave. If this voltage is recorded and played through a good audio system, the loudspeaker will respond to the amplified voltages and reproduce a sound that is identical to the one input to the microphone.

So a person can speak a word into a microphone which creates a unique voltage for that word and that particular person's voice. The voltage is fed into an electronic circuit, and the pattern is digitized and stored in the computer. If several words are spoken, the circuit will digitize each one of them and store them. Each one of them will have a distinct pattern. Later, when the computer hears a word, it will search through the patterns that it has stored to see if the input word matches any one of its stored words.

Of course, once the computer is able to recognize a word, you can have it perform some useful work. You could command it to load and run a program or perform any of several other tasks. Since every person's voice is different, the computer would not recognize the voice of someone who had not trained it. Training the computer may involve saying the same word several times so that the computer can store several patterns of the person's voice.

Voice data input is very useful whenever you must use both hands for doing a job but still need a computer to perform certain tasks. One area where voice data is used extensively is in the new military fighter planes. They move so fast that the pilot does not have time to manipulate computer keys. But he can have the computer do hundreds of jobs by just telling it what he wants done.

Voice data is also useful on production lines where the person does not have time to enter data manually. It can also be used in a laboratory where a scientist is looking through a microscope and cannot take his eyes off the subject to write down the findings or data. There might be times when the lighting must be kept too dim to manually input data to a computer. There are other instances where the person might have to be several feet from the computer and still be able to input data through the microphone lines. The person might even be miles away and be able to input data over a telephone line.

In most of the systems in use today, the computer must be trained to recognize a specific word, so the vocabulary is limited. But every word that can be spoken can be derived from just 42 *phonemes.* Several companies are working on systems that will take a small sample of a person's voice that contains these phonemes. Using the phonemes from this sample, the computer could then recognize any word that the person speaks.

The technology continues to improve. Eventually a person will be able to communicate with a computer without a keyboard. The boss can write his own letters with no secretary involved. Soon we will have computers, robots and other devices that will be able to understand and perform thousands of mundane tasks that will make life easier for us. And this will give us more time to play with our computers.

Chapter 11

Printers

Several years ago, a vice-president of a large corporation decided that there was too much printed paper work in the company. He advocated a ''paperless society'' and believed that it could be achieved with computers. He had several installed throughout the company and immediately the amount of printed paper work doubled. The reason was that there was a printer attached to each one of those computers.

Just seeing an electronic message on a computer screen is not enough for most people. They need printed hard copies that they can read, then file away for future reference if necessary. Computers or not, the printed word is here to stay.

PRINTER CONSIDERATIONS

For the vast majority of applications, a computer system is not complete without a printer. Choosing a printer for your system can be a difficult task because there are so many options. There are several types of printers and hundreds of manufacturers.

There are several factors that should be considered before purchasing a printer. The type of printer needed will depend primarily on what the computer will be used for. The following are some factors that should be considered when shopping for a printer.

Type Quality. If the printer to be used for business correspondence, a *daisy wheel* or a *laser printer* can provide the best letter quality type. A good 24-pin dot matrix can provide *Near Letter Quality* (NLQ) type. For most purposes, an NLQ printer will be sufficient.

It is possible to buy a very low cost 9-pin dot matrix. But if you do any serious printing at all, you will be unhappy with it. There are some that have 18 pins in the head, but the print is not as good as a good 24-pin dot matrix.

Again, depending on what you want to do with your printer, the laser will give the best print. But there are some things you can do with a dot matrix that can't be done with a laser. For instance, I need a wide carriage quite often; however, the lasers are limited to 8.5 by 11. More about lasers later.

Fonts. Font designs can be copyrighted. Many large corporations, such as IBM, have their own copyrighted fonts. There are several major types of fonts such as Roman, Times, Courier, Helvetica and others. Each of these types from different companies will be slightly different in shape. If there are going to be several printers in a company or office, it might be worthwhile to consider buying all the same brand of printers because of the font differences.

Most daisy wheel manufacturers provide several different daisy wheels with different type fonts. The better dot matrix printers also have several font options. Many printers are now equipped with a couple of slots that will accept cartridges for several different font styles. If you do any fancy printing, they can be valuable.

There are several software programs that can be used with dot matrix printers to print out large type, such as headlines, signs, banners, and all sorts of graphics. Most lasers have a large variety of fonts.

Pitch. The number of characters that can be printed in one inch is the character pitch. The better printers are usually capable of printing at least three different pitches. Ten characters per inch is called *pica*. Most typewriters use this spacing which is 80 characters per line. Twelve characters per inch is called *elite*. It is also possible to have *semi-condensed* type at 15 characters per inch and *expanded* type at five characters per inch. Many of the printers can be switched from one pitch to another with application software such as a word processor or with a simple BASIC program.

Proportional Spacing. Typewriters and most printers give each character the same amount of space no matter how wide it is. Pica pitch gives an "M" and an "I" each 1/10 of an inch even though the "M" may be two or three times wider than the "I". Proportional spacing can be a critical consideration if the printer is going to be used for desktop publishing. Most daisy wheels cannot support proportional spacing. Proportional spacing is possible with the better dot matrix printers and lasers.

Subscripts and Superscripts. If you are going to be doing any kind of scientific writing, you will probably need this capability. The printer should also be capable of variable line spacing.

Bold Face and Underline. These capabilities are very important to stress or emphasize a point or to set a group of words apart.

Speed. The characters per second (CPS) is a factor to be considered when deciding on a printer. Of course, you want one that is as fast as possible. It can be frustrating having to wait for a long document to print out. Depending on the type of printer and your software, your computer may be tied up for as long as it takes to print out a document. In a business office, this could be expensive if the employee has to sit there and do nothing until the printing is finished.

Draft quality is often sufficient for such things as informal notes, memos, and preliminary reports. A quick draft copy makes proofreading and editing much easier than trying to do it on the computer. Most monitors display twenty five lines only. Many word processors use 10 to 15 of those lines for menus and help, which means you can only see a portion of the page at any one time. You might make a correction or amendment on the portion of the page that is showing on the screen, then completely forget about it when the other half of the page comes up. So, it's best to print out a quick rough draft and do your proofing on a hard copy.

Some manufacturers advertise draft speeds as high as 400 CPS in draft mode but few claim more than 160 CPS in NLQ mode. You should be aware that many vendors tend to exaggerate a bit on their CPS claims. One reason is that there is no standard speed test and it takes less time to print certain characters than others. So a printer might achieve 400 CPS in a burst of speed during the middle of a line, but the time required to print every character of the alphabet and for the carriage returns and line feeds would reduce the figure somewhat.

A full page might have about 4000 characters. In draft mode at 400 CPS, a page could be printed in 10 seconds, or about six pages per minute. A laser can print six to ten pages per minute of good letter quality print. So, in draft mode a good dot matrix can print about as fast as some lasers. For NLQ print, the dot matrix slows down to 100 to 150 CPS. So to print a sheet of 4000 characters would take from 27 to 40 seconds. The daisy wheel printers are rated from 15 CPS up to 60 CPS. So at 15 CPS, it would take about 4.5 minutes to print 4000 characters. At 60 CPS, it would take a little over 1 minute.

The Output Technology Corporation claims over 800 CPS for their printer. They use three print heads, each with a 9-pin matrix. One of their machines, the 850 PrintNet, has five built-in connectors and the capability to be shared by five different computers.

Compatibility. There are absolutely no standards for printers. Drivers are usually needed to take advantage of the capabilities offered. Software packages such as word processors, spreadsheets, database, and graphics programs have to supply hundreds of different drivers with their software packages to try to make them compatible with whatever printer you happen to have. The closest thing to a standard is the character and graphics set first used by Epson. IBM bought the small Epson graphics dot matrix printers and put their own IBM logo on them. This helped to establish somewhat of a standard. Most of the printer makers are still installing their own operating systems, but many of them are including emulation firmware for the IBM and Epson standard.

Graphics Capability. The printer should be able to emulate the IBM and Epson standard. If possible get a demonstration of it printing out a simple graphics pie chart or something similar. Note the speed and the fineness of lines, the shape of curves and circles and uniform density of filled in areas.

Parallel or Serial. parallel printer should be no more than ten feet away from the computer. If the cable is much longer, the signals can be degraded and possibly lose some data. A serial cable can be up to 50 feet long without causing any degradation of the signal.

IBM chose the parallel system and it has become the closest thing to a standard that we have. Many printers will only accept parallel signals. Some of the better printers will accept either parallel or serial. This capability could be very important if the printer is located more than ten feet from the computer.

Wide Carriage. Most printers come in at least two different widths. I prefer the wide carriage. Quite often I have to address a large manila envelope which requires a wide carriage. If you are in a business office, there may be times when you will need to do graphics or need the wide paper for a spreadsheet printout. The wide carriage models may cost $100 to $200 more than the standard size. Otherwise, they usually have the same specifications as to speed and letter quality.

Tractors. The tractors are the sprockets that engage the holes in the margins of continuous feed paper. Most printers have standard friction feed for printing individual cut sheets. Several of them have built-in tractors. But some offer the tractor only as an added cost option which may cost $75 to $100 extra. Tractors are essential, especially if you are going to be printing labels or other types of work where the paper must be controlled. Most friction feeds will not hold the paper straight, or provide accurate and consistent line feed spacing, especially after the platen gets a bit old and hardened. I would recommend that you get a printer with a tractor.

Paper Advance. Most of the printers have a couple of buttons that advance the paper. One may be marked Top Of Form and the other one marked Paper Feed. The Top Of Form will move a sheet of paper forward to the top of the next sheet. The Paper Feed will advance the paper one line at a time as long as the button is held down.

Most printers also have a large knob attached to the platen which can be turned to position the paper. You should not use this knob whenever the power is on because it works against the electric clutches that advance the paper. This could damage and wear out the clutches. If you want to use the knob to position the paper, switch off the power, then switch it back on.

Buffers. Even a very high speed printer is very slow compared to how fast a computer can feed data to it. If the printer has a large memory buffer, the computer can dump its data into the buffer, then be free for other work. Some printers may have a buffer as small as 1k, but the better ones have 8K or more. Many of them have an option to add more memory to the buffer. If the printer is in a large office, it might even be worth the cost to install a large standalone buffer between the printer and computer.

Print Spoolers. Print spoolers are similar to buffers, except that they use a portion of your computer's RAM memory to store the data that is to be printed. Some programs will even store the data on your hard disk and spool it out to the printer as needed. The computer will then be free for doing more important things than just sitting idle most of the time while the printer is doing its thing. Several of the LIM EMS boards come with software for using expanded memory for print spooling. Incidentally, *Spool* is an acronym for Simultaneous Peripheral Operations On Line.

Multiple Bins. Some printers will allow you to attach several different paper bins to them. A standard size cut sheet paper could be in one bin, the long legal size in another, and perhaps an envelope feeder also. In a busy office it can save a lot of time. But some of the bins are rather expensive, especially those designed for laser printers.

Ribbons. Most dot matrix printers use a nylon cloth ribbon. The ribbons are relatively inexpensive and can last for quite a long time. Most ribbons cost between $4 and $10. There are kits available that can be used to re-ink the ribbons. After the kit is paid for, it costs only pennies to re-ink a ribbon. And they can be used over and over until the fabric wears out.

Many of the letter quality printers use a carbon film type of ribbon. This gives good crisp letters that are truly print quality. It is possible to use the cloth type ribbons, but cloth ribbons cannot produce the same quality print, no matter how good the printer is.

The carbon film ribbons are good for a single pass only. And there is no way that they can be re-inked or used again. Some printers use a wide ribbon in a cartridge. The ribbon carriage moves the ribbon up and down so that three characters can be struck across the width of the ribbon. One of these ribbons will allow several thousand characters to be printed in a single pass.

Color. Both cloth and carbon film ribbons are available in various colors for most printers. Most ribbons are on cartridges that are very easy to change. It is quite simple in most word processors to insert a print pause, change ribbons, then resume printing. A little color can be a great way to call attention to a certain portion of a letter or an important report to the CEO.

Some printers can use a wide ribbon that has three or more colors on it. The printer can shift the ribbon to the desired color and actually blend the colors to achieve all the colors of the rainbow. Hewlett-Packard has an ink-jet type of printer that can print seven color graphics.

Paper. Paper is a very important element. But there is a sea of confusion as to paper specifications such as weight, brightness, and thickness. Different printers and different applications need various kinds of paper. Some specialty printers, such as thermal printers, require a special paper. Here are a few definitions:

Bond. Early government bonds were printed on high quality paper with a watermark. Nowadays, almost anything can be called bond paper. But the better bond will have a watermark and at least 25 percent rag content. The better quality papers may also have terms like linen, wove, and laid. Linen has a regular weave pattern and a sheen. Laid paper has a sculpted feeling.

Brightness. There are many shades of white. The better paper is rated as to the brightness. For best results from laser printers, the paper should have a uniform surface, anti-curl, anti-static, and a brightness rating above 85.

Continuous Sheet. The continuous sheets have perforations to separate each sheet. They also have a removable strip along each side for the pin feed sprocket holes of the printer tractor. Most of the continuous sheet paper is now laser cut so that the pages and pin strips tear off evenly.

Cut Sheets. This would be single sheets that would require the use of friction feed by the printer's platen. Cut sheets are also used for laser printers.

Weight. The weight is determined by weighing 500 sheets (1 ream) of 17 × 22 inch paper. The most common weight is 20 pounds. But the 17 × 22 inch sheets are cut in half to give 8.5 × 11 after they are weighed. Some very thin low priced computer paper may weigh as little as 12, 15, or 18 pounds. This thin paper might be suitable for draft type printing or interoffice memos. It would not be very good for correspondence or for important data.

Sound Proofing. Printers can be very noisy. In a large office the noise can be disruptive. Several companies manufacture sound proofing enclosures. These are usually made from plywood and then lined with foam rubber. They usually have a clear plastic door so that you can see what is going on inside. These enclosures can be rather expensive though, costing from $150 to over $200. If you don't have that kind of money, you might even take a large cardboard box and put it over the printer.

You can eliminate a lot of the printer noise by simply placing foam rubber beneath the printer. Most printers have covers that protect the head and other internal parts of the printer. The cover helps to cut down on the noise. Most of the printers have microswitches that will not allow the printer to operate without the cover.

I have a Star NB 24-15, a wide carriage, 24-pin dot matrix. It has several controls under the plastic protective cover. One control is the paper thickness. For a single sheet of paper it should be at the minimum. For an envelope it should be moved out. Every time I wanted to address an envelope, I had to lift the cover off, set the lever, then close the cover again. Then, hopefully, remember to reset it before I printed my next single page letter. I got tired of this, so I just leave the cover off. I defeated the microswitch with a paper clip. I suppose that I am violating all kinds of warranties and safety precautions, but it sure is easier to operate. Star should have made these important controls a bit more accessible. Otherwise, I have been quite pleased with the printer.

Stands. There are several stands that you can buy to raise the printer up off the table so that a stack of fanfold computer paper can be placed beneath it. They will cost from $20 up to $75. I have mine sitting on a couple of bricks. I put foam rubber on top of the bricks to eliminate some of the noise.

Cost. The cost of a dot matrix printer can range from $200 up to over $2000 depending on the speed, special features and other extras. The cost of the daisy wheels range from $400 up to $3000 depending on speed, buffers and other accessories.

SOURCES

Listed below are the names and telephone numbers of some of the Dot Matrix Printers. Many of them also manufacture daisy wheel printers. Call them for their latest models and prices.

Advanced Matrix Technology	(805) 499-8741
Alps America	(800) 828-2557

Brother International	(201) 981-0300
C. Itoh Digital Products	(213) 327-2110
Canon U.S.A.	(516) 488-6700
Citizen America	(213) 453-0614
Dataproducts Corp.	(603) 673-9100
Datasouth Computer Corp.	(800) 222-4528
Epson America	(213) 539-9140
Fujitsu America	(408) 946-8777
Genicom Corp.	(703) 949-1000
IBM Corp.	(800) 426-2468
Infoscribe	(800) 233-4442
JDL Inc.	(805) 495-3451
Mannesman Tally	(206) 251-5500
NEC Information Systems	(800) 343-4418
Newbury Data Inc.	(213) 372-3775
Nissho Information Systems	(714) 952-8700
Okidata	(800) 654-3282
Olympia	(201) 722-7000
Output Technology Corp.	(800) 422-4850
Panasonic Industrial Co.	(201) 348-7000
Printronix	(714) 863-1900
Seikosha America	(201) 529-4655
Star Micronics	(212) 986-6770
Tandy/Radio Shack	(817) 390-3011
Texas Instruments	(800) 527-3500
Toshiba America	(714) 730-5000

LASER PRINTERS

Laser printers combine laser technologies and copy machine technologies. A laser uses synchronized, multifaceted mirrors and sophisticated optics to write the characters or images on a photosensitive rotating drum. This drum can then print a whole sheet of paper in one rotation.

The drum and its associated mechanical attachments is called an *engine.* Canon, a Japanese company, is one of the foremost makers of engines. They manufacture them for their own laser printers and for dozens of other companies such as Hewlett-Packard and Apple.

The Hewlett-Packard LaserJet was one of the first low cost lasers. It was a fantastic success and became the de facto standard. There are now hundreds of laser printers on the market. Most of them emulate the LaserJet standard, and most software adheres to this standard. If you are buying a laser, check for this feature.

The competition has been a great benefit to us consumers. It has forced many new improvements, and the discount price for some models is now down to under $1500. I have no doubt that the prices will drop even more as the competition increases and the economies of scale in the manufacturing process becomes greater.

EXTRAS FOR LASERS

Don't be surprised if you go into a store to buy a $1500 laser printer and end up paying about twice that much. The laser printer business is much like the automobile, the computer, and most other businesses. The $1500 advertised price may be for a barebones model without several of the essential items needed to do any productive work. Such items as cartridge plug-in fonts, memory, controller boards, and software may all cost extra. Some sheet bin paper feeders may cost as much as a basic printer.

Memory. If you plan to do any graphics or desktop publishing (DTP), you will need to have at least one megabyte of memory in the machine. Of course, the more memory, the better. It will cost about $500 extra for 1.5 megabytes of memory and about $2000 for an extra 4.5 megabytes.

Page-Description Languages. If you plan to do any desktop publishing you will need a page-description language (PDL) controller board. As we pointed out in Chapter 8, text characters and graphics images are two different species of animals. Monitor controller boards usually have all of the alphabetical and numerical characters stored in ROM. When we press the letter A on the keyboard, it dives into the ROM chip, drags out the A and displays it in the block on the screen wherever the cursor happens to be. It has another set of chips where it stores the symbols it uses to create graphics displays. Some of the early monitor drivers were capable of producing text only.

Laser printers are similar to the monitors and drivers. They need a special controller, a PDL, to be able to mix and print images or graphics and text on the same page. Several companies have developed their own PDLs. Of course, none of them are compatible with the others. This has caused a major problem for software developers because they must try to include drivers for each one of these PDLs.

Speed. Laser printers can print from 6 to over 10 pages per minute depending on the model and what they are printing. Some complex graphics may require more than one minute to print a single page.

Color. Several companies are working to develop a color laser printer. But there are some large problems, and it is not expected that they will be easily overcome. If and when color is available, the cost will probably be from $15,000 to $25,000.

Resolution. Almost all of the lasers have a 300 × 300 dots per inch resolution (DPI). This is very good, but not nearly as good as 1200 × 1200 dots per inch typeset used for standard publications. Several companies are working to develop 600 × 600 DPI machines.

Maintenance. Most of the lasers use a toner cartridge that is good for 3000 to 5000 pages. The original cost of the cartridge is about $100. Several small companies are now refilling the spent cartridges for about $50 each.

Of course there are other maintenance costs. Since these machines are very similar to copy machines, they have a lot of moving parts that can wear out and jam up. Most of the larger companies give a mean time between failures (MTBF) of 30,000 up to 100,000 pages. But remember that these are only average figures and not a guarantee.

SOURCES

Here are the telephone numbers of a few laser printer companies. Call them for their product specifications and latest price list.

Apple Computer	(408) 973-2222
AST Research	(714) 863-1333
Brother International	(210) 981-0300
Canon USA	(516) 488-6700
C. Itoh	(213) 327-2110
Epson GQ-3500	(800) 421-5426
Hewlett-Packard LaserJet II	(800) 367-4772
IBM Corp.	(800) 426-2468
Kyocera Unison	(415) 848-6680
Mannesman Tally Corp.	(206) 251-5500
NEC Information Systems	(800) 343-4418
Office Automation Systems (OASYS)	(619) 452-9400
Olympia USA	(201) 231-8300
Okidata	(800) 654-3282
Panasonic Office Automation	(201) 348-7000
Personal Computer Products	(619) 485-8411
Quadram Corp.	(404) 432-4144
QMS Inc.	(205) 633-4300
Ricoh PC Laser	(201) 892-2000
Sharp Electronics	(201) 529-9500
Star Micronics	(212) 986-6770
Texas Instruments	(800) 343-4418
Toshiba America	(714) 380-3000

LIQUID CRYSTAL SHUTTER PRINTERS

At least two companies, Taxan and Data Technology, are manufacturing *Liquid Crystal Shutter* (LCS) printers. They use an engine that is similar to that used by the lasers. But instead of using a laser beam to write on the photosensitive drum, they use high-intensity lights that are turned on and off with a liquid crystal shutter. There are 2400 lights that are mounted in a line on a print bar.

The speed, resolution, and cost is about the same as the laser printers. But they have fewer moving parts than a laser, so they should have fewer mechanical problems. They should cost less to manufacture so the price should come down to less than the lasers. For more information, contact: Taxan USA Corp. at (800) 772-7491 and Data Technology at (408) 727-8899.

INK JET PRINTERS

Ink jet printers spray ink onto the paper to form characters. They are quiet since there is no impact. Hewlett-Packard is the major manufacturer of these printers. They are small, quiet and are capable of printing in various colors.

The Hewlett-Packard DeskJet is an ink jet printer that costs less than $1000. It can produce 300 DPI resolution that approaches that of a high cost laser. But it does not use the laser type engine. Instead it has a head that is similar to that of the dot matrix printer. Ink is forced through a matrix of tiny ink holes to form characters on plain paper.

The DeskJet's output looks very much like a laser. But it has many of the limitations of a dot matrix printer. It is limited in its graphics capabilities and fonts. A laser can print about 8 sheets per minute. The DeskJet can only print about 2 per minute. Hewlett-Packard can be contacted at 1820 Embarcadero, Palo Alto, CA, 94303.

OTHER TYPES OF PRINTERS

There are several other types of printers that are available. *Thermal* printers are relatively inexpensive. They use heat to darken a specially treated paper. They are quieter than the impact type dot matrix printers but the quality may be rather poor.

PLOTTERS

Plotters are devices that can draw almost any shape or design under the control of a computer. A plotter may have from 1 to 8 or more different colored pens. There are several different types of pens for various applications, such as writing on different types of paper or on film or transparencies. Some pens are quite similar to ball point pens, others have a fiber type point. The points are usually made to a very close tolerance and are very small so that the thickness of the lines can be controlled. The line thicknesses can be very critical in some design drawings.

The plotter arm can be directed to choose any one of the various pens. This arm is attached to a sliding rail and can be moved from one side of the paper to the other. A solenoid can lower the pen at any predetermined spot on the paper for it to write.

While the motor is moving the arm horizontally from side to side, a second motor moves the paper vertically up and down beneath the arm. This motor can move the paper to any predetermined spot and the pen can be lowered to write on that spot. The motors are controlled by predefined X-Y coordinates. They can move the pen and paper in very small increments so that almost any design can be traced out. The computer can direct the plotter to move the pen to any point on the sheet.

Plotters are ideal for such things as printing out circuit board designs, for architectural drawings, for making transparencies, for overhead presentations, for graphs and charts, and many CAD/CAM drawings. All of this can be done in as many as seven different colors.

There are several different sized plotters. Some desk top units are limited to only A and B sized plots. There are other large floor standing models that can accept paper as wide as four feet and several feet long. A desk model might cost as little as $200 and up to $2000. A floor standing large model might cost from $4000 up to $10,000. If you are doing very precise work, for instance designing a transparency that will be photographed and used to make a circuit board, you will want one of the more accurate and more expensive machines.

There are many very good graphics programs available that can use plotters. But there are several manufacturers of plotters. And again, there are no standards. Just like the printers, each company has developed its own drivers. Again, this is very frustrating for software developers who must try to include drivers in their programs for all of the various brands.

Hewlett-Packard is one of the major plotter manufacturers. Many of the other manufacturers now emulate the HP drivers. Almost all of the software that require plotters include a driver for HP. If you are in the market for a plotter, try to make sure that it can emulate the HP. Houston Instruments is also a major manufacturer of plotters. Their plotters are somewhat less expensive than the Hewlett-Packards.

One of the disadvantages of plotters is that they are rather slow. There are now some software programs that will allow a laser printer to act as a plotter. Of course, the laser is limited to 8 ½ by 11 inch sheets of paper. Here is a list of some of the plotter manufacturers. Call them for a product list and latest prices.

Alpha Merics	(818) 999-5580
Bruning Computer Graphics	(415) 372-7568
CalComp	(800) 225-2667
Hewlett-Packard	(800) 367-4772
Houston Instruments	(512) 835-0900
Ioline Corp.	(206) 775-7861
Roland DG	(213) 685-5141

It is important that a good supply of plotter pens, special paper, film, and other supplies be kept on hand. Plotter supplies are not as widely available as printer supplies. A very high priced plotter may have to sit idle for some time if the supplies are not on hand. Most of the plotter vendors provide supplies for their equipment. Here is the name of one company that specializes in plotter pens, plotter media, accessories and supplies:

Plotpro, P.O. Box 800370, Houston, TX, 77280, 1-800-223-7568.

PORTS

The computer allows for four ports, two serial and two parallel. No matter whether it is a plotter, dot matrix, daisy wheel, or laser printer, it will require one of these ports. If you have a serial printer, you will need a board with a RS232C connector. The parallel printers use a Centronics type connector. When you buy your printer, buy a cable from the vendor that is configured for your printer and your computer.

Many of the 386 motherboards have built-in parallel and serial ports on them. But these ports are usually just a couple rows of pins soldered to the motherboard. To use them you will need a cable with connectors that will plug in to these pins. These motherboards usually have a switch or shorting bar that enables or disables the on-board ports. Make sure you get a manual or some sort of documentation showing the various ports and shorting switches on your motherboard.

INTERFACES

Printers can be very difficult to interface. In the serial system, the bits are transmitted serially, one bit at a time. The parallel system uses an 8-line bus and 8 bits are transmitted at a time, one bit on each line at a time. It takes 8 bits to make one character. So with the parallel system, a whole character can be transmitted on the eight lines at one time.

The parallel system was developed by the Centronics Company. IBM adopted the parallel system as the default mode for their PC and PC-XT. Of course the clones followed suit, so parallel inputs are the standard on most printers sold today. Many printers will accept either parallel or serial. You can buy printer boards with a parallel or serial output port. Some multifunction boards provide both.

PRINTER SHARING

Ordinarily, a printer will sit idle most of the time. There are some days when I don't even turn my printer on. There are usually several computers in most large offices and businesses. Almost all of them are connected to a printer in some fashion.

But it would be a waste of money if each one had a separate printer that was only used occasionally. It is fairly simple to make arrangements so that a printer or plotter can be used by several computers. If there are only two or three computers, and they are fairly close together, it is not much of a problem. There are manual switch boxes that cost from $45 to $150 that can allow any one of two or three computers to be switched on line to a printer.

But with a simple switch box, if the computers use the standard parallel ports, the cables from the computers to the printer should be no more than 10 feet long. Parallel signals will begin to degrade if the cable is longer than 10 feet and could cause some loss of data. A serial cable can be as long as 50 feet. If the printer has a parallel only input, it is possible to buy a serial to parallel converter. A fairly long serial cable can be used, then the signals can be converted to parallel just before the cable is connected to the printer.

If the office or business is fairly complex, then there are several electronic switching devices available. Some of them are very sophisticated and can allow a large number of different types of computers to be attached to a single printer or plotter. Many of them have built-in buffers and can allow cable lengths up to 250 feet or more. The costs range from $160 up to $1400.

Of course there are several networks that are available to connect computers and printers together. Many of them can be very expensive to install. One of the least expensive methods of sharing a printer is for the person to generate the text to be printed out on one computer, record it on a floppy diskette, then walk over to a computer that is connected to a printer. If it is in a large office, a single low cost XT clone could be dedicated to a high priced printer.

Here are the names and phone numbers of some of those companies that provide switch systems. Call them for their product specs and current price list:

Logical Connection
Fifth Generation Systems
(800) 225-2775

EasyPrint
Server Technology
(800) 835-1515

Buffalo XL-256
Buffalo Products
(800) 345-2356

Auto Six Shooter
Black Box Corp.
(412) 746-5530

Crosspoint 8
Crosspoint Systems
(800) 232-7729

PrintDirector MS-1
Digital Products
(800) 243-2333

ShareSpool ESI-2076
Extended Systems
(208) 322-7163

Caretaker Plus
Rose Electronics
(713) 933-7673

Western Telematic PSU-81B
Western Telematic
(800) 854-7226

Quadram
Microfazer VI
(404) 564-5566

Chapter 12

Communications

The communications capability of the computer is one of its most important aspects. There are thousands of software programs and hardware components that can allow you to communicate with millions of other computer owners. You can also use much of this software and hardware to link up and share the hard disks, data, and resources of other computers. In this chapter, I will briefly discuss some of the important communications methods. This will include both hardware and software that involves modems, electronic mail (E-Mail), and facsimile (or FAX) systems.

MODEMS

A *modem* is an electronic device that allows a computer to use an ordinary telephone line to communicate with other computers that are equipped with a modem. Modem is a contraction of the words *mo*dulate and *dem*odulate. The telephone system is analog, and computer data is usually in a digital form. The modem modulates the digital data from a computer and turns it into analog voltages for transmission. At the receiving end, a similar modem will demodulate the analog voltage back into a digital form.

Baud Rate. Telephone systems were originally designed for voice and have a very narrow bandwidth. They are subject to noise, static, and other electrical disturbances. The original modems could only operate at about

50 baud, or about 5 characters, per second. There have been some fantastic advances in the modem technologies. About one third of the modems today operate at a 1200 baud rate, or at about 120 characters per second. Another one third are operating at 2400 baud. Thousands of others are operating at 4800 and 9600 baud. The 9600 baud rate will no doubt become the standard.

Of course both the sending and receiving modem must operate at the same baud rate. Most of the faster modems are downward compatible and can operate at the slower speeds. The faster the baud rate, the less time it will take to download or transmit a file. If the file is being sent over a long distance line the length of time can be critical. If the modem is used frequently, the telephone bills can be very substantial.

Besides the phone line charges, the major on-line service companies, such as CompuServe, Dataquest, and Dow Jones News/Retrieval, charge for connect time to their service. The connect time is much less with some of the high speed modems. But in order to keep their revenue up, some companies are charging more for the higher speed modems.

As of this date, there is no standard for baud rates higher than 2400. There is still a lot of squabbling among the various manufacturers. Hayes has developed a 9600 baud machine, and since they are the leader, it will more than likely set the standard. Some of the 9600 baud modems may cost up to $3000. Unless you perform extensive file transfers, you would probably be better off buying a 2400 baud machine. These modems may cost from $175 up to $700. Many of them come with bundled software.

Software. In order to use a modem, it must be driven and controlled by software. There are dozens of communication programs that can be used.

One of the better ones is Relay Silver from VM Personal Computing, (203) 798-3800. Their Relay Gold is one of the most versatile of the communications software packages. It has features that allow remote communications, accessing main frames, and dozens of utilities not found on the usual communications programs. Crosstalk, (404) 998-3998, was one of the earlier modem programs. ProComm, (314) 474-8461, is one of several low cost shareware programs. There are also several public domain programs such as QModem that will do almost everything that the high cost commercial packages do.

Besides using a faster baud rate, another way to reduce phone charges is to use file compression. Bulletin Boards have been using a form of data compression for years. There are several public domain programs that squeeze and un-squeeze the data.

Firmware. Several new advances have recently been made in some of the newer modems. They use a system for the compression of data before it is transmitted, then decompression after it is received. The methods are similar to the algorithms used to compress data on some hard disk systems. Some schemes can compress a file and make it smaller by as much as 100 and up to 200 percent. Again, the smaller the file the less time on the telephone line. Squeezed or compressed files also take up less room when recorded on a hard disk or floppy.

Basic Types. There are two basic types of modems, the external desktop and the internal. Each type has some advantages and disadvantages. The bad news is that the external type requires some of your precious desk space and a voltage source. It also requires a COM port to drive it. The good news is that most external models have LEDs that light up and let you know what is happening during your call. Both the external and the internal models have speakers that let you hear the phone ringing or if you get a busy signal. Some of the external models have a volume control for the built-in speaker.

The internal modem is built entirely on a board, usually a half or short board. The good news is that it doesn't use up any of your desk real estate, but the bad news is that it uses one of your precious slots. And it does not have the LEDs to let you know the progress of your call.

Hayes Compatibility. One of the most popular early modems was made by Hayes Microcomputer Products. They have become the IBM of the modem world and have established a defacto standard. There are hundreds of modem manufacturers. Except for some of the very inexpensive ones, almost all of them emulate the Hayes standard.

Connection. The modem plugs into your phone line. You can have a dedicated line, or you can buy a Y connector and run an extension off your regular line. It is not very difficult to install. You can buy the extension cable and Y connectors at most hardware stores or stores that sell telephones and equipment.

Using an extension off your regular phone will cause no problems unless someone tries to make a call at the same time that you are transmitting or receiving data. If the modem is going to be used frequently, it would probably be best to install a dedicated phone line.

BULLETIN BOARDS

If you have a modem, you have access to several thousand computer bulletin boards. There are over one hundred in the San Francisco Bay area and about twice that many in the Los Angeles area. Most of them are free of any charge. You only have to pay the phone bill if they are out of your calling area. Some of them charge a nominal fee to join, and some just ask for a tax deductible donation.

Some of the bulletin boards are set up by private individuals and some by companies and vendors as a service to their customers. Others are set up by users groups and other special interest organizations. There are over one hundred boards nationwide that have been set up for doctors and lawyers. Most of the bulletin boards are set up to help individuals. They usually have lots of public domain software and a space where you can leave messages for help, for advertising something for sale, or for just plain old chit-chat.

If you are just getting started you probably need some telecommunications software. There are public domain software packages that are equivalent to almost all of the major commercial programs. And the best part is that they are free. Some of the programs are in the Shareware category such as PC Write, QModem, and ProComm. You can download them and use them, but the originator asks that you send a nominal donation or fee for the program. This is not unreasonable considering that many of these programs are as good or better than some of the commercial programs that cost hundreds of dollars. They cannot force you to pay for these programs, but if you don't, your conscience will probably bother you.

The bulletin boards are a two-way system. They ask that you contribute public domain software that you may have written or acquired so that it can be shared by other users. Most people are glad to share what they have with others.

VIRUSES

There are all kinds of people in this world. Some of them are sick and sadistic psychos who seem to derive a certain pleasure out of hurting others. There have been several reports that some of these sick individuals have hidden *viruses* in some public domain and even in some commercial software. This software appears to be something that is functional and useful. It may perform for some time, then a hidden command in the software may erase an entire hard disk, or it may gradually erase portions of the disk each time the machine is turned on or in some other way damage your data. Any time a copy is made of this program, it will attach itself to the copy and spread. One form of virus attaches itself to the boot-up portion of the COMMAND.COM and slightly increases the number of bytes in this vital command each time the computer is booted up. One way to detect this virus is to do a check on your version of COMMAND.COM every so often to be sure that it remains the same. Just type DIR COMMAND.COM and it will display the amount of bytes in the file.

There are now several public domain and commercial software "vaccine" programs that will check for viruses. Here is a short list:

Asky Inc.	(408) 943-1940
Data Physician	(800) 221-8091
Flu-Shot	(212) 889-6438
Sophco	(303) 444-1542

Most bulletin board operators are now screening their programs, although it is almost impossible to find some of the viruses. It is advisable to download programs on a floppy diskette and run them for a while before putting them on a hard disk. If a floppy is ruined, you won't be hurt too much.

ILLEGAL ACTIVITIES

Some of the bulletin boards have also been used for illegal and criminal activities. Stolen credit card numbers and telephone charge numbers have been left on the bulletin boards. Because of these few low-life vermin, many of the *sysops*, bulletin board system operators, are now carefully checking any software that is uploaded onto their systems. Many of them are now restricting access to their boards. Some of them have had to start charging a fee because of the extra time it takes to monitor the boards.

There are several local computer magazines that devote a lot of space to bulletin boards and user groups. In California the *MicroTimes* and *Computer Currents* magazines have several pages of bulletin boards and user groups each month. One of the magazines that I write for occasionally is the *Computer Shopper*. It has the most comprehensive listing of bulletin boards and user groups of any national magazine. See the chapter on Sources for the addresses of this and other magazines.

The Bulletin Board listings in the Computer Shopper is compiled by Gale Rhoades, P.O. Box 3474, Daly City, CA 94015, (415) 755-2000. She works with an international nonprofit computer user group called FOG. If you know of a bulletin board or user group that should be listed, contact her. She can also supply you with a listing of boards.

ON-LINE SERVICES

There are several large national bulletin boards, information, and reference services such as CompuServe, Dataquest, Dow Jones, and Dialog. These companies have huge databases of information. A caller can search the databases and download information as easily as pulling the data off his own hard disk. The companies charge a fee for the connect time.

Many of the national bulletin boards offer electronic mail, or E-Mail, along with their other services. These services can be of great value to some individuals and businesses. E-Mail subscribers are usually given a "post office box" at these companies. This is usually a file on one of their large hard disk systems. When a message is received, it is recorded in this file. The next time the subscriber logs on to this service he or she will be alerted that there is mail in their in-box.

E-Mail is becoming more popular every day and there are now several hundred thousand subscribers. The cost for an average message is about one dollar. By comparison, the cost for overnight mail from the U.S. Post Office, Federal Express, and UPS is $11 to $13.

Some of the companies who provide E-Mail at the present time are:

AT&T Mail	(800) 367-7225
CompuServe	(800) 848-8990
DASnet	(408) 559-7434
MCI Mail	(800) 444-6245
Western Union	(800) 527-5184

LAN E-MAIL

Most of the larger Local Area Network (LAN) programs also provide an E-Mail utility in their software. For those packages that do not provide this utility, there are programs available that work with installed LANs. Contact the following companies for more information:

Action Technologies	(800) 624-2162
Lotus Express	(800) 345-1043
PCC Systems	(415) 321-0430

OTHER SERVICES

Many banks offer systems that will let you do all your banking with your computer and a modem from the comforts of your home. You would never again have to drive downtown, hunt for a parking space, then stand in line to do your banking.

If you don't own a modem, many cable TV services offer hookups to personal computers that provide news, stock quotations, airline schedules, and many other services for a small monthly fee.

FACSIMILE BOARDS AND MACHINES

Facsimile (FAX) machines have been around for quite a while. Newspapers and businesses have used them for years. They were the forerunners of the scanning machines. A page of text or a photo is fed into the facsimile machine. it scans it, digitizes it, and transmits it over the telephone lines.

The early machines were similar to the early acoustic modems. Both used foam rubber cups that fit over the telephone handset for coupling. They were very slow and subject to noise and interference. FAX machines and modems have come a long way since those early days.

Over 500,000 facsimile machines were sold in 1987. It is expected that over one million will be sold in 1988. There are very few businesses that cannot benefit from the use of a FAX. A FAX machine can be used to send documents, such as handwriting, signatures, seals, letterheads, graphs, blueprints, photos, and other types of data, around the world, across the country, or across the room to another FAX machine.

I mentioned earlier that it costs $11 to $13 to send an overnight letter but that E-Mail only costs about $1. A FAX machine can deliver the same letter for about 45 cents and do it in less than three minutes. Depending on the type of business, and the amount of critical mail that must be sent out, a FAX system can pay for itself in a very short time.

Stand-Alone Units

There are still several facsimile machines that are stand-alone devices that attach to a telephone. They have been vastly improved in the last few years but they still accept and produce paper images only. So the stand-alone units cannot compare to a versatility and convenience of a computer equipped with a FAX board. Some overseas companies are making stand-alone units that are fairly inexpensive, some for as little as $400. Several large American companies are building more sophisticated ones that cost up to $2000.

FAX Computer Boards

Several companies have developed FAX machines on circuit boards that can be plugged into computers. Special software then allows the computer to control the FAX machines and gives them a magnitude of versatility over the stand-alone units. The FAX boards cost from $395 to $1500 depending on their capabilities.

I have installed a GAMMAFAX card from the Gamma Technology Company, so I will talk about it. But there are several other companies who manufacture similar cards. The GAMMAFAX card can be plugged into any slot in an IBM PC, XT, AT compatible, or 80386. With this card, a computer can send and receive FAX files to or from any Group III FAX machine in the world. Text files can be created from the keyboard, or a scanner can be used to input graphics or an exact copy of a document to a file. The file can be sent from a floppy disk, hard disk, or from any other input to the computer. Incoming FAX files can be captured by the computer and sent to a printer or stored on disk.

The GAMMAFAX software allows the files to be sent or received in the background so that the computer can be concurrently used for other tasks. It is also possible to have the computer automatically send files at night when traffic on the telephone lines is less and the rates are lower.

FAX files must be converted to the proper format before they can be transmitted or printed out. The GAMMAFAX software performs all necessary conversions such as ASCII to the FAX format, FAX to ASCII, FAX to a display format, or FAX to a print format. The software also supports conversion between the FAX format and Dr. Halo and the PC Paintbrush.

The GAMMAFAX software comes with a Microsoft Windows compatible printer driver. It can be configured so that pages can be printed from any Windows application to a FAX format file. This allows the use of PageMaker or Ventura, or other desktop publishing programs to make up FAX files that can be transmitted.

Incoming FAX messages can be printed on several different types of printers. The software converts and coordinates incoming and outgoing FAX traffic and spools the data out as necessary. A windowing file manager is used to set up and control background operations. This software can also be used to set up and control an automatic dialing directory. A log can be set up and maintained of the FAX schedules and activity.

The GAMMAFAX PLUS is an optional Hayes compatible modem card that can be attached piggyback to the GAMMAFAX card. This configuration allows the FAX and a modem to be installed in a single slot. The card has two telephone line connectors. One is for the incoming line from the wall socket, the other is for a standard handset telephone. This allows the use of the telephone, the modem, or the FAX.

Modems and facsimile machines are quite similar and related in many respects. But there are times when one or the other is needed. Both units are never in use at the same time, so the same phone line can be used for both of them.

Scanners

Scanners are not absolutely essential to operate a PC based FAX. But there may be times when it is necessary to transmit photographs, blueprints, documents, or handwritten signatures on contracts, and a host of other needs. So a scanner is needed to get the most utility from a FAX.

There are several scanners available that will operate with FAX machines. The scanners range in price from $700 to $7000. Of course the higher the cost, the more sophisticated and versatile the machine will be. These machines can scan a sheet of text, a graph, or a blueprint into a computer, then allow it to be changed, manipulated, updated, edited or re-arranged as necessary. Some of the low cost scanners do not allow any manipulation of the data after it has been input. Most of the scanners listed in the previous chapter will work with FAX boards.

Depending on the type of business, it would be possible to get by with just the GAMMAFAX board, a PC, and a dot matrix printer. Such a system could cost less than $2500. But a scanner, a modem, a laser printer, and several other options could drive the price up to $6000 or more. But still, in any business that does a lot of communicating, a good FAX system would pay for itself in a very short time.

Sources

Most FAX boards are very easy to install and easy to operate. A person can be up and doing simple communications within a few minutes. Of course, for the more sophisticated type of communicating, it will take some time and study of the manuals to learn all the intricacies involved. Here are the phone numbers of just a few FAX board manufacturers. Call them for spec sheets and prices.

ADTech SMARTFAX	(818) 578-1339
Advanced Vision MegaFax	(408) 434-1115
Asher JT Fax	(800) 334-9339
Brooktrout Fax-Mail	(617) 235-3026
Carterfone DATAFAX	(214) 634-2424
Datacopy MicroFax	(800) 821-2898
GammaLink GAMMAFAX	(415) 856-7421
GMS Corporation EZ FAX	(800) 443-0500
KoFax Image Products	(714) 474-1933
Microtek Lab MFAX96	(213) 321-2121
OAZ Communications XAFAX	(714) 259-0909
Panasonic Fax Partner	(201) 348-7000
Pitney-Bowes PATH II & III	(203) 356-5000
Ricoh FB-1	(201) 882-2000
Spectrafax FAXCARD	(813) 775-2737

Chapter 13

Local Area Networks

One of the better business uses for the marvelous 386 is in *Local Area Networks* (LANs). The powerful features of the 386, such as the ability to handle massive amounts of data, speed as well as its multitasking and multiuser capabilities, makes it a natural for this very important business function.

Xerox was among the first to investigate the benefits of local area networks in 1978 when they developed Ethernet. But LANs didn't really become popular until about 1982 when the era of the Personal Computer really took off. Since that time it seems that there has been at least one article on networking in every issue of every major computer magazine.

Many of these articles emphasize the simplicity and ease of installing a network system. But unless the person knows what they are doing, and is very careful, a network system can be a nightmare. I don't mean to discourage anyone from using these fantastic tools. Some of them are simple and easy to install and maintain. But these simple systems are usually rather limited in what they can do. Most of the more sophisticated and complex systems are rather expensive. Most will need professionals to install them, and many of those systems will require professional maintenance after installation.

A LAN system might even require drilling holes through walls and stringing unsightly cables. But there is at least one company, Raynet, that makes a wireless LAN. It is quite similar in operation to a TV remote control. It has a small transmitter and receiver that can be mounted above the cubicle walls in a large office and can communicate with any other machine that is so equipped as long as there is a clear line of sight.

On the positive side, a LAN can be well worth the trouble and under the proper circumstances more than pay for its cost. A LAN can allow multi-tasking, multiusers, security, centralized backup, and shared resources such as printers, modems, FAX machines and other peripherals.

WHAT IS A LAN?

A LAN can be several dumb terminals tied to a large server, or it can be two or more computers tied together so that they may share and process files. This would be called a *shared CPU system* since all the terminals share the same CPU. This can work well if there are only a few terminals on line. But if there are several vying for attention at the same time, there will usually be some delay.

A LAN can also consist of a combination of dumb terminals, low cost PCs and 386s. Ordinarily the PCs will have a floppy disk drive, but there are some installations that have diskless PCs. Usually the reason for not having disks is for security purposes. For instance a bank would not want to risk having an employee downloading information about their customers onto a floppy disk.

Most systems require a plug-in board and software to drive them. Some of the more sophisticated boards may cost from $300 to $1000 each. This means that you would need one of these boards installed in each station terminal and a more expensive master in the server. If you have several nodes, it can become quite expensive.

LOW-COST SWITCHES AND LANS

You might just want to be able to have two computers share a printer, or perhaps have a computer be able to output to a laser printer or a dot matrix. This could be done very easily with mechanical switches. Some switch boxes can handle the switching needs for as many as four or five systems. These boxes may cost from $50 to $500. Here are some vendors of mechanical switchers:

Black Box Corporation	(412) 746-5530
Global Computer Supplies	(800) 845-6225
Inmac Supplies	(408) 727-1970
Lyben Computer Systems	(313) 589-3440
R + R Direct	(800) 654-7587

There are some electronic switch boxes that are a bit more sophisticated and have more capabilities and functions. Some offer buffers and spooling. Here are a few vendors:

Bravo Communications	(408) 270-4500
Digital Products	(800) 243-2333
Fifth Generations	(800) 225-2775
Novotek Corp.	(415) 492-3393
Qubit Corp.	(408) 747-0740

Here are some companies who provide low cost LANs that use the RS232 serial port:

Applied Knowledge	(408) 739-3000
IDEAssociates	(617) 663-6878
Server Technology	(800) 835-1515
Software Link LANlink	(404) 448-5465

SERVERS

Quite often there will be one computer that will act as the server for one or more workstations. For instance, an 80386 computer could have an 80 megabyte, or larger, hard disk system. The disks could store a large database of the company's customers, their account numbers, their addresses, and other pertinent information. The database might also include a list of the company's products, part numbers, and inventory. It could also include the accounts payable, accounts receivable, employee payroll information, company assets and liabilities, computerized forecasts, budgets, and other financial information.

The server hard disk could have several software programs such as WordStar4 for word processing, dBASE III Plus for database users, Quattro or SuperCalc4 for financial and spreadsheet needs, Windows, and several application specific programs. This software and the files on the hard disk could be available to anyone with a workstation tied to the system.

Printers sit idle much of the time. It would not be cost effective to have a printer at each workstation. The server could be attached to one or more printers such as a dot matrix, a laser, or perhaps a good letter quality daisy wheel. These printers would then be available to anyone on the network and be much better utilized.

The same server, or a different one, could also hold the records of a company's work scheduling, the work in progress (WIP), overhead costs, and statistical and quality control trends. It might also have programs and software for computer aided design/computer aided manufacturing/computer integrated manufacturing (CAD/CAM/CIM). It might also be used to design and implement programs for numeric controlled (NC) machines.

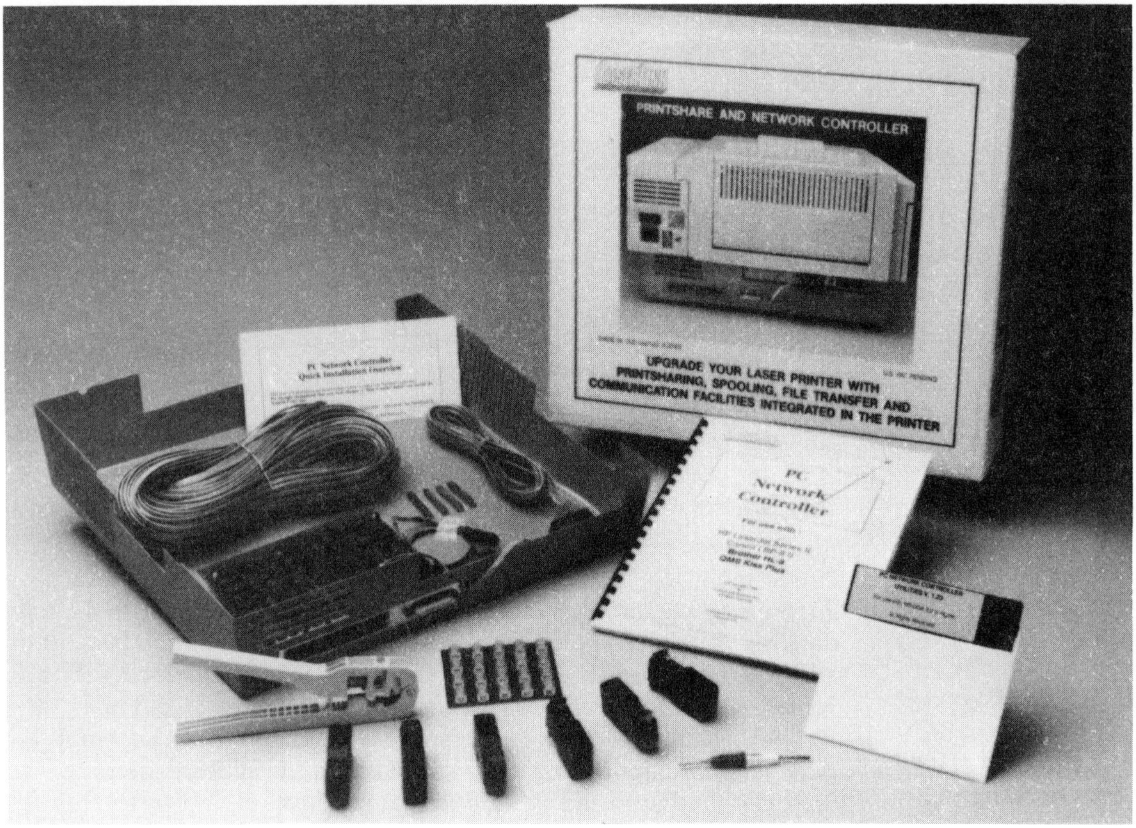

Fig. 13-1. A network controller for printer sharing. (Photo courtesy Novotek Corp.)

BAR CODES

The network could have a bar code system to keep track of the time that each employee spent on a job. The laser printer could be used to print up bar coded work orders and labels. A bar coded label could be attached to each part. Each employee could have a bar code on his or

Fig. 13-2. A printer sharing plug-in board for the HP Laser Jet. (Photo courtesy Qubit Corp.)

her badge with their name. When they began a job, they would use a scanner to read the label on the part, the bar code on the work order and the bar code on their badge. When they finished the operation they were performing, they would again scan the bar codes and log off. The computer would have an absolute record of the time charged against the job, where the part was in the production cycle and where it was located.

There are thousands of other ways that network systems can be used for greater productivity and resource sharing. And there are thousands of different types of networks. And of course, many different price levels for the cost of the systems.

STANDARDS

One of the problems is standardization. There have been some achievements in this area but not nearly enough. There are still a few companies who have their own proprietary network systems that will not work with any other network. If you start out with one of those systems, you have to stay with them. Since the Ethernet system was first, it became somewhat of a standard. Life could have been a lot easier for the networking industry if IBM and AT&T had joined them.

The International Standards Organization (ISO) has tried for sometime to establish the Open System Interconnection (OSI). This is a standard that has seven layers concerning the physical types, the transmission, and the protocols. Groups from the Institute of Electrical and Electronic Engineers (IEEE) and American National Standards Institute have had some success in formulating a few standards for hardware for the two lower levels of OSI.

There are four major types of LANs: Xerox's Ethernet, IBM's Token AT&T's StarLAN, and Datapoint's ARCnet. The IEEE standards are in 802.1 through 802.7. These standards cover the description of the relationship among the various systems and how they should operate.

TOPOLOGIES

There are three major types of LAN Topology as exemplified by AT&T's StarLAN, the linear ARCnet bus and IBM's Token-Ring. (See Figs. 13-3, 13-4, and 13-5.)

There are some advantages and disadvantages to each system. In a star system, each station has it own cable and is unique. If a station goes down it doesn't affect any of the other stations. But a disadvantage is that it requires a lot of cable.

The linear bus topology has a single length of cable, or trunk. Each device is connected to the bus by stubs and not connected to each other. The wiring is simple, but there may be a limit in the distance allowed

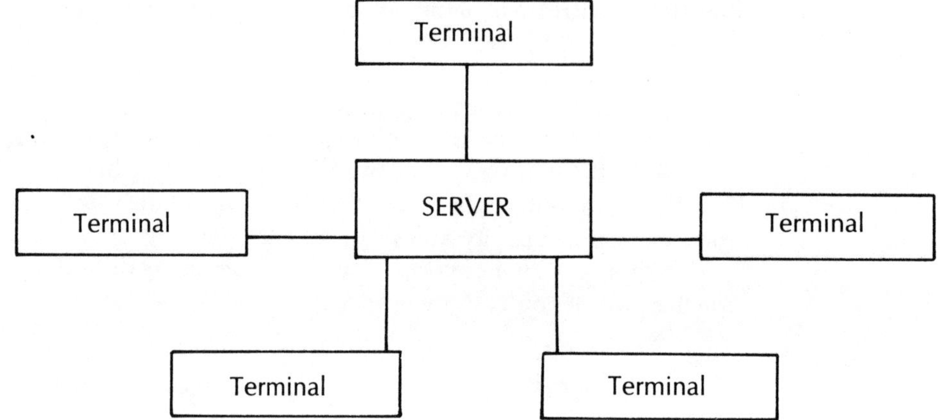

Fig. 13-3. AT&T's StarLAN topology.

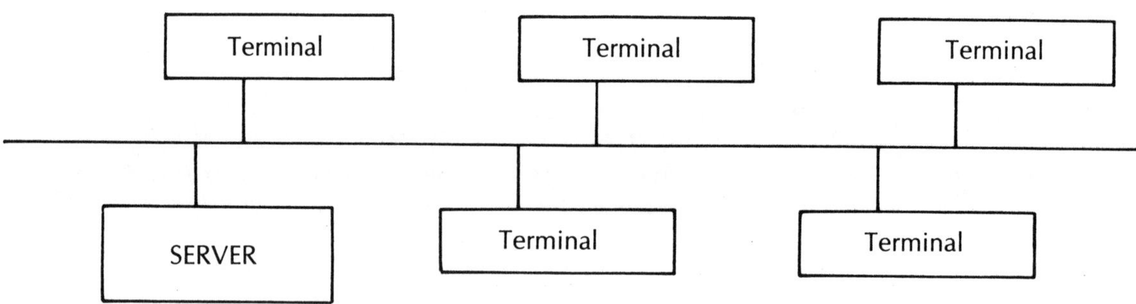

Fig. 13-4. ARCnet bus topology.

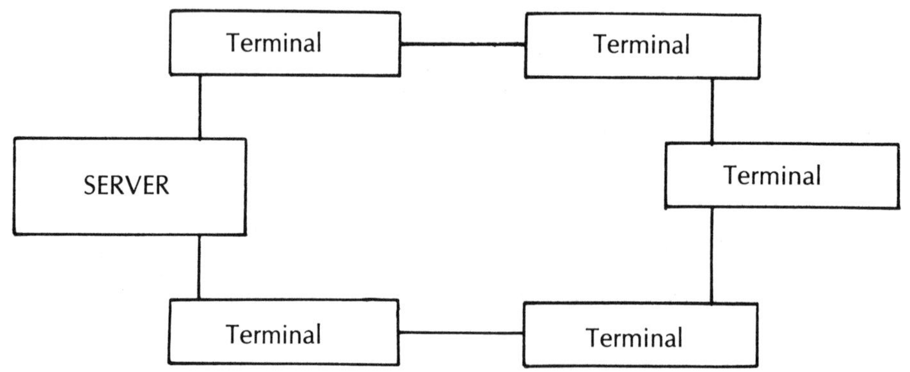

Fig. 13-5. IBM's Token-Ring topology.

between each station. Another disadvantage is that a break in the bus can cause a segment of the network to go down.

A ring topology has all the stations connected in a loop in series with the server. All data passes through all stations. A breakdown of any station causes the whole system to go down. There are variations of all these systems. Some systems may include parts of all these topologies.

MANUFACTURING AUTOMATION PROTOCOL (MAP)

General Motors uses a lot of computers for CAD/CAM/CIM, robots and computerized machinery. It has had great difficulty interfacing with their various computers, components, and machinery. They suggested a set of standards called Manufacturing Automation Protocol (MAP). Several large industries have joined General Motors in pushing for such standards, but they have not had a whole lot of success.

I doubt that you will ever be faced with the type of problems that General Motors has. Networking can be a very valuable and productive tool. But if you plan on installing a fairly large system, you probably should do some research, some comparison shopping, and maybe even hire a reputable consultant, before spending a lot of money.

LAN SOFTWARE AND HARDWARE VENDORS

Some companies manufacture boards, or hardware only, some make both hardware and software, some make software only. Novell is one of the better known companies that makes some hardware, but they primarily provide software. Their software will operate on the boards and hardware of dozens of other manufacturers. You can even buy IBM software to operate many of the hardware boards.

The software may cost from $100 up to $500 per node or workstation. In addition to the software, each station will require a board which may cost from $250 up to over $1000 each. There will also be a cost for cabling between each station. There are several types of cables available, from twisted pairs to coax. The type required will depend on the type of board and system installed.

Here are some LAN system vendors:

3COM Corp.	(408) 562-6400
Alloy Computer Products	(617) 875-6100
Asher Technologies	(404) 564-2353
AST Research Corp.	(714) 863-1333
AT&T	(800) 247-1212
Banyan Systems	(617) 898-1000
Bridge Communications	(415) 969-4900
CBIS Inc.	(404) 446-1332

Computer Pathways	(206) 487-1000
Corvus Systems	(408) 281-4100
Digital Equipment	(617) 897-5111
Excelan Inc.	(800) 392-3526
Gateway Communications	(800) 367-6555
IBM	(800) 447-4700
Kimtron Corp.	(800) 828-8899
Micom-Interlan	(617) 263-9929
NetWorth Inc.	(800) 544-5255
Novell Inc.	(800) 453-1267
NTI Group	(408) 739-2180
Orchid Technology	(415) 683-0300
Quantum Software	(613) 591-0931
Tiara Computer Systems	(800) 638-4272
TOPS	(415) 549-5900
Torus Systems	(415) 594-9336
Ungermann-Bass	(408) 496-0111
Univation Inc.	(408) 263-1200
Western Digital Corp.	(800) 638-5323

If you need a network system, I would suggest that you subscribe to the *LAN Magazine.* Novell publishes a free magazine to qualified subscribers called *LAN Times. PC Week* is an excellent weekly magazine that is sent free to qualified subscribers. Each issue includes a supplement called *Connectivity* that deals specifically with networking. See the Appendix for the addresses of these and other magazines. It would also be helpful to study some of the articles on LANs that appear in other computer magazines.

There are also several books that have been published on Networking. Some that TAB publishes are *Networking with the IBM Token-Ring* (No. 2829), *Network Synthesis* (No. 1402), and *Networking with the IBM Network and Cluster* (No. 1929).

Chapter 14

Desktop Publishing

I attended a desktop publishing conference and seminar a short time ago. There were over 1000 persons who paid $595 each to attend the several seminars. Over 10,000 people paid $25 each to view the products displayed at the 170 exhibition booths. Over 200 writers and reporters from the press also attended the conference. There is definitely a lot of interest in this technology.

A couple of years ago it was fairly easy to choose a desktop publishing (DTP) system because there were very few choices. For a high end system the only choice was the Macintosh with PageMaker software and the Apple LaserWriter. Xerox with its Ventura software and a few other companies had just started to get into the business. But Apple had the biggest slice of the pie at the time and still has today. Apple had a headstart of at least a year over the PC/MS-DOS world. The PC/MS-DOS world is working overtime to try to catch up.

PageMaker and Ventura are still the leading DTP software packages. But there are literally hundreds of other packages now available. There are also hundreds of new laser printers, new larger monitors, and other hardware that has been developed for DTP. These new software and hardware systems are proliferating like bunnies in springtime. So it is now much more difficult to make a choice as to which system to buy.

THE BIRTH OF DESKTOP PUBLISHING

The term Desktop Publishing was coined by Paul Brainerd, president of Aldus Corporation, at an Apple stockholders meeting in January of 1985. Aldus had originated PageMaker, a composition program for the Macintosh. PageMaker allows graphics and text to be imported, edited and manipulated. This was something that no other PC software could do at that time. But this fantastic achievement wasn't of much use unless it could be printed out.

Adobe Systems just happened to be there with their *Page Description Language* (PDL), PostScript. With firmware installed in an Apple LaserWriter, the text and graphics generated by PageMaker could easily be printed out.

Like the basic research for the mouse and icons, the first PDL, Interpress, was developed at the Xerox Palo Alto Research Center (PARC). But there really wasn't too much need for it in the early 1980s. Charles M. Geschke and John E. Warnock helped develop the language. They left Xerox and in 1982 set up Adobe Systems.

When they got together in 1985 with Steve Jobs of Apple and Paul Brainerd of Aldus, Desktop Publishing was born. Brochures, newsletters, manuals, magazines, professional proposals, and a host of other printing projects could be accomplished in just minutes. The quality of the printed output was very near to that of a professional print shop. People no longer had to go to the art department, cut and paste, manage several people, then send it out to the printer and sometimes wait weeks to get it back. Instant composition and printing was now available for most needs.

The Apple world was very excited. The PC/MS-DOS world didn't pay it too much attention. Most agreed that the Macintosh was easy to use, but it had a dinky little screen and closed architecture. And there was not nearly as much software available for it as for PC/MS-DOS machines. But the toy-like Mac made the PC/MS-DOS people sit up and take notice when the DTP market took off like a rocket.

THE PROLIFERATION OF DTP

It didn't take long for the IBM and MS-DOS world to realize what a fantastic tool desktop publishing could be. And profitable also. There is now a tremendous amount of DTP interest in the PC/MS-DOS world. Hundreds of new DTP products are popping up every day. It has been estimated that the DTP industry will be worth $6 billion by 1990. It is almost like the early days of clones. Because of the intense competition, prices are coming down on some components of the DTP systems.

Companies can now publish their own manuals, documents, management directives, and training aids in house. They can print up professional looking proposals in just hours. They no longer have to send pasted up material out to a printshop, wait for a week for it to come back, then find out that it had several errors. They now have control and can change or edit any of the documents in just minutes, then print out a clean copy. It is great for newsletters, for pamphlets, brochures, books, and even in politics.

David Bunnel is chief editor of *PC World* and *Publish!* In a column he wrote for the February 1988 issue of *Publish!*, he reported that Art Agnos, a candidate for mayor of San Francisco, was way behind in the polls. One of his aides suggested that he write a book stating his goals and philosophy and send it out to the voters. His aide used a desktop software package to put together an 80 page brochure for Agnos. He copied it onto diskettes and took them to a service shop that rented time on a PostScript laser. He made a copy of each page, then had a print shop turn out 250,000 copies of it. It only cost $60,000 to produce the 250,000 copies. It would have cost about $250,000 for a similar TV campaign. Agnos won by a large majority. Don't be surprised if you start getting tons of junk mail, created with DTP, from politicians.

HOW PDL FIRMWARE AND DTP SOFTWARE WORK

A PDL is an interpreter which executes page descriptions generated by software such as PageMaker and Ventura. Computers store pre-formed individual letters, numerals, characters and symbols in ROM. When we press the letter A on the keyboard, the computer goes to its A address, picks up the code for the preformed A and sends it to the monitor screen, the printer, modem, or whatever. Most printers have firmware in ROM that can recognize an A when it is sent to them. They pick up the instructions for making an A from their ROM storehouse and print it out.

But suppose we want to print out a photo with text around it. With most common word processors we couldn't even get the text and graphics on the screen at the same time, but with the desktop publishing programs it is an easy matter. They allow the mixing of text, line drawings, photos, graphics, and many other utilities for page composition.

Once the page of text and graphics is laid out on the computer screen, we would like to print it. But most printers, like word processors and computers, only recognize the ASCII character set and perhaps a few special fonts.

PostScript can take the page that was composed with the DTP program and make the printer print it. But the printer must have a lot of memory, about 2 megabytes. At this time, the lasers are about the only printers that can do this. A PDL might be compared to a high level language such as BASIC which will accept English words and commands. It then goes off into the bowels of the computer and matches these words and commands to the low level bits of 1s and 0s to carry out the required functions.

A standard page is 8.5 inches wide and 11 inches long. The laser printers have a resolution of 300 dots per square inch. 8.5 × 11 × 300 × 300 is 8,415,00 dots that can appear on a printed page. A PDL, along with quite a lot of memory, controls where these individual dots are placed.

A page is usually composed on a computer display screen using software such as PageMaker or Ventura, then it is sent to the PDL in the laser printer. The PDL stores the full page in memory then modulates the laser beam accordingly. If the page has complex graphics, some of the PDLs may take up to a half hour just to interpret and store the page. But once the page has been initially stored it can be printed out at the normal rate of 6 to 8 pages per minute. Each PDL printer actually has a computer inside it. The Apple LaserWriter Plus has a Motorola 68000 CPU, 1.5 megabytes of RAM and 1 megabyte of ROM. The PostScript language is in ROM.

Most word processors use routines to send special instructions to a printer such as one for bold face, or underline. When the word processor is installed, a number of questions are asked about your printer. There are hundreds of different types of printers. Each one may have several different features and require special routines in order to take full advantage of all its capabilities. Once the word processor has been installed with the printer requirements, the word processor will know what codes to send to the printer for the special features.

PostScript and other PDLs are similar to the ROM in dot matrix printers. The PDL must be told by the software what to do. Adobe has put their PostScript documentation in the public domain so that it is easily accessible to programmers who write software that addresses PostScript.

FONTS

PostScript only has 30 different fonts. Softcraft, Bitstream, and several other companies have developed many other fonts than can be used with PostScript. Font generators can be very expensive. They may cost as much as $100 for each font. Most fonts are copyrighted, and each vendor must either design their own fonts or pay someone else a license fee to use theirs. Mergenthaler, one of the early lintoype machine manufacturers, has one of the largest libraries of fonts. They license their styles to several vendors.

POSTSCRIPT CLONES

Incidentally, one of the reasons for the high cost of PostScript printers is because Adobe charges a very high rate for their license. It may add as much as $200 to the cost of the printer. Because of this, several companies are working on PostScript clones. There will probably be several on the market by the time you read this.

Some major companies have developed PDLs, all of which are incompatible with each other. Some of these companies are: Xerox with Interpress, Imagen with Document Description Language (DDL), Hewlett-Packard with H-P Graphics Language (HPGL), and Adobe with PostScript.

Hewlett-Packard originally decided to offer the Imagen DDL along with their HPGL. IBM has decided to go with PostScript so it will undoubtedly become the standard. Hewlett-Packard has recently announced that they will also offer the LaserJet II with PostScript.

The Imagen Company is a manufacturer of high end lasers. They have decided to offer their own DDL and PostScript on their printers. The QMS Corporation, a manufacturer of low cost lasers, and Imagen have recently merged. They are now one of the largest of the laser printer companies.

The addition of PostScript capability to a printer can increase the cost of the basic printer by as much as $3000. The required additional memory is one reason for the high cost. About a year ago the AST Corporation entered the DTP arena. They offered a PostScript equipped laser for $3995 and claimed that it was the least expensive of any equivalent laser printer. They have recently increased their price to $5495. One reason given was the higher cost of memory. It comes equipped with three megabytes of RAM and one megabyte of ROM.

The Conographic Corporation offers an alternative to conventional PostScript printer. Their Conodesk 6000 board plugs into a PC, XT, AT, or 386 and controls the laser printers. Their board costs $2995. They claim that their board is much faster than PostScript. If you need PostScript compatibility, they have a software package that can translate files that have been created for PostScript so that they can be printed out with their Conodesk 6000.

WHAT IS NEEDED FOR A DESKTOP PUBLISHING SYSTEM?

A good system will have the DTP software, a scanner, a laser printer, a computer, a high resolution display, and a mouse. A fairly good system can be assembled for $10,000. A more elaborate system may cost from $15,000 to $30,000 depending on the components chosen.

Look for the program to accept the text and data from a word processor, spreadsheets, and databases. It should be able to place text of all sizes and varieties on the screen, as well as to place the text in columns and use kerning to permit the professional spacing of words and characters for the purpose of justification.

Also look for automatic hyphenation and pagination. Some programs are able to place graphs, charts, and symbols on the screen, along with photos and drawings, and be able to move, rotate, crop, reduce or enhance them. Another useful feature is a WYSIWYG (What You See Is What You Get) system that will print out exactly as it is laid out on the screen.

COST OF A DTP SYSTEM

The cost of a system depends of course on what you want it to do. Here are some of the things you will need for a basic system:

ITEM	COST
A computer, PC, XT, AT or 386	$ 600- 3500
A monitor, large, high resolution, EGA adapter	1000- 3000
Software, word processor	200- 500
Software, for DTP	200- 900
Scanner, for OCR and Image input	1000- 4000
A mouse	60- 120
A modem	200- 500
A laser printer	1500- 7000
Total	$4760-19520

As you can see there can be almost $15,000 difference depending on what you want. Let's look at each item:

Computers. The new Macintosh II is a good machine, but it costs $5000 to $6000. You can build, or assemble an 80386 for much less than the cost of a Macintosh II. Incidentally, there are about 400,000 original small-screen Macintoshes in existence. There are over 10 million PCs, XTs, ATs, and compatibles in use. There will soon be over a million 386s in use. Guess which type of computer will have the most DTP hardware and software available in the next few months.

You can put together an 80386 system with a color monitor and a 40M hard disk for about $3500. It is possible to use a smaller system with a 20 megabyte drive, depending on the requirements of the particular project. A clone PC, XT, or AT could very well be used for low end DTP projects.

Monitors. The monitor should be a large screen, monochrome or high resolution color. Wyse Technology sells a high resolution 15-inch monochrome monitor with an adapter for $999. However, many of the DTP software programs need the Windows environment in order to use the mouse, and Windows needs a color monitor and EGA. A large high resolution monitor or display is almost essential to DTP. Nineteen inches seems to be the better size. There were very few manufacturers of this type monitor a couple of years ago, but because of the demand of the DTP industry, there are now dozens of manufacturers. Color is not necessary for DTP, but several manufacturers are providing them. Color is pleasing to the eyes and helps to delineate the various graphics and objects on the screen. Large screen color monitors range from $1500 to $3500. Adapter cards for large monitors range from $400 to $1500.

Software. You might think that you wouldn't need a word processor and desktop software. But in most cases, both are important. The DTP software can let you enter text, edit, and re-arrange it. But its primary function is to allow the formatting of the page on the screen of your monitor. It is much better to use a word processor, like WordStar4, to create your text files. These files can then be copied over to the DTP program for page layout and formatting.

PageMaker was originally developed for the Macintosh, but they now have a version for PC/MS-DOS machines. Ventura from the Xerox Corporation was developed for PC/MC-DOS only. Of course, there are some small utilities and functions found in one program that is not included in the other. They are both good programs, and it would be difficult to say which is the better. Here are some functions found in both programs:

- WYSIWYG (What-You-See-Is-What-You-Get) screen displays.
- Cut and paste, rulers, column guides, and design aids.
- Mouse based pull down menus.
- Importing of text and graphics and integrating and editing.
- Several fonts and font sizes.
- Text wrap around and automatic formatting.

There are dozens of other features found in these publishing programs that you won't find in most word processors. Many of the word processor companies are hurriedly revising and adding desktop publishing functions to their packages. Spellbinder now offers a full fledged desktop publisher package. WordStar 2000 Release 3 has almost everything that you need for DTP. Look for many others to follow.

There are many other companies that provide DTP software. Some packages may be slightly less expensive but may not offer as many features. There are many companies who offer supporting and adjunct software for publishing packages. some offer add-on items such as extra font types, pre-formed illustrations and drawings and logos.

Scanners. It is almost essential that you have a scanner that can read both text and graphic images and input them to the computer. Once the text or image is in the computer, it can be edited and manipulated.

There are some companies, Canon for one, who are manufacturing a scanner that is also a FAX machine. FAX machines have been around for quite a while, but this device can scan images or text and send them to the computer or across the country over ordinary telephone lines. Or images and text stored in the computer can be sent to the FAX which then sends it out over the telephone lines.

Scanners may cost from $1000 to $14,000 for some of the more sophisticated ones. Some of the less expensive scanners may be able to read only certain type fonts and sizes and they may not be able to digitize images or photos.

The Dest Corporation was one of the early pioneers in scanning. But there are now dozens of companies who are manufacturing scanners including Hewlett-Packard, Kurzweil, Xerox, Cannon, Microtek, Datacopy, and many others. Again, due to the competition, the prices are coming down.

The BioScan Company of Seattle sells a system that can capture and digitize a video frame from a VCR or a video camera. A plug-in board is used in a PC, XT, 286, or 386 to capture images or photos of people or objects. These digitized photos can then be cropped, enhanced, or manipulated in several ways and printed out with a publishing software program.

Mouse. One of the biggest reasons that the Macintosh became so popular was because the mouse made using the computer much easier to learn. A mouse is essential to moving the cursor around in cutting and pasting to format a page. Except for doing text word processing, the keyboards are used very little in DTP. In many cases, the text is scanned in with a scanner. Once the data is in the system, almost all of the manipulation is done with a mouse or some other pointing device.

Modem. A modem is necessary to send or receive data from other computers. It is possible to even send DTP formatted data over a modem to a printer at some other location.

Laser Printers. Basically, a laser printer is quite similar to a xerographic copy machine. They have a rotating drum that is scanned by a laser beam. The laser printer industry is no different than the dot matrix industry in the area of standards. There are none. Software developers had to create drivers in their programs that would work with all of the PDLs on the market.

PostScript controllers are rather expensive. In many cases they may cost up to twice as much as the whole laser printer. The Laser Connection, Box 850296, Mobile, Al 36685, offers a PostScript controller for the Hewlett-Packard LaserJet and other laser printers that use the Canon engine, for $2995. The Laser Connection is a subsidiary of the QMS Corporation which manufactures the Kiss and Big Kiss laser printers. The Laser

Connection publishes a catalog that lists several other products for laser printers and adjuncts for DTP.

Most of the present day lasers are capable of 300 dots-per-square-inch resolution. There are some very expensive ones that can lay down a resolution of 600 dots-per-inch. As the technology improves we will probably see more of these machines.

Some of the more expensive lasers will have lots of memory, up to two megabytes or more, a built in controller and a PDL in ROM.

Liquid Crystal Shutter Printer. The Taxan Corporation has developed a printer using a liquid crystal shutter (LCS) technology. They claim that their machine has fewer moving parts than the laser printers and will therefore have a longer life and provide greater reliability. They have also developed a scanner and a high resolution 19-inch monitor. They offer all three units for a price of $6995. A PC, XT, AT, or 386 added to these components would provide a fairly good low cost DTP system.

They claim that their PC based plug-in controller can allow a complex graphic to be printed out in 15 seconds that would require up to 20 minutes on other printers. They didn't mention names, but they were probably referring to PostScript equipped printers.

LOW-COST DTP

It is not absolutely necessary to have a large monitor, a high priced PDL laser, and a scanner to do some types of DTP. It is possible to use a good 24-pin dot matrix printer to do low end types of DTP. Of course, it will not have the same quality as the high end laser produced material. But if you are on a tight budget, it might be a good alternative. Some of the newer word processing programs, such as WordStar 2000 Release 3, PFS:First Choice and several others can do a fairly decent job of controlling the printout.

The Lebaugh Software Company, (800) 532-2844, produces a program called LePrint that will allow a page formated data to be printed on a laser or a dot matrix. They have several versions from $175.00 to $325.00.

SERVICE SHOPS

There are now service shops in some of the larger cities. They will rent time on their PostScript lasers, computers, and DTP facilities. Some of them offer expert help in generating the brochure or whatever the DTP project is. Or some of them will do the whole job for you. This service costs of course, but if you don't need it very often it is probably a lot less than what it would cost to own a PDL laser printer.

You can use one of the DTP software packages, design your newsletter, brochure, or other work, put it on a diskette and run it down to a service shop. You can even send the work out over a modem to some shops. It will only take a few minutes to print out a copy of your masterpiece. You can then take the copy to the nearest copier store or printer and have all the copies you need made up. This can be a very cost effective alternative to the expensive laser route. For some applications you many not need to spend $10,000 to $20,000 for DTP needs.

CONSULTANTS

The DTP industry is still in its infancy. Not too many people have had a chance to become expert in this field. If a consultant tells you that he or she has been in the Desktop Publishing business for ten years, you should probably take a good look at his or her credentials. This is not meant to be a reflection on all consultants; after all, I also do a bit of consulting now and then. There are many good consultants who have done their homework and can save you some money. If you are contemplating installing a large system, it might be worthwhile to check with one.

OTHER SOURCES OF INFORMATION

If you get an opportunity, by all means visit some of the DTP conferences, Computer Faires, or COMDEX shows and see some first hand demonstrations. At a show you can compare the various features of several different systems, often side by side. If you are in a large city you can probably visit several dealer show rooms for demonstrations.

TAB Books publishes several books on DTP. The *Ventura Publisher* explains all you need to know about this best selling software. The author, Elizabeth McClure, takes the reader through an actual Desktop Publishing application from start to finish. Another TAB Book is *BYLINE: A Creative Approach.* BYLINE is the name of a DTP software package that was developed by Ashton-Tate, the originators of dBASE II and dBASE III. Leo J. Scanlon, the author of this book shows the readers directly and systematically how BYLINE can help them in DTP.

Another book that is very interesting is *Publishing From the Desktop,* by John Seybold and Fritz Dressler. It is published by the Bantam Book Company. The book gives a lot of the history of printing and publishing. The book also explains many of the printing terms and jargon that are foreign to most of us.

A national association of desktop publishers has been formed. They have issued a *Desktop Publishers Journal* which contains a series of articles on DTP. The Association provides group discounts on books, newsletters, and magazines pertinent to the DTP industry. For more information write to the NADTP, P.O. Box 508, Kenmore Station, Boston, MA 02215-9919.

Almost every major computer magazine has at least one article on DTP in every issue. There are at least four magazines that are now dedicated to the DTP industry (Publish!, PC Publishing, Personal Publishing, and EP&P). These magazines usually have some very good articles and tips on how to do the job better and easier. There are lots of ads from the vendors who supply DTP components and products.

Desktop publishing is a new and exciting part of the computer age in which we live. There is a definite need for it, whether in a large corporation or for a small church newsletter.

Chapter 15

Needed Software

Much of the software that will take full advantage of your new 386 has not yet been written. The capabilities of this machine are so vast that its full potential will probably never be realized. But not to worry. There is more software already written and immediately available than you can use in a lifetime. There are off-the-shelf programs that can do almost everything that you could ever want to do with a computer. Yet thousands and thousands of software developers are working overtime to design new programs. It is almost like the soap business, they constantly issue new and improved versions. In some cases, the old version can do all you need to do.

For most general applications, there are certain basic programs that you will need. (Speaking of basic, BASIC is one that is needed. GW-BASIC from Microsoft is more or less the standard. Many applications still use BASIC. Even if you are not a programmer, it is simple enough that you can design a few special applications yourself with it.) There are six categories of programs that you will need to do any kind of productive work with your computer: operating system, word processor, database, spreadsheet, utilities, disk management, and communications. Depending on what you intend to use your computer for, there will be other specialized needs.

Software can be more expensive than the hardware. The prices may also vary from vendor to vendor. Few people pay the list price; it will

Fig. 15-1. Stacks of software. With diskettes and manuals, some of the packages weigh over ten pounds.

pay you to shop around. I have seen software that had a list price of $700 advertised from a discount house for as little as $350. Also, remember that there are excellent public domain programs that are free that can do almost everything that the high cost commercial programs can do.

I can't possibly list all of the thousands of software packages available. Again, I suggest that you subscribe to the magazines listed in the Appendix. Most of them have detailed reviews of software in every issue. The following sections list some of the essential software packages that you will need.

OPERATING SYSTEM SOFTWARE

DOS to a computer is like gasoline to an automobile. Without it, it won't operate. DOS is an acronym for Disk Operating System, but is does much more than just operate the disks. In recognition of this, the new OS/2 has dropped the D.

You can use any version of DOS on your 386. I don't know why anyone would want to, but you can even use version 1.0. Of course, you would be severely limited in what you could do. I would recommend version 3.3 or 3.2. Version 3.3 adds a few utilities that are not in 3.2 such as the ability to use hard disks larger than 32M. Of course, the higher DOS versions can operate any software that was written for an earlier

Fig. 15-2. A novel project management software package.

version. The list price for DOS 3.3 is $125. The long awaited OS/2 is finally here. But the general consensus seems to be that not too many people care. Unless you have some special need for multitasking or multiusing, you can probably get by with DOS. Besides, there isn't that much software available yet to take advantage of OS/2. Cost can be another factor in staying with DOS and the time that it will take to learn OS/2. Also, there will be slight variations in versions released by different companies. IBM will have a version, Compaq has theirs, and several other companies will have their own versions. But if you just have to have it, it will allow you to more fully utilize your fantastic 386. It will do almost everything that you always wanted DOS to do. List price for version 1.0 is $325. Later versions will cost about $725.

DESQview is an excellent alternative to OS/2. It allows multitasking and multiusers. You can have up to 50 programs running at the same time and have as many as 250 windows open. It runs all DOS software. It is simple to learn and use. List price is $129.95.

Concurrent DOS 386 is another excellent alternative to OS/2. It also is a multitasking and multiuser operating system. It takes advantage of the 80386 virtual 8086 mode and allows simultaneous processing of DOS applications. It is easy to install and operates with familiar DOS commands. List price is $395.

Wendin-DOS is still another alternative to OS/2. It allows multitasking and multiuser operations. It runs PC-DOS programs and supports DOS commands. It is easy to install and to use. List price is $99.

WORD PROCESSORS

The most used of all software is word processing. There are literally hundreds of word processor packages, each one slightly different than the others. It amazes me that they can find so many different ways to do the same thing.

I started off with WordStar on my little CP/M Morrow with a hefty 64K of memory and two 180K single-sided disk drives. It took me some time to learn how to use WordStar. I have tried several other word processors since then and found that most of them would require almost as much time to learn as WordStar did originally. I don't have a lot of free time, and WordStar does all I need. So I have not learned too many other processors.

There are probably more copies of WordStar in existence than any other word processor. Most magazine and book editors expect their writers to send manuscripts to them on a diskette in WordStar. WordStar 2000 Release 3 can do just about all you need to do in word processing and in desktop publishing. Like WordStar 4, it has a spelling corrector, an excellent thesaurus, an outline program, communications program and about 400 improvements over earlier versions.

By the time you read this MicroPro will have released WordStar 5.0. Version 4.0 was called WordStar Professional, version 5.0 will be called WordStar Classic. It will have most of the new features found in WordStar 2000. Some of the new features that have been added are the ability to do as many as eight columns on the screen, laser printer support, font selection, automatic text alignment, editing of two windows and the ability to move text from one window to the other, graphics pull down menus, improved thesaurus and spelling corrector, and the ability to import files from dBASE and Lotus and several other features.

MicroPro's educational division offers an excellent discount to schools, both for site licenses and for student purchases.

Educational Division
15 Loudon SW
Leesburg, VA 22075
(703)777-9110

MicroPro Corp.
33 San Pablo Ave.
San Rafael, CA 94903
1-800-227-5609

For registered owners, the upgrade will be $89. This list price is $495.

WordPerfect is one of the hottest selling word processors, so it must be doing something right. One thing they are doing right is giving free unlimited toll-free support.

The newest version is version 5.0. It can select fonts by a proper name, has simplified printer installation, and can do most desktop publishing functions, columns and several other useful functions. The list price is $495.

WordPerfect Corp.
228 W. Center St.
Orem, UT 84057
(801) 225-5000

Microsoft Word was developed by the same people who gave us MS-DOS. It has lots of features and utilities. It is about number three among the best selling word processors in the country. The list price is $450.

Microsoft Corp.
16011 N.E. 36th Way
Redmond, WA 98073
(206) 882-8080

PC-Write is the least expensive of all the word processors. It is shareware and is free if copied from an existing user. They ask for a $16 donation. Full registration with manual and technical support is $89. It is easy to learn and is an excellent personal word processor.

Quicksoft Inc.
219 First N. #224
Seattle, WA 98109
(800) 888-8088

Most of the word processor programs come with a spelling checker. Some of them come with a thesaurus which can be very handy. One of the better ones is WordFinder that comes with WordStar. WordFinder will also work with most other word processors.

Microlytics' WordFinder
300 Main St.
East Rochester, NY 14445
(800) 828-6293

The Funk and Wagnalls Standard Desk Dictionary has been put on disk by the Inductel Company. This dictionary has over 100,000 entries and full definitions of words that requires about five megabytes of hard disk space. It can be very handy. The list price is $79.95

Inductel's Funk and Wagnalls Dictionary
18661 McCoy Ave.
Saratoga, CA 95070
(800) 367-4497

If you want to learn more about word processors, subscribe to almost any computer magazine. Most of them will have a review of a package almost every month. The February 29, 1988, issue of *PC Magazine* was devoted almost entirely to word processors. It had in-depth reviews of 55 different packages.

DATABASE PROGRAMS

Database packages are very useful for business purposes. They allow you to manage large amounts of information. Most programs allow one to store information, search it, sort it, do calculations and make up reports, and several other very useful features.

At the present time there are almost as many database programs as there are word processors. Few of them are compatible with others. There is a strong effort in the industry to establish some standards under the Structured Query Language (SQL) standard. Several of the larger companies have announced their support for this standard. The average price for the better known database packages is almost twice that of word processors.

Ashton-Tate with their dBASE II was one of the first with a database program for the personal computer. dBASE III Plus is the current version. It is a very powerful program and has hundreds of features. It is a highly structured program and can be a bit difficult to learn.

dBASE IV was released recently. It is about ten times faster than dBASE III, has a built-in compiler, SQL and an upgraded user interface along with several other enhancements. The list price for dBASE III Plus is $695, and for dBASE IV, $795.

Ashton-Tate
20101 Hamilton Ave.
Torrance, CA 90502.
(213) 329-8000

AskSam 4.0 is an acronym for Access Knowledge via Stored Access Method. It is a free form, text oriented database management system. It is almost like a word processor. Data can be typed in randomly, then sorted and accessed. Data can also be entered in a structured format for greater organization. It is not quite as powerful as dBASE III, but is much easier to use. It is ideal for personal use and for the majority of business needs. The list price is $295.

Seaside Software
Box 1428
Perry, FL 32347
(800) 327-5726

DataEase is another program that is very easy to use. It is more powerful and a bit more structured than askSam. It is also more expensive, but for a large business it can be well worth it. The list price is $700.

DataEase Inc.
7 Cambridge Dr.
Trumbull, CT 06611
(800) 243-5123

SPREADSHEETS

Spreadsheets are primarily number crunchers. They have a matrix on by formulas and mathematical equations. If the data in the cell acted on affects other cells, re-calculations are done on them. Several of the affects other cells, re-calculations are done on them. Several of the tax software programs use a simple form of spreadsheet. The income and all the deductions can be entered. If an additional deduction is discovered, it can be entered and all the calculations will be done over automatically.

Spreadsheets are essential in business for inventory, expenses, accounting, forecasting, making charts, and dozens of other vital business uses. There are a large number of spreadsheet programs. I will only list a few of them.

For years Lotus 1-2-3 has been the premier spreadsheet but it appears that Microsoft Excel will take the top spot and honors. It is a very powerful program, with pull-down menus, windows and dozens of features. It can even perform as a database. For $10 you can get a videotape showing what Excel can do. If you later decide to buy Excel, they will refund the $10. Call (800) 323-3577, Ext. A95. The list price is $495.

Microsoft
16011 N.E. 36th Way
Redmond, WA 98073
(206) 882-8080

The Quattro spreadsheet looks very much like Lotus 1-2-3, but is has better graphics capabilities for charts, calculates faster, has pull-down menus, can print sideways, and has several other features not found in Lotus 1-2-3. One of the better features is the suggested list price of $195. Lotus costs $495.

Borland International
4585 Scotts Valley Dr.
Scotts Valley, CA 95066
(408) 438-8400

SuperCalc was one of the pioneer spreadsheets. It has never enjoyed the popularity of Lotus, though it has features not found in Lotus. It is an excellent spreadsheet. Computer Associates has also developed several excellent accounting packages costing from $595 to $695. The list price for SuperCalc is $495.

Computer Associates
120 McKay Dr.
San Jose, CA 95131
(408) 432-1727

Adam Osborne started the Paperback Software Company after his Osborne Computer Company went bankrupt. He developed several low cost software clones including VP-PLANNER Plus, a Lotus 1-2-3 style spreadsheet. Lotus sued him because his VP-Planner had the ''look and feel'' of Lotus 1-2-3. As of this time, the case is still pending. VP-Planner has several features not found in Lotus 1-2-3, such as the fact that it has pull-down menus, mouse support, an undo command, macro library, and others. The list price is $179.95.

Paperback Software
2830 Ninth St.
Berkeley, CA 94710
(415) 644-2116

UTILITIES

Utilities are essential tools that can un-erase a file, detect bad sectors on a hard disk, diagnose, un-fragment, sort and many others. We briefly reviewed several in Chapter Six under Hard Disks. Norton Utilities was the first and is still foremost in the utility department. Mace Utilities has several functions not found in Norton. The two of them complement each other. Steve Gibson's SpinRite and Prime Solution's Disk Technician are both excellent hard disk tools.

Norton Utilities
2210 Wilshire Blvd., Suite 186
Santa Monica, CA 90403
(213) 453-2361
List price $75.

Mace Utilities
123 N. First St.
Ashland, OR 97520
(503) 488-0224
List price $99.

Gibson Research
SpinRite
Box 6024
Irvine, CA 92716
(714) 830-2200
List price $59.

Prime Solution
Disk Technician
1940 Garnet Ave.
San Diego, CA 92109
(619) 274-5000
List price $99.

DIRECTORY AND DISK MANAGEMENT PROGRAMS

There are dozens of disk management programs that help you keep track of your files and data on the hard disk, find it, rename it, view it, sort it, copy, delete it, and many other useful utilities. They can save an enormous amount of time and make life a lot simpler.

Executive Systems
15300 Ventura Blvd. Suite 305
Sherman Oaks, CA 91403
(800) 634-5545
List price $129.

Gazelle Systems
42 North University Ave., Suite 10
Provo, UT 84601
(801) 377-1288
List price $69.

Bourbaki
P.O. Box 2867
Boise, ID 838701
(208) 342-5849

Tree86
Aldridge Co.
2500 CityWest Blvd., Suite 575
Houston, TX 77042
(713) 953-1940
List price $49.95.

Here are some other good programs:

LaSabre's L-Dir II
4364 Indigo Dr.
San Jose, CA 95136
List price $49.95.

Individual Software's Directory Assistance
1163-I Chess Dr.
Foster City, CA 94404
(415) 341-6116

SoftLogic Solutions' DoubleDOS
One Perimeter Rd.
Manchester, NH 03103
(603) 644-5555

OTHER UTILITIES

I have about 3000 files on my hard disk in several subdirectories. You can imagine how difficult it is to keep track of all of them. I sometimes forget in which sub-directory I filed something. But there are a couple of programs than can go through all of my directories and look for a file by name. But since you are only allowed eight characters for a file name, it is difficult to remember what is in each file. I have tried programs that can search through all the files and find almost anything that you tell them to. You don't even have to know the file that you are looking for. They will accept wild cards and tell you when there are matches.

Here are three programs that are very similar. The Text Collector is a bit faster than Gofer and has a few more features. Dragnet works under the Windows environment.

O'Neill Software's Text Collector
P.O. Box 26111
San Francisco, CA 94126
(415) 398-2255
List price $69.

Microlytic's Gofer
300 Main St.
East Rochester, NY 14445
(800) 828-6293
List price $59.95.

Access Softek's Dragnet
3204 Adeline St.
Berkeley, CA 94703
(800) 222-4020
List price $145.

SIDEKICK PLUS

Sidekick is in a class by itself. It was first released in 1984 and has been the most popular pop-up program ever since. It has recently been revised and enlarged so that it does much more than the simple calculator, notepad, calendar, and other utilities it had originally. It now has all of the original utilities plus scientific, programmer and business calculators, an automatic phone dialer, a sophisticated script language, and much more.

Sidekick loads into memory and pops up whenever you need it, no matter what program you happen to be running at the time.

Borland International
4585 Scotts Valley Dr.
Scotts Valley, CA 95066
(408) 438-8400.
List price $199.95.
Upgrade for registered owners of original Sidekick is $69.95.

WINDOWS/386

Your new 386 machine would not be complete with a copy of Windows. It will run Windows 2.0, but only one program at a time. If you really want to take advantage of more of the fantastic features of the 386, then you need Windows/386. Windows works best with a mouse. It brings Macintosh type screens and ease of use to the DOS world. There are several application and utility programs built into Windows that are similar to the utilities in Sidekick.

Microsofts Windows
16011 N.E. 36th Way
Redmond, WA 98073
(206) 882-8080
List price of Windows 2.0 is $99; Windows/386 is $199.

In addition there are many third party application programs that have been developed to run in the Windows environment. They take advantage of the windows and pull down menus of this vital tool.

Windows Graph is a presentation graphics program that uses Windows. Data from spreadsheets, and other files can be ported to the program to make all sorts of graphs.

Micrografix
1820 Greenville Ave.
Richardson, TX 75081
(800) 272-3729
List price $395.

Blythe Software has developed Omnis Quartz, a database program that works in the Windows environment with a mouse. It takes full advantage of the Windows capabilities in the screens and multiple windows.

Blythe Software
1065 E. Hillsdale Blvd. #300
Foster City, CA 94404
(800) 843-8615

The hDC Computer Corp. has developed ClickStart, an applications organizer for Windows. It allows you to customize Windows and your applications, design your own icons and help screens, password protect confidential files and many more useful utilities.

hDC Computer Corporation
8405 165th Ave. N.E.
Redmond, WA 98052
(206) 885-5550
List price $79.95.

GROUPWARE

The Information Research Corporation has developed an unusual software package for project control. This would be very useful for a manager who had responsibility for a large number of people working on a special project. The software helps track budgeted time and/or dollars and provides analysis reports. It can interface with several spreadsheets and database programs.

Information Research Corp.
P.O. Box 7644
Charlottesville, VA 22906

MENU CREATION

VM Personal Computing, the creators of the Relay series of communications programs, has developed Beyond Bat. It allows someone who has a bit of computer experience to create complex batch files and design menus. It can be used to create many useful applications that can make using a computer much easier. Menus can be created so that the novice has only to point and click. It can also set up the function keys for easy data input and file manipulation.

VM Personal Computing
41 Kenosia Ave.
Danbury, CT 06810-9990
(800) 222-8672

TAX SOFTWARE

Congress recently revised our tax laws. Among other things, it was supposed to simplify them. But most people say that they have complicated them by a magnitude. The laws that Congress passed are going to benefit tax preparers more than anyone else. The laws have guaranteed them an excellent income. Most people are now going to have to use the services of a tax preparer for anything more than the simplest return. And to top it off, except in certain cases, you can't even deduct the cost of having it done.

Many of the tax preparers are now charging $100 an hour or more. If you are thinking about going into some kind of business, you could do a lot worse than being a tax preparer. But there are some alternatives. There are several companies who provide tax software that can help you through this miserable chore. Most of the companies put out an upgrade each year. Once you have bought an original program, the updates are fairly inexpensive.

Best Programs publishes several different tax programs. PC/TaxCut is a $75 program for the person who does not have too many complications. It even comes with IRS approved forms with pinfeed perforations so that you can print out your return on a printer.

Best also publishes a Professional TaxPartner package for professional tax preparers. It has a couple of large manuals that cover just about every aspect of the law. Of course it is a bit more expensive at $495. But if you have a complicated return, it might be less than what you would have to pay a preparer.

Best Programs
2700 S. Quincy St.
Arlington, VA 22206-2205
(703) 820-9300

HowardSoft is one of the earliest and best known of the computer tax programs. It is a bit expensive at $295 for their Tax Preparer. It has an excellent bound manual, a very good tutorial, and is easy to use. They also have a professional package called Tax Preparer: Partnership Edition for $495. HowardSoft is one of the few companies who also offer state packages for most states. The California Supplement is only $125. HowardSoft is the next best thing to having a hundred dollar an hour preparer do it for you.

HowardSoft
1224 Prospect St., Suite 150
La Jolla, CA 92037
(619)454-0121

Several of the larger tax preparer companies now have a direct line to the IRS. As soon as they have finished your returns they can send it directly from their computer to the IRS computer by modem. Eventually, the same service will probably be extended to individuals who have computers.

Chapter 16

Troubleshooting

So you finally finished putting it together, and you turned it on for the smoke test. Of course you hopefully didn't see any smoke. Most of the components in your computer are fairly low power, and low voltage. The only high voltage in your system is in the power supply, and it is pretty well enclosed. Even if your system is working perfectly now, it is possible that sooner or later you could have some problems. You can minimize those possibilities by taking good care of your baby. If you have a hard disk, be very careful in moving or jarring it, especially while it is running. It could cause a head crash.

THE FIRST THING TO DO

The chances are if your computer is going to break down, it will do it at the most inopportune time. I think this is one of the basic tenets of Murphy's laws. If it breaks down, try not to panic. Ranting and cussing won't help. Remember, it is only a pile of sheet metal, plastic, and silicon. Under no circumstances should you beat on it with a ball bat. Instead, get out a pad and pencil and write down all the problems as they happen. It is very easy to forget. You may get error messages on your screen. Use the PrtSc (for Print Screen) key to print out the messages.

If you can't solve the problem, call your vendor for help. Have all the written information before you. Try to be near your computer when you call, if possible as it is acting up. It is also a good idea to join a users group and become friendly with all the members. They can be one of your best sources of troubleshooting. Most of them have had the same problems and are glad to help.

POWER SUPPLY

Most of the power supplies have short circuit protection. If too much of a load is placed on them, they will drop out and shut down, similar to what happens when a circuit breaker is overloaded. The fan in the power supply should provide all the cooling that is normally needed. But if you have stuffed the computer into a corner and piled things around it, shutting off all its circulation, it could possibly overheat. Heat is an enemy of semiconductors, so try to give it plenty of breathing room.

Table 16-1 shows the pin connections and wire colors from the power supply.

Table 16-1. Power Supply Pin Connections and Wire Colors.

Disk Drive Power Supply Connections

Pin	Color	Function
1	Yellow	+12 Vdc
2	Black	Ground
3	Black	Ground
4	Red	+5 Vdc

Power Supply Connections to the Motherboard

	Pin	Color	Function
P8	1	White	Power Good
	2	No connection	
	3	Yellow	+12 Vdc
	4	Brown	−12 Vdc
	5	Black	Ground
	6	Black	Ground
P9	1	Black	Ground
	2	Black	Ground
	3	Blue	−5 Vdc
	4	Red	+5 Vdc
	5	Red	+5 Vdc
	6	Red	+5 Vdc

The eight slotted connectors on the motherboard have 62 contacts, 31 on the A side and 31 on the B side.The black ground wires connect to B1 of each of the eight slots. B3 and B29 has +5 Vdc, B5 −5 Vdc, B7 −12 Vdc, and B9 has +12 Vdc. These voltages go to the listed pins on each of the eight plug-in slots.

INSTRUMENTS AND TOOLS

There are different levels of troubleshooting. A person would need some rather sophisticated and expensive instruments to do a thorough analysis of a system. You would need a good high frequency oscilloscope, a digital analyzer, a logic probe and several other expensive pieces of gear. You would also need a test bench with a power supply, disk drives and a computer with some empty slots so that you could plug in suspect boards and test them.

You would also need a voltohmmeter, some clip leads, a pair of side cutter dikes, a pair of long nose pliers, various screwdrivers, nutdrivers, a soldering iron and solder, and lots of different size screws and nuts.

You will need plenty of light over the bench and a flashlight, or a small light to light up the dark places in the case.

And most importantly, you will need quite a lot of training and experience. But for many problems, just a little common sense will tell you what is wrong.

COMMON PROBLEMS

For most of the common problems, you won't need a lot of test gear. I have found that a large percentage of my problems is due to my own stupid errors. Many are caused by not taking the time to read the manual or instructions, or not being able to understand them.

Often a problem can be solved by using our eyes, ears, nose and touch. If we look closely, we can see a cable that is not plugged in properly. Or a board that is not completely seated. Or a switch that is not set right. And many other obvious things. We can use our ears for any unusual sounds. The only sound from your computer should be the noise of your drive motors and the fan in the power supply. If you have ever smelled a burned resistor or a capacitor, you will never forget it. If you smell something very unusual, try to locate where it is coming from. If you touch the components and some seem to be unusually hot, it could be the cause of your problem. It is always best to be cautious, except for the insides of your power supply, there should not be any voltage above 12 volts in your computer. So it should be safe to touch the components.

ELECTROSTATIC DISCHARGE

Before you touch any of the components or handle them, you should ground yourself and discharge any static voltage that you may have built up. You can discharge yourself by touching an unpainted metal part of the case of a computer or other device that is plugged in. It is possible for a person to build up a charge of 4000 volts or more of electrostatic voltage. If you walk across some carpets, and then touch a brass door knob you can sometimes see a spark fly and often get a shock. On most electronic assembly lines, the workers wear a ground strap whenever they are working with any electrostatic discharge sensitive components. When I am installing memory chips, or handling other ICs, I often use a clip lead to ground myself. I clip one end to my metal watch band and the other end to the computer case.

RECOMMENDED TOOLS

Here are some tools that you should have around the house, even if you never have any computer problems.

- Several sizes of screwdrivers. A couple of them should be magnetic for picking up and starting small screws. You can buy magnetic screwdrivers, or you can make one yourself. Just take a strong magnet and rub it on the blade of the screwdriver a few times. Be careful of any magnet around your floppy diskettes; it can erase them.
- You should also have a small screwdriver with a bent tip that can be used to pry up ICs. Some of the larger ICs are very difficult to remove.
- You should have a couple pairs of pliers. You should have at least one pair of long nose pliers.
- You will need a pair of side cutter dikes for clipping leads of components and cutting wire. You might buy a pair of cutters that also have wire strippers.
- A soldering iron comes in handy around the house many times. And, of course, some solder.
- No home should be without a voltohmmeter. They can be used to check for the correct wiring in house wall sockets. (The wide slot should be ground.) They can be used to check switches, wiring continuity in your car, house, stereo, phone lines, etc. And you could check for the proper voltages in your computer. There are only four voltages to check for, +12 volts, −12 volts, +5 volts and −5 volts. You can buy a relatively inexpensive voltohmmeter at any of the Radio Shack stores or electronic stores.

- You should also have several clip leads. You can buy them at the local Radio Shack or electronic store.
- You need a flashlight for looking into the dark places inside the computer.

HOW TO FIND THE PROBLEM

If it seems to be a problem on the motherboard or a plug-in board, look for chips that have the same number. Try swapping them to see if the problem goes away or worsens. If you suspect a board, and you have a spare, or can borrow one, swap it. If you suspect a board, but don't know which one, take the boards out to the barest minimum. Then add them back until the problem develops. Always turn off the power when plugging in or unplugging a board or cable. Wiggle the boards and cables to see if it is an intermittent problem. Many times a wire can be broken and still make contact until it is moved.

Check the ICs and connectors for bent pins. If you have installed memory ICs and get errors, check to make sure that they are seated properly and all the pins are in the sockets. If you swap an IC, make a note of how it is oriented before removing it. There should be a small dot of white paint or a U shaped indentation at the end that has pin 1. If you forgot to note the orientation, look at the other ICs. Most of the boards are laid out so that all of the ICs are oriented the same way. The chrome fillers that are used to cover the unused slots in the back of the case make very good tools for prying up ICs.

You might also try unplugging a cable or a board and plugging it back in. Sometimes the pins may be slightly corroded or not seated properly. Or if the problem could be in a DIP switch, you might try turning it on and off a few times.

Always make a diagram of the wires, cables and switch settings before you disturb them. It is easy to forget how they were plugged in or set before you moved them. You could end up making things worse. Make a pencil mark before turning a knob or variable coil or capacitor so that it can be returned to the same setting when you find out that it didn't help. Better yet, resist the temptation to reset these types of components. Most were set up using highly sophisticated instruments. Most of them do not change enough to cause a problem.

If you are having monitor problems, check the switch settings on the motherboard. There are several different motherboards. Some have dip switches or shorting bars that must be set to configure the system. Most monitors also have fuses. You might check them. Also check the cables for proper connections.

Printer problems, especially serial type, are so many that I will not even attempt to list them here. Many printers today have parallel and serial interfaces. The IBM defaults to the parallel system. If at all possible, use the parallel port. There are very few problems with parallel as compared to serial. Most printers have a self test. It may run this test fine, but then completely ignore any efforts to get it to respond to the computer if the cables, parity and baud rate are not properly set.

Sometimes the computer will hang up. You may have told it to do something that it could not do. You can usually do a warm reboot of the computer by pressing the Ctrl, Alt, and Del keys. Of course, this would wipe out any file in memory that you might have been working on. Occasionally the computer will not respond to a warm boot. You can pound on the keyboard all day long and it will ignore you. In that case, you will have to switch off the main power, let it sit for a few seconds, then power up again.

DOS has several error messages that will be displayed if you try to make the computer do something it can't do. But many of the messages are not very clear. The DOS manual explains some of them, but you might want to get a book that goes into more detail.

If you find the problem is a board, a disk drive, or some component, you might try to find out what it would cost before having it repaired. With the flood of low-cost clone hardware that is available, it is often less expensive to scrap a defective part and buy a new one. Sometimes finding the cause of a problem can be a real headache. Rather than try to find it, maybe you should do the next best thing. Just take a couple of aspirins and call a repair shop.

Appendix

Sources

The computer industry is one of the most volatile of all businesses. New products, discoveries, technologies, and changes are introduced daily. If you want to try to keep up with the latest in the computer business, or if you need sources of supplies, then you should be subscribing to several or all of the magazines listed in this appendix The magazines publish articles on software, hardware, systems, and all of the latest developments in the field.

Many of the magazines try to find a niche in the business and differentiate themselves from the others. Several new magazines have been introduced in just the last few months to address new technologies such as *Publish!* for desktop publishing and *LAN* for local area networks. All of the magazines have something to offer. They are educational, informative and well worth the money. Some of them are even sent to you completely free of any charge.

MAIL ORDER

These magazines are full of advertisements for computer components and systems. You can use the advertisements to do comparison shopping without leaving home. You can plan your system and have a fairly good idea of how much it will cost you. If you don't live in a large city where there are lots of computer stores, you can order your system through the mail from the advertisements. Most of the larger mail-order stores have developed a fairly good reputation for delivering as advertised. A recent article in *PC Week* said that about $2.1 billion worth of PC equipment would be sold through the mail during 1987.

SOME MAIL-ORDER CONSIDERATIONS

You should read the advertisements very carefully. Some of them may show a complete system and a very low price. But if you read the advertisement carefully, you may find that all that is shown in the ad is not included. If the price looks like it is too good to be true, it probably is. Compare prices of similar products of other vendors who have ads in the magazine. They should all be fairly close. You should also have a fairly good idea of what it is you are buying. Some copywriters get carried away, and the description that they provide may not match the article exactly.

You should have a fairly good idea of the cost of the item. Many of the advertisements are made up a month or so in advance, so the price in the advertisement may have changed since the advertisement was placed. Call the advertiser to verify the price, the model, and to get as many other details as possible. Ask about the shipping costs. It is possible that shipping and handling could make the article more expensive than what it would cost to buy locally.

Many of the companies will take an order over the telephone and allow you to charge it to your charge card. But you should be aware that the Federal Trade Commission offers some protection if you order by mail, but it can't help much if the order is placed by telephone.

MAGAZINES

Here is a list of magazines that you should be subscribing to. This is only a partial listing. There are many other good magazines on the market.

PC Computing
P.O. Box 58229
Boulder, CO 80321

Computer Shopper
407 S. Washington Av.
Titusville, FL 32796

MicroTimes Magazine
5951 Canning St.
Oakland, CA 94609

PC World Magazine
501 Second St.
San Francisco, CA 94107

PC Magazine
One Park Av.
New York, NY 10016

Personal Computing
10 Mulholland Dr.
Hasbrouck Hts., NJ 07604

Business Software
P.O. Box 27975
San Diego, CA 92128

PC Tech Journal
P.O. Box 2968
Boulder, CO 80321

Byte Magazine
70 Main St.
Peterborough, NH 03458

Publish!
P.O. Box 55400
Boulder, CO 80321-5400

LAN
12 West 21 Street
New York, NY 10010

Computer Currents
5720 Hollis St.
Emeryville, CA 94608

CD-ROM Review
P.O. Box 921
Farmingdale, NY 11737-9621

PC Resource
P.O. Box 950
Farmingdale, NY 11737-9650

Computer Living
5795 Tyndall Av.
Riverdale, NY 10471

Texas Computing
17818 Davenport, #119
Dallas, TX 75252

The following magazines are free to qualified subscribers.

PC Week
P.O. Box 5920
Cherry Hill, NJ 08034

Circulation Dept.
Electronics
McGraw-Hill Bldg.
1221 Avenue of the Americas
New York, NY 10020

InfoWorld
1060 Marsh Rd.
Menlo Park, CA 94025

Computer Systems News
600 Community Dr.
Manhasset, NY 11030

Information Week
600 Community Dr.
Manhasset, NY 11030

Computer+Software News
P.O. Box 3119
Grand Central Station
New York, NY 10164-0659

Utah Access
P.O. Box 1952
Orem, Utah 84057

Mini-Micro Systems
P.O. Box 5051
Denver, CO 80217-9872

Computer Products
P.O. Box 14000
Dover, NJ 07801-9990

Circulation Dept.
Machine Design
Penton Publishing
1100 Superior Av.
Cleveland, OH 44114

Computer Technology Review
924 Westwood Blvd. Suite 650
Los Angeles, CA 90024-2910

The Processor
P.O. Box 85518
Lincoln, NE 68501

Computer Dealer
Gordon Publications
P.O. Box 14000
Dover, NJ 07801-9939

ID Systems
174 Concord St.
Peterborough, NH 03458

The free magazines listed above are sent only to qualified subscribers. The subscription price of a magazine usually does not come anywhere near covering the costs of publication, mailing, distribution, and other costs. Most magazines depend almost entirely on advertisers for their existence. The more subscribers that a magazine has, the more it can charge for its ads. Naturally they can attract a lot more subscribers if the magazine is free.

To get a free subscription, you must write to the magazine for a qualifying application form. The form will ask several questions such as how you are involved with computers, the company you work for, whether you have any influence in purchasing the computer products listed in the magazines, and several other questions that give them a very good profile of their readers. Many of these magazines also make money by selling this specialized mailing list of names to direct mail order advertisers.

The MicroTimes Magazine listed above is distributed free to most of the computer stores and at computer shows throughout California. It is an excellent magazine. If you can't get to one of the computer stores in time to pick up your free copy before they are all gone, or if you don't live near one, you can have it delivered to your home for just $12 a year.

The list of magazines above is not nearly complete. There are hundreds of trade magazines that are sent to qualified subscribers. The Cahners Company alone publishes 32 different trade magazines. Many of the trade magazines are highly technical and narrowly specialized.

MAIL-ORDER MAGAZINES

There are some magazines that are strictly mail order. One example is 47 St. Photo. At one time, they dealt mostly in photo and camera equipment. I recently ordered some camera equipment from them and am now on their mailing list. They publish a monthly catalog of the wares they have for sale. The May issue had 226 pages, over half of them were for computers and computer related products. The catalog has a cover price of $2.95, but once you have ordered something from them, you are put on their mailing list. I am sure you can subscribe to the catalog, or order a single copy. The address is:

47 St. Photo
36 East 19th St.
New York, NY 10003
(212) 260-4410

Another magazine that is filled with ads from companies and individuals is *Nuts & Volts*. It is given away free at most computer swaps. But you can subscribe to it $10 for one year, or $50 for a lifetime subscription. The address is:

Nuts & Volts
P.O. Box 1111
Placentia, CA 92670
(714) 632-7721

A weekly magazine that deals strictly with buy and sell ads is the *Computer Hot Line Weekly*. Subscription is $29 for 52 issues. The address is:

Computer Hot Line Weekly
Box 1373
Fort Dodge, IA 50501
(800) 247-2000

Here is a list of mail order firms who sent out their catalogs that cover the following items: Office Supplies, Paper, Ribbons, Diskettes, Cartridges, Toner, Pens, Software, and Electronic Supplies.

Lyben Computer
1050 E. Maple Rd.
Troy, MI 48083
(313) 589-3440

Jameco Electronics
1355 Shoreway Rd.
Belmont, CA 94002
(415) 592-8097

Jade Computer
4901 W. Rosecrans Ave.
Hawthorne, CA 90250
(213) 973-7707

Priority One
21622 Plummer St.
Chatsworth, CA 91311
(818) 709-5464

Inmac Computer Furniture
2465 St. Augustine Dr.
Santa Clara, CA 95054

800-SOFTWARE
940 Dwight Wy. #14
Berkeley, CA 94710
(800) 227-4587

Public Brand Software
Box 51315
Indianapolis, IN 46251
(800) IBM-DISK

Selective Software
903 Pacific Ave.
Santa Cruz, CA 95060
(800) 423-3556

Nebs Computer Forms
500 Main St.
Groton, MA 01470
(800) 225-9550

Power Up!
2929 Campus Dr.
San Mateo, CA 94403
(800) 851-2917

Inacomp Computer
20717 Kelly Rd.
Birmingham, MI 48021-2702
(800) 999-9898

This is not a complete listing, but it will give you an idea of what is available. Thumbing through these magazines is a great way to be aware of what is available and do some price comparisons without leaving home. You should be aware that some of the magazines listed above are not discount houses. They may have slightly higher prices than those you may see advertised in some of the computer magazines.

COMPUTER SHOWS

In the larger cities, there is a computer swap or show going on somewhere almost every weekend. Most of the computer dealers, especially the clone vendors, set up booths and display their wares. I enjoy the shows. There are always large crowds and a circus-like atmosphere. I often go even when I don't need anything.

There are several large shows held in San Francisco every year. One of the best is the West Coast Computer Faire that is held in early spring each year. The Interface Group sponsors this show which has exhibitors from all over the nation. The Interface Group also sponsors a Computer Faire in Boston, the Spring COMDEX (COMputer Dealers EXposition) in Atlanta and the Fall COMDEX in Las Vegas each year. The Las Vegas COMDEX is the largest show in the country. It usually has about 1200 exhibitors and 80 to 100 thousand visitors.

COMDEX publishes a Program & Exhibits Guide for their shows. This guide gives a brief description of each exhibitor and their address and phone number. The guide alone is worth the price of the show. I constantly refer to it. It is an excellent resource for finding products and the addresses of suppliers.

USER GROUPS

If you live in a large city, chances are that there are several personal computer user groups (PCUGs) in your area. The groups are usually made up of people who own computers. Ordinarily, they meet once or twice a month and discuss computers, software, and problems. Some of them hold their meetings in a wing of a public library, at a public school, at company facilities, or at the home of one of the members.

There are several different kinds of user groups. Some may be set up for one particular kind of computer such as Apple or Atari. Some are set up within corporations and sponsored by them. These companies realize that the more their people know about computers, the more valuable they are as an employee. If it is a fairly large user group, quite often they can contact local computer, software vendors and suppliers and arrange for volume discounts and other benefits for the club.

If you have a problem, there is usually someone at the meeting who can help you. Most groups publish a list of the members so that you can possibly call one of them at home if you have a problem. Most of the members are usually more than happy to help you. I would recommend that you join a group. If there are none in your area, perhaps you could start one. There are no set rules or regulations as to how the club should be run. Several of the magazines listed above publish a list of user groups as a public service.

PUBLIC DOMAIN SOFTWARE

Here is a short list of companies that provide public domain and low cost software:

PC-Sig
1030D East Duane Ave.
Sunnyvale, CA 94086
(800) 245-6717

MicroCom Systems
3673 Enochs St.
Santa Clara, CA 95051
(408) 737-9000

Software Express/Direct
Box 2288
Merrifield, VA 22116
(800) 331-8192

Selective Software
903 Pacific Ave. Suite 301
Santa Cruz, CA 95060
(800) 423-3556

The Computer Room
P.O. Box 1596
Gordonsville, VA 22942
(703) 832-3341

Softwarehouse
3080 Olcott Dr. Suite 125A
Santa Clara, CA 95054
(408) 748-0461

PC Plus Consulting
14536 Roscoe Blvd. #201
Panorama City, CA 91402
(818) 891-7930

Micro Star
P.O. Box 4078
Leucadia, CA 92024-0996
(800) 443-6103

International Software Library
511 Encinitas Blvd. Suite 104
Encinitas, CA 92024
(800) 992-1992

National PD Library
1533 Avohill
Vista, CA 92083
(619) 941-0925

Most of the companies listed above can provide a catalog listing of their software. Some of them charge a small fee for their catalog. Write to them or call them for details and latest prices. The above list is not complete. You may find several other companies advertised in some of the magazines listed earlier.

MAIL-ORDER BOOKS

One of the better ways to learn about computers is through books. There are several companies who publish computer books. One of the companies is TAB BOOKS Inc., Blue Ridge Summit, PA 17294-0850, (717) 794-2191. Call or write to them for a listing of the many books they publish.

I must admit that I am a bit prejudiced of course, since I write for TAB Books, who published the book you have in your hands.

Another book that would be helpful in putting together a system is the *386 COMPUTER BUYER'S GUIDE AND HANDBOOK*. It was written by a friend of mine, Edwin Rutsch, 431 Ashbury St., San Francisco, CA 94117.

Glossary

access time—The amount of time it takes the computer to find and read data from a disk or from memory. The average access time for a hard disk is based on the time it takes the head to seek and find the specified track, the time for the head to lock on to it and the time for the head to spin around until the desired sector is beneath the head. See Chapter 4 for fuller explanation.

active partition—The partition on a hard disk that contains the boot and operating system. A single hard disk can be partitioned into several logical disks such as drive C:, drive D:, and drive E:. This can be done at the initial formatting of the disk. Only one partition, usually drive C:, can contain the active partition.

adapter boards or cards—The plug-in boards needed to drive monitors. Most monitor boards are Monochrome Graphic Adapters (MGA), or Color Graphic Adapters (CGA), or Enhanced Graphic Adapters (EGA). The EGA boards give a higher resolution than the CGA when used with a high resolution monitor. The Video Graphics Adapters (VGA) can give an even higher resolution than the EGA.

algorithm—A step by step procedure, scheme, formula, or method used to solve a problem or accomplish a task. May be a subroutine in a software program.

alphanumeric—Data that has both numerals and letters.

analyst—A person who determines the computer needs to accomplish a given task. The job of an analyst is similar to that of a consultant. Note that there are no standard qualifications requirements for either of these jobs. Anyone can call themselves an analyst or a consultant. They should be experts in their field, but may not be.

ANSI—Abbreviation for American National Standard Institute. A standard adopted by MS-DOS for cursor positioning. It is used in the ANSI.SYS file for Device drivers.

ASCII—Abbreviation for American Standard Code for Information Interchange. Binary numbers from 0 to 127 that represent the upper and lowercase letters of the alphabet, the numbers 0-9, and the several symbols found on a keyboard. A block of eight 0s and 1s are used to represent all of these characters. The first 32 characters, 0 to 31, are reserved for noncharacter functions of a keyboard, modem, printer, or other device. Number 32, or 0010 0000, represents the space, which is a character. The numeral 1 is represented by the binary number for 49, which is 0011 0001. Text written in ASCII is displayed on the computer screen as standard text. Text written in other systems, such as WordStar, has several other characters added and is very difficult to read. Another 128 character representations have been added to the original 128 for graphics and programming purposes.

ASIC—Acronym for Application Specific Integrated Circuit.

assembly language—A low-level machine language, made up of 0s and 1s.

asynchronous—A serial type of communication where one bit at a time is transmitted. The bits are usually sent in blocks of eight 0s and 1s.

AUTOEXEC.BAT—If present, this file is run automatically by DOS after it boots up. It is a file that you can configure to suit your own needs, can load and run certain programs, or configure your system.

.BAK files—Any time that you edit or change a file in some of the word processors and other software programs they will save the original file as a backup and append the extension .BAK to it.

BASIC—Abbreviation for Beginners All Purpose Symbolic Instruction Code. A high level language that was once very popular. There are still many programs and games that use it. It comes standard on the IBM BASICA. Some of it is in ROM.

batch—The batch command can be used to link commands and run them automatically. The batch commands can be made up easily by the user. They all have the extension .bat.

baud—A measurement of the speed or data transfer rate of a communications line between the computer and printer, modem, or another computer. Most present day modems operate at 1200 baud. This is 1200 bits per second or about 120 characters per second.

benchmark—A standard type program against which similar programs can be compared.

bidirectional—Of or relating to both directions. Most printers print in both directions, thereby saving the time it takes to return to the other end of a line.

binary—Binary numbers are 0s and 1s.

BIOS—An acronym for Basic Input Output System. The BIOS is responsible for handling the input/output operations.

bits—A contraction of Binary and digITs.

boot or bootstrap—When a computer is turned on, all the memory and other internal operators have to be set or configured. The PC takes quite a while to boot up because it checks all the memory parity and most of the peripherals.

A small amount of the program to do this is stored in ROM. Using this the computer pulls itself up by its bootstraps. A warm boot is sometimes necessary to get the computer out of an endless loop, or if it is hung up for some reason. A warm boot can be done by pressing Ctrl, Alt, and Del.

bubble memory—A non-volatile type memory that is created by the magnetization of small bits of ferrous material. It held a lot of promise at one time. But it is rather expensive to make and is slower than semiconductor memory.

buffer—A buffer is usually some discrete amount of memory that is used to hold data. A computer can send data thousands of times faster than a printer or modem can utilize it. But in many cases the computer can do nothing else until all of the data has been transferred. The data can be input to a buffer, which can then feed the data into the printer as needed. The computer is then freed to do other tasks.

bug—The early computers were made with high voltage vacuum tubes. It took rooms full of hot tubes to do the job that a credit card calculator can do today. One of the large systems went down one day. After several hours of troubleshooting, the technicians found a large bug that had crawled into the high voltage wiring. It had been electrocuted, but had shorted out the whole system. Since that time any type of trouble in a piece of software or hardware is called a bug. To debug it, of course, is to try to find all of the errors or defects.

bulletin boards—Usually a computer with a hard disk that can be accessed with modem. Software and programs can be uploaded or left on the bulletin board by a caller, or a caller can scan the software that has been left there by others and download any that he likes. The BB's often have help and message services. A great source of help for a beginner.

bus—Wires or circuits that connect a number of devices together. It can also be a system. The IBM PC bus is the configuration of the circuits that connect the 62 pins of the 8 slots together on the motherboard. It has become the de facto standard for the clones and compatibles.

byte—A byte is 8 bits, or a block of 8 0s and 1s. These 8 bits can be arranged in 256 different ways. This is $2 \times 2 \times 2 \times 2 \times 2 \times 2 \times 2 \times 2 = 256$, or 2 to the eighth power. Therefore, one byte can be made to represent any one of the 256 characters in the ASCII character set. It takes one byte to make a single character.

cache memory—A high speed buffer set up in memory to hold data that is being read from the hard disks. Often a program will request the same data from the disk over and over again. This can be quite time consuming depending on the access speed of the disk drive and the location of the data on the disk. If the requested data is cached in memory it can be accessed almost immediately.

cell—A place for a single unit of data in memory, or an address in a spreadsheet.

Centronics parallel port—A system of 8-bit parallel transmission first used by the Centronics Company. It has become a standard and is the default method of printer output on the IBM.

character—A letter, a number or an eight bit piece of data.

chip—An integrated circuit, usually made from a silicon wafer. It is microscopically etched and has thousands of transistors and semiconductors in a very small area. The 80286 CPU used in the AT has an internal main surface of about one-half-inch-square. It has 120,000 transistors on it.

clipboard—A holding place for temporarily storing text or graphics.

clock—The operations of a computer are based on very critical timing, so they use a crystal to control their internal clocks. The standard frequency for the PC and XT is 4.77 million cycles per second, or MHz. The turbo systems operate at 6 to 8 MHz.

cluster—Two or more sectors on a track of a disk. Each track of a floppy disk is divided into sectors.

composite video—A less expensive monitor system that combines all the colors in a single input line.

console—In the early days a monitor and keyboard was usually set up at a desk like console. The term has stuck. A console is a computer. The command COPY CON allows you to use the keyboard as a typewriter. Type COPY CON PRN or COPY CON LPT1 and everything you type will be sent to the printer. At the end of your file, or letter, type Ctrl-Z or F6 to stop sending.

consultant—Someone who is supposed to be an expert who can advise and help you determine what your computer needs are. Similar to an analyst. There are no standard requirements or qualifications that must be met. So anyone can call themselves an analyst or consultant.

Coprocessor—Usually an 8087 or 80287 that works in conjunction with the CPU and vastly speeds up some operations.

copy protection—A system that prevents a diskette from being copied.

CPU—Acronym for Central Processing Unit. For example, the 8088 or 80286.

crop—To trim the edges of a photo or graphics image to make it fit in an allotted space, for artistic purposes or to emphasize a certain portion.

current directory—The directory that is in use at the time.

cursor—The blinking spot on the screen that indicates where next character will be input.

daisy wheel—A round printer or typewriter wheel with flexible fingers that have the alphabet and other formed characters.

database—A collection of data, usually related in some way.

DATE command—Date will be displayed anytime DATE is typed at the prompt sign.

dialog box—A window or full-screen display that pops up in response to a command.

DMA—Acronym for Direct Memory Access. Some parts of the computer, such as the disk drives, can exchange data directly with the RAM without having to go through the CPU.

documentation—Manuals, instructions, or specifications for a system, hardware or software.

double density—At one time, most diskettes were single sided and had a capacity of 80 to 100K. Then the capacity was increased and technology was advanced so that the diskettes could be recorded on both sides with up to 200K per side double sided, double density. Then quad density was soon introduced with 400K per side. Then, of course, the newer 1.6M high-density diskettes. All of the above figures are before formatting. Most double density is the common

360K formatted. The quad ends up with 720K formatted and the high density is 1.2M. The 3.5-inch diskette standard format is 720K. The high density 2M 3.5-inch diskettes will format to 1.44M.

DRAM—Acronym for Dynamic Random Access Memory. A type of memory that must constantly be refreshed, or recharged. Primary type of memory used in PCs.

dumb terminal—A terminal that is tied to a mainframe or one that does not have its own microprocessor.

ECHO—A command that causes information to be displayed on the screen.

EEMS—Acronym for Enhanced Expanded Memory Specification. A specification for adding expanded memory put forth by AST, Quadram and Ashton-Tate (AQA EEMS).

EEPROM—An Electrically Erasable Programmable Read Only Memory chip.

EGA—Acronym for Enhanced Graphics Adapter. Board used for high resolution monitors. Can provide a resolution of 640 × 350 pixels. EEGA is an enhanced EGA or Super EGA. These boards will usually provide a resolution of 640 × 480.

EMS—Acronym for Expanded Memory Specification. A specification for adding expanded memory put forth by Lotus, Intel, and Microsoft (LIM EMS).

EPROM—An Erasable Programmable Read Only Memory chip.

Ergonomics—The study and science of how the human body can be the most productive in working with machinery. This would include the study of the effects of things such as the type of monitor, the type of chair, lighting and other environmental and physical factors.

errors—DOS displays several error messages if it receives bad commands or there are problems of some sort.

ESDI—Acronym for Enhanced Small Disk Interface. A hard disk interface that allows data to be transferred to and from the disk at a rate of 10 megabits per second. The older standard ST506 allowed only 5 megabits per second.

expanded memory—Memory that can be added to a PC, XT or AT. It can only be accessed through special software.

expansion boards—Boards that can be plugged into one of the 8 slots on the motherboard to add memory or other functions.

extended memory—Memory that can be added to an 80286 or 80386 that is addressable with the OS/2 operating system.

external commands—DOS commands that are not loaded into memory when the computer is booted.

FAT—An acronym for the File Allocation Table. This is a table on the disk that DOS uses to keep track of all of the parts of a file. A file may be placed in sector 3 of track one, sectors 5 and 6 of track ten and sector 4 of track twenty. The FAT keeps track of where they are and directs the read or record head to those areas.

fonts—The different types of print letters such as Gothic, Courier, Roman, Italic and others.

fragmentation—If a diskette has several records that have been changed several times, there are bits of the files on several different tracks and sectors. This slows down writing and reading of the files because the head has to move back and forth to the various tracks. If these files are copied to a newly formatted diskette, each file will be written to clean tracks that are contiguous. This will decrease the access time to the diskette or hard disk.

friction feed—A printer that uses a roller or platen to pull the paper through.

game port—An Input/Output (I/O) port for joysticks, trackballs, paddles, and other devices.

gigabyte—One billion bytes. This will be a common size memory in a very short time. In virtual mode, the 80286 can address this much memory.

glitch—An unexpected electrical spike or static disturbance that can cause loss of data.

global—A character or group of characters that appears throughout an entire document or program.

H and J—Short for hyphenation and justification. Some programs can do these things automatically using a large dictionary.

handshaking—A protocol between systems, usually the printer and the computer, to indicate readiness to communicate with each other.

Header—One or two lines of text that appears at the top of each page.

hexadecimal—A number system that uses the base 16. The binary system is based on 2, our decimal is based on 10. The hexadecimal system goes from 00 to 09 and continues with 0A, 0B, 0C, 0D, 0E, and 0F. Ten would be 16 decimal, and it starts over so that 20 would be 32 in decimal. Most of the memory locations are in hexadecimal notation.

hidden files—The files that do not show up in a normal directory display.

high-level language—A language such as BASIC, Pascal, or C. These program languages are fairly easy to read and understand.

IC—Acronym for Integrated Circuit.

icon—A graphic representation of a file or a command that is displayed on the screen. A mouse can be pointed to an Icon and clicked and the command will be performed. An example is the trash can used on the Apple programs. When this Icon is invoked, characters or blocks are deleted or erased.

interface—A piece of hardware or a set of rules that allows communications between two systems.

internal commands—Those commands that are loaded into memory when DOS boots up.

interpreter—A program that translates a high level language into machine readable code.

kilobyte—1024 bytes or 2^{10}.

LAN—Acronym for Local Area Network; a system in which several computers are tied together or to a central server.

low level format—Most hard disks must have a preliminary low level format performed on them before they can be formatted for DOS. Low level formatting is also sometimes called initializing.

low-level language—A machine-level language. Usually in binary digits that would be very difficult for the ordinary person to understand.
LQ—Acronym for letter quality, the type from a daisy wheel or formed type printers.

mainframe—A large computer that may serve several users.
megabyte—1M; 1,048,576 bytes (2^{20}). It takes a minimum of 20 data lines to address 1M, a minimum of 24 lines to address 16M, and a minimum of 25 lines to address 32M.
menu—A list of choices or options. A menu driven system makes it very easy for beginners to choose what they want to run or do.
MFM—Acronym for Modified Frequency Modulation, the scheme for the standard method of recording on hard disks. See RLL.
mode—A DOS command that must be invoked to direct the computer output to a serial printer.
modes—The 80286 and 80386 will operate in three different modes: the real, the protected, and the virtual.
mouse—A small pointing device that can control the cursor and move it anywhere on the screen. It usually has two or three buttons that can be assigned various functions.
MTBF—Acronym for Mean Time Before Failure. An average of the time between failures, usually used in describing a hard disk or other components.

NLQ—Acronym for Near Letter Quality. The better formed characters from a dot matrix printer.

null modem cable—A cable with certain pairs of wires crossed over. If the computer sends data from pin 2, the modem will receive it on pin 3. The modem sends data back to the computer from its pin 2 and is received by the computer on pin 3. Several other wires would also be crossed.

OS/2—The long awaited operating system that allows the 80286 and 80386 machines to directly address huge amounts of memory. It removes many of the limitations that DOS imposes. OS/2 will not benefit the PCs or XTs to any great degree.

parallel—A system that uses 8 lines to send 8 bits at a time, or one whole byte.
plotter—An X-Y writing device that can be used for charts, graphics, and many other functions that most printers can't do.
prompt—The > sign that shows that DOS is waiting for an entry.

QIC—Acronym for Quarter Inch Cartridge tape. A width of tape used in tape backup systems. Some standards using this size tape have been developed, but there are still several nonstandard systems in use.

RAM—Acronym for Random Access Memory. A volatile memory. Any data stored in it is lost when the power is turned off.

RGB—For Red, Green, and Blue, the three primary colors that are used in color monitors and TVs. Each color has its own electron gun that shoots streams of electrons to the back of the monitor display and causes it to light up in the various colors.

RLL—Acronym for Run Length Limited. A scheme of hard disk recording that allows 50% more data to be recorded on a hard disk than the standard MFM scheme. ADRT or ERLL, for Advanced and Enhanced RLL will allow twice as much data to be recorded on a hard disk. The older MFM system divided each track into 17 sectors of 512 bytes each. The RLL format divides the tracks into 26 sectors with 512 bytes each. The ADRT and ERLL divides them into 34 sectors per track.

ROM—Acronym for Read Only Memory. It does not change when the power is turned off.

SCSI—Acronym for Small Computer System Interface. A fast parallel hard disk interface system developed by Shugart Associates and adopted by the American National Standards Institute (ANSI). The SCSI system allows multiple drives to be connected. It supports a transfer rate of 1.2 megabytes per second. Since a byte is 8 bits, this is about the same as the ESDI 10 megabit per second rate.

sector—A section of a track on a disk or diskette.

serial—The transmission of one bit at a time over a single line.

SIMM—Acronym for Single In-line Memory Module. A row of nine small memory modules with a single row of pins. They are similar to the standard IC chip, but instead of having leads on each side, these have all their pins or leads on one side. They are smaller than the standard IC, so more memory can be installed in a given amount of space. Up to four megabytes of RAM can be installed on some of the 386 motherboards.

source—When copying a diskette, the origin, or diskette to be copied from.

spool—Acronym for Simultaneous Peripheral Operations On Line. A spooler acts as a storage buffer for data which is then fed out to a printer or other device. In the meantime the computer can be used for other tasks.

SRAM—Acronym for Static Random Access Memory. It is made up of transistors that remain in whatever state they are placed in, either on or off, until changed or power is removed. SRAM can be very fast and does not need to be refreshed. But it is bulky and expensive.

target—The diskette to be copied to.

time stamp—The record of the time and date that is recorded in the directory when a file is created or changed.

tractor—A printer device with sprockets or spikes that pulls the computer paper with the holes in the margins through the printer at a very precise feed rate. A friction feed platen may allow the paper to slip, move to one side or the other and not be precise in the spacing between the lines.

turbo—Usually means a computer with a faster than normal speed.

user friendly—Usually means bigger and more expensive. It should make using the computer easier. Memory is now less expensive, so large programs are being developed to use more memory than ever before.

user groups—Usually a club or a group of people who use computers. Often the club will be devoted to users of a certain type of computer. Usually though anyone is welcome to join.

vaporware—Products that are announced, usually with great fanfare, but are not yet ready for market.

VGA—Acronym for Video Graphics Array. An analog board for interfacing and driving an analog type monitor.

virtual—Something that may be essentially present, but not in actual fact. If you have a single disk drive, it will be drive A, but you also have a virtual drive B if your DIP switches on the motherboard are set properly.

virtual memory—A unique feature of the 80386 that allows it to run memory up to 64 terabytes, which is much larger than physical memory. It can remove bits of the program from a disk and process it automatically. Sixty-four terabytes is 64 trillion.

virus—Destructive code that is embedded in a computer program. It is often done by a disgruntled employee or a sick person who just wants to hurt others. The virus is usually self-replicating and will often copy itself onto other programs. It may lie dormant for some time, then completely erase a person's hard disk.

volatile—Refers to memory units that lose stored information when power is lost. Nonvolatile memory would be that of a hard disk or tape.

wait state—Slower devices on the bus may not be able to respond at the same speed as the CPU. For instance, if a memory access by the CPU requires more than one clock cycle, then the CPU is slowed down by having the CPU sit idle for one or more cycles while the procedure is accomplished.

windows—Many new software packages are now loaded into memory. They stay in the background until they are called for, then they will pop up on the screen in a window. The Microsoft company has a software package called *Windows*. It provides an operating environment for many DOS programs.

WYSIWYG—Pronounced "wizzywig." An acronym for What You See Is What You Get. Many of the better DTP programs and word processors let you see on screen what the printout will look like.

Index

Edited by Jonathan L. Mayo/David Gauthier